ONE THING LEADS TO ANOTHER...

THE TURBULENT YOUTH OF DAN MCCALL

A Memoir by

DANIEL F. MCCALL

With assistance from Pat Morgan, Edna Bay and George Brooks

authorHOUSE®

AuthorHouse™
1663 Liberty Drive
Bloomington, IN 47403
www.authorhouse.com
Phone: 1-800-839-8640

First published by AuthorHouse 9/16/2009

ISBN: 978-1-4490-1757-6 (e)
ISBN: 978-1-4490-1755-2 (sc)
ISBN: 978-1-4490-1756-9 (hc)

Library of Congress Control Number: 2009909439

Printed in the United States of America
Bloomington, Indiana

This book is printed on acid-free paper.

Contents

PROLOGUE

Who was Mame Burke?

"Do you know who this is?" the voice of the woman standing beside me asks. Apparently I say nothing. The object of the query, an elderly woman with silver-rimmed eyeglasses and a dark cloche hat from under which wisps of gray hair escape, says, "How could he? He was just a baby."

The voice beside me says, "This is Mame Burke, who took care of you when your mother died."

That is all there is to the memory, two short utterances from the unidentifiable woman standing beside me, and a brief response from Mame Burke. The visual part of the memory is an essentially immobile cameo of the head of the woman named Mame Burke. I can't even see the rest of her but I suppose she is dressed in something dark in keeping with her hat. And I can't see the woman next to me who asks the question.

Childhood memories do not come packaged in chronological order. Each stands alone in an unorganized past. To place them in a sequence, a memory must contain something that is in some way datable. Meeting Mame Burke I can place, on this basis, in my late eighth or early ninth year – just before the break-up of my family following the bankruptcy of my father's business.

I have no surprise at the mention of my mother's death, so it must be just before we left Beckwith Street, because it was at about that time that a neighbor woman, mother of one of my playmates, told me that Irene, my father's wife, whom I called "mama," was not my birth mother.

The woman who is quizzing me in this hazy memory should be my Aunt May, my father's older sister, because it was she who guided me in so many ways in my early life, but it could not be she – or why can I not recall her presence? The questioner does not seem really familiar.

She might be Aunt Gertrude, my mother's sister, but I think not. My mother's family was wroth with my father for marrying soon after my mother's death, and I do not remember seeing any of my mother's family until I was in high school.

So it has to be someone in my stepmother Irene's family. It might be Ella, Irene's older sister. That has a certain probability: the occasion was likely one when family and friends were gathered for a marriage, christening, or funeral, and there was a funeral at about this time for one of Irene's brothers.

Irene had three brothers. Eddie, a short but burly policeman with strands of light brown hair on a shiny pate, had a merry smile. He was married to a rotund, cheerful woman whom the family said was Bohemian, and who delighted me by pronouncing the strange Czech names of pastries she baked and served when we visited. The second, Willy, is never in my recollection of that period, but I knew him later as an aging bachelor living with his mother. The third brother, a handsome dark-haired young man, was a salesman. He was called Tom and owned a car, which made him appear successful, but he committed suicide. I was not told but overheard, probably at his funeral, that he sat in his car and smoked a great number of cigarettes before shooting himself in the head. The floor of the car was covered with butts and the gun fell on his lap. He was in some trouble about money. I didn't understand what the problem was. But if it was at his funeral that I was asked to identify Mame Burke, then Tom had money troubles on the run-up to the '29 stock market crash. Maybe he was caught short in the market, perhaps having invested money that was the company's, not his own. That would have been around the time my father's fortunes were on the downturn – though for a different reason. I liked Tom because he had once come to Nantasket beach while we were there on summer vacation. He took me down a long slide at the amusement park, holding me on his lap, and was criticized by Irene for taking me on a scary ride. I had loved it.

My mother, née Marguerite Sweeney, died in the influenza epidemic of 1918, when I was eight months old. They told me that I, too, almost died. No one ever gave me any details of my mother's illness, just the simple statement that she died of influenza. I imagined her lingering in bed growing slowly but increasingly weak and finally expiring. My model for this image probably was the time I was confined in a darkened room with one of my childhood diseases while a sulfur candle was kept burning. But the influenza of 1918 was not like the flu of later years. Its victims died within days of being infected. The disease was first reported in the U.S. in September 1918 in various army camps (Fort Devens, Massachusetts, being one of them) where soldiers were being readied to join those already in France. My mother, about a hundred miles west of Fort Devens, died in October.

It is not surprising that I caught the disease, being a baby at my ill mother's breast, but it is surprising that I survived; children under five were a category of high mortality. The epidemic took mainly young adults, leaving children over five and the elderly unscathed.

My father remarried shortly afterwards. His new wife, Irene Sheehan, had been his bookkeeper, and so she might have helped find a caretaker for her boss's children -- me and my two-year-old sister, Ruth. Mame Burke may have been a friend or relative of the Sheehan family. Whoever she was, I never saw or heard of her again, perhaps because after my father's bankruptcy we all left Westfield, where apparently this event, partly preserved in my memory, occurred.

CHAPTER ONE

BANKRUPT IN BRIGHTSIDE

In 1927, just after my ninth birthday, my father's business went bankrupt. This catastrophic shock shattered my family. We had been a unity in a home on Beckwith Avenue in Westfield, Massachusetts, but were then splintered into three disparate locations. We were not really far apart – we were all in the Connecticut River valley in south central Massachusetts. Ruth, my older sister, and I found ourselves in Holyoke. My other siblings and stepmother were in West Springfield, and Dad was in Springfield. To me it seemed that the only adults I knew were out of reach and suddenly I was in a strange place among strangers. I did not anticipate that it would soon get worse.

Dad closed the door of D.F. McCALL, SHOES, on Main Street. The remaining stock had been confiscated. He lost his home and its fine furnishings and his Pierce Arrow touring car. Penniless and in debt, he returned to Springfield, where he had been born and reared, to look for a job. He ended up as a door-to-door salesman for shirts and socks and perhaps some other items. Earnings were uncertain and not enough to provide a home for his wife and children.

The failure of my father's business preceded the Crash of '29. It was a harbinger of coming events. Dad had bought shoes on credit from factories in Lynn and Brockton. He sold them on credit, as was then the custom. This was fine so long as he competed only with shoe stores like his own, but when a chain store opened in Westfield, it could, with economies of scale, undersell him.

A man would come into D.F.McCall's Shoe Store and buy shoes for himself, his wife and however many children he had. Each payday he would come by and make a payment of an agreed amount on his bill. That was one reason Dad needed a bookkeeper. Once the chain store sold cheaper shoes, Dad's customers bought what they needed in the new store for cash, but now having put out money for new shoes, they were short of what they should pay Dad for the shoes they had bought previously. Some paid something; many paid nothing. Even if he were to start requiring cash on delivery, his price would have to be higher than the chain store's. It didn't take long before Dad couldn't pay for the shoes he had bought on credit from the factories. Bankruptcy was inevitable.

It was devastating for him. Once he had been a successful small businessman, a member of the group that was the backbone of the community. He had a store on Main Street. People looked up to him, were happy to greet him. Subsequently he was a failure nobody wanted to notice, some because they owed him money that was never going to be repaid. Some felt pity for his fall, but others considered bankruptcy a disgrace. He had been an important person, albeit in a small town. Then he became a nobody.

Actually Dad had owned very little except his Pierce Arrow automobile, more impressive than a Model T Ford, and an expensive suit of clothes. He rented his house and rented his store; his inventory was not really his, being obtained on credit and not paid for till the stock was sold. If there had not been a merchandizing revolution with the coming of chain stores, he would have continued to prosper, but he began his career when an epoch was coming to an end. I am sorry for Dad because he always afterward thought he might "get back on his feet" and open another store, but that was never possible. But I am not sorry to have missed what might have been one of the consequences of a continued success. Being the oldest son, I would have inherited the business (or some part of it) had father prospered. I would have been brought up to expect it, educated in the way the business was organized, and probably been content to succeed in my progenitor's foot steps. From my perspective now, I am glad to have had an academic, rather than a commercial, career.

Dad later told me he had worked in a shoe store in Springfield, learned the business, saved some money, borrowed a bit more, and opened the store in Westfield. He didn't start up in Springfield because he considered his former employer, who had taught him what he needed to know, as his benefactor and didn't wish to compete with him. I accepted this story without question; I still think it essentially correct, but maybe there is a different proportion to be seen in the amount of money saved and the "bit more" that was borrowed. How much could he have saved on his wages? He contributed something to his parental household once he began to work. First as a stock boy, he wouldn't have been paid very much, then as a salesman, not an enormous increase. It is likely that the amount borrowed was considerably greater than the amount saved. Who would lend to an immigrant Irishman's son with an eighth-grade education?

Who else but his bride's family, my mother's kin? They were not filthy rich but owned some properties in Springfield and West Springfield and a farm in Easthampton, and had white-collar jobs. My mother's father was Chief of Police in West Springfield. Her only brother, Raymond, was Tax Collector. Her older sister, Gertrude, was married to an optician. Two other sisters were married, one to an engineer and the other to a businessman. They would have credit, if not spare cash. I have a vague recollection of having heard from the husband of one of my maternal aunts what was probably an allusion to an unpaid debt. It could be, then, that some of the animosity against my father was over the consequences of his bankruptcy and not only to his precipitous remarriage. They may have granted that Marguerite's children needed a "mother" and that remarriage would provide one, but the loss of their investment in the shoe store would have rankled.

Irene, the woman I had always called "Momma," went back to her mother's house in West Springfield and took her children with her. Grandma Sheehan told our stepmother that she and her children could move in with her in West Springfield, but "Dan's other children will have to go elsewhere." Irene's mother was a widow and elderly, and could barely manage to take in her own descendants. She had no room for "Dan's other children."

That left Ruth and me behind. The early loss of our mother, which I had been too young to remember, seemed to foreshadow the bereft condition that my sister and I now confronted. Grandma Sheehan had told our stepmother that Ruth and I would have to go "elsewhere." Elsewhere, briefly, was Uncle Jack's, Dad's younger brother, who was a typesetter living in Holyoke.

John (Jack) and Mary McCall had four children, three girls and a seriously retarded boy. The girls are faceless in my mind's eye. My images of them are as they were later when we were grown up. The boy, John, was a burden to the entire family. Though older than me, he was still in diapers, and had to be spoon-fed. No sound that came out of his mouth was an intelligible word. He was large-framed and thrashed about. To me he seemed scary. All the family was involved in his care. John had been put in an institution for the disabled but taken out because his mother thought the treatment there was insensitive to his needs. Aunt Mary had her hands full, and no one can blame her if she did not happily view the arrival of two additional young children into her care.

I suppose Uncle Jack was not completely a stranger to me at that moment when we, Ruth and I, were taken to Holyoke to be given refuge in his home. We knew he was Dad's brother, but had we ever met him? I have no image of Uncle Jack before or even during my brief stay at his home. I must have seen him, but he made only a fleeting impression. No doubt he was absent much of the time at work, but there were evenings and weekends when he must have been around, yet I have no recollection of him being present. Aunt Mary ran the household. I do have a clear picture of Aunt Mary, a tall, robust woman with graying hair, an apron over a flowered housedress, and -- at least when she looked at me -- a stern face.

As it happened, Grandma Sheehan soon changed her mind about us, at least with regard to Ruth. When not in school, eleven-year-old Ruth could help take care of seven-year-old Robert, five-year-old Phillip, and year-old Dorothy, while Irene, their mother, was away during the day at work as a salesperson for S.S. Kresge's Five Cents to a Dollar Store in Springfield. But Grandma Sheehan saw no use for me, and I remained in Holyoke, an irritant in Aunt Mary's burdensome life.

Ruth had always looked out for me, and I especially missed her. Now I felt completely alone even though in the midst of cousins and uncle and auntie.

I didn't stay there long, but long enough to be enrolled in the local parochial school, which I remember only because as the new kid on the block, I had to fight my way to and from school. On the way to school, I was set upon by a gang of boys who felt they had to test a newcomer's stuff before he was permitted on their turf. A scuffle on the way in, waylaid in another fight on the way home, and I would arrive mussed up and not in the best of moods, to the annoyance of Aunt Mary. And not being in the best mood after these tussles, I may have been nasty to my girl cousins, or at least the one about my age, whose hair I've been told I pulled. Probably so, but I do not remember, and neither did she when I asked her after decades of separation. But if -- in the perception of Aunt Mary -- I was a hair-puller, that might have encouraged thoughts of transferring me somewhere.

My time at Uncle Jack's was brief. Uncle Jack must have reconsidered his generous offer to help with his older brother's difficulty. I was dumped in Brightside, a Catholic orphanage. There must have been some discussion over the decision to move me to the orphanage, but I was totally unaware of it. I didn't remain in Holyoke long after Ruth's departure. Some weeks? A couple of months? I can't pin down a precise length of time.

Brightside was a Catholic orphanage. Some of the cost was supposed to be paid for a child if a relative could do so, but the Church bore the greater part of the expenses. Probably in my case the orphanage absorbed all the expense; what could Dad afford to give? Now I was completely on my own, in the midst of other homeless boys, corralled by stern-faced nuns who looked formidable in head-to-foot black costumes with only starched white cowls around their faces.

The buildings were atop a hill in view of the road between Holyoke, the direction from which I had arrived, and West Springfield, very close to the line between these two towns. Holyoke was a mill town on the Connecticut River. I had not been happy there, so the orphanage, where there were no gangs commanding a turf, was actually a respite of comparative tranquility. I should have been content to stay. I was not.

How can an orphanage control a large number of boys 24 hours a day without regimentation? Perhaps there is a way. Brightside hadn't found it. I suppose my discontent was largely that which I later felt in the military in World War II: regimentation. We were lined up in the dormitory in the morning after we were dressed and marched to breakfast in the dining hall, then marched to classrooms. At noon we were marched back to the dining hall for lunch, then back to classrooms, and finally marched to the playing fields and allowed to break ranks to run about free or play ball. Assembled again in our ranks, we were marched to a washroom, then marched to dinner with clean hands. Allowed to read or play checkers or whatever for an hour or so, and we were then marched to the dormitory.

A dreary routine, but merely humdrum. Saturday there was no schooling. It was bath day. This was a ridiculous procedure. One class was ushered into the bathhouse. We entered an undressing room where we removed our shirts, draped them around our waists, removed our pants and underwear, put on bath trunks, then took our shirts and put them with the other clothes in a laundry bin. We would get our next week's clothes after we bathed. We did not get into bathtubs. In the adjoining room was a cement floor with a raised ridge about a foot or two high around an area of several square yards that was filled with water. We all got in and sat down in this common pool and washed ourselves "by the numbers." The nun in charge would command, "Wash your faces." We soaped our washcloths and scrubbed our faces. "Wash your necks." We did so. "Wash your ears." Hair, chests, arms, armpits, legs. Then each boy scrubbed the back of his "buddy" (the one he walked beside in the line of march). Then we were told to wash inside our trunks, and, "Don't play with yourselves."

Washing completed, we were commanded to stand up. Towels were handed out to each of us. By the numbers we dried our faces, hair, chests, arms, backs, legs and then wrapped the towel around our waists, removed our trunks, and stepped out of the pool. In a dressing room, clean underwear was handed out and when it was put on, the towel was removed on command, not before. The rest of dressing was more haphazard.

Class dismissed. Next class entered on the heels of the preceding class and progressed via the three function rooms before being released cleansed and reclothed. We were then all free to go to the playground.

One Saturday after I had been there for a while, I walked across the playground, which was quite wide, and as the weather was cold, not very many boys were outside, most preferring to be in the game room inside. No one apparently noticed that I kept on walking. Soon in the shelter of some trees I began to run. In short order I was out of the grounds of the orphanage, and I reached the road to West Springfield. Afraid of a search party looking for me, I kept away from the road, going parallel to it, but trying to keep out of sight, sometimes going through backyards, but there were not many houses then along that stretch of road. As dusk settled in, headlights forewarned me of the approach of cars, and I hid behind trees.

How I knew how to find my way is a mystery to me. True, the way was not difficult, but I had never been over it before. The road led to the town of West Springfield and there I crossed the North End Bridge to Springfield. I was then in an unknown city. I knew only Westfield and not much of that, and my brief stay in Holyoke enabled me to learn only the way from Uncle Jack's to school and back. But I had the address of the rooming house where Dad was staying. My possession of this information must have been due to having to write a letter regularly, probably as a classroom assignment, to a relative. Having the address allowed me to inquire from people in the street until I reached my goal and found my father. If I hadn't found him, I would have had to cope with the cold night alone, huddling in some alley. I had made good time, on legs shorter than they were to become, dodging imaginary pursuers, for there were none, and with the luck that often accompanied me, I got there. It did not do me much good; Dad returned me to the orphanage.

Dad was surprised to see me. He hadn't taken me seriously when I told him I would run away if he didn't take me out. His answer had been that he was living in a rooming house and that was not good for a young boy; the nuns would take better care of me. But I had persisted, begging him when he came to see me every other Sunday. Aunt May alternated with him. They always brought candy, fruit, and the funny papers. Both of them counseled me to be patient. Times would get better and the family would be reunited. I was not patient.

Dad called Brightside and told the nuns that I was with him. He fed me a good meal in a restaurant, "talked sense" to me, and took me to the movies. What I had done was foolish. There was no alternative at the moment. I should decide to put up with the situation – which would save me grief. It was late when we arrived at Brightside. A nun was waiting. She took me up to the dormitory, told me to be sensible and not even think of running away again.

As soon as she was down the stairs, I crept down, found a way out and ran down the hill. Dad was standing by the road waiting for the next interurban trolley. He was not pleased. He was, however, gentle but firm and brought me back up the hill and into the hands of the surprised nun who hadn't realized I had escaped.

The nun who was the porter that evening, stationed at the door, escorted me to the dormitory and waited while I changed into a nightgown so she could take away my clothes. She notified the nun who was the teacher of my class, who came up and knelt beside the bed. My teacher, who was younger than most of the nuns, seemed very sympathetic to my distress. She promised to pray for me and suggested that I should pray to God for guidance. She gave me an apple, and told me to come to her if I felt sad. I prayed, but not for guidance. I prayed to get out.

I prayed that my family would be reunited, and I spent a lot of time daydreaming about the home that no longer existed. Exactly what my memories were at that time I cannot now be sure, but there are some scenes I feel must have been included. Our home was a house in Westfield with 16 peach trees lining two sides of a large lawn on one side of the house. On the other side of the house where Dad parked his Pierce Arrow automobile, there were two apple trees, one of which gave us Russet apples, a variety I've never found again.

Current and gooseberry bushes were behind the house. At least once, I climbed out the window of my bedroom at the back of the house, early on a summer morning while everyone else was asleep, and fed myself on berries from these bushes. I was told, when my bed was found empty and a search of the house did not produce me, that I should not climb out windows.

There was plenty of room for kids to play. This western section of Westfield, on the edge of Woronoko, was sparsely populated at that time. The house where we lived was the only one on the out-of-town side of the street. I think there were two, maybe three, houses on the other side, and that was about as much space that existed to allow building between the road to Woronoko and the Westfield River. A hill nearby was great for sledding in winter and for gatherings of kids at any time of the year.

A path along the river bank was familiar to me because whenever Aunt May came to visit, she would take us children for a walk there, and as we walked she would recite poetry to us. May was Dad's older sister, never married but beloved by all her nephews and nieces. She declaimed one poem that she said was especially for me. *My* poem begins:

> *Blessings on thee, little man,*
> *Barefoot boy, with cheek of tan!*
> *With thy turned-up pantaloons,*
> *And thy merry whistled tunes;*
> *With thy red lip, redder still*
> *Kissed by strawberries on the hill;*

With the sunshine on thy face,
Through thy torn brim's jaunty grace;

I didn't know what a pantaloon was, and I didn't know how to whistle, nor did the rest of the picture particularly fit me, but I never doubted that that the poem was *for* me. There were many other poems that she recited from memory. I can still see the picture her voice created of Longfellow's village blacksmith's doorway open to children looking in at the flying sparks from the mighty smith's forge. Aside from a selected bit from "Hiawatha" and Shelley's "Ode to a Nightingale," I can no longer identify the many other poems she recited, but I know that her voice, unhesitatingly running over the mellifluous stanzas of long verse stories, awakened my lifelong feeling for poetry.

The length and complexity of "Hiawatha" surprised me when I finally saw it in a book; Aunt May skipped over a lot of introductory verses and started with:

By the shores of Gitche Gumee,
By the shining Big-Sea-Water,
Stood the wigwam of Nokomis,
Daughter of the Moon, Nokomis.

Aunt May had a sense of the dramatic in focusing on the beginning of the action in the long, stodgy poem. Her recitations conjured vivid pictures like the images of Longfellow:

Under a spreading chestnut tree
The village smithy stands;
The smith, a mighty man is he,
With large and sinewy hands;
And then:
And children coming home from school
Look in at the open door;

They love to see the flaming forge,
And hear the bellows roar,

Aunt May owned a millinery shop in Springfield. On alternate Sundays she came by interurban trolley to Westfield. On intervening Sundays she went to Holyoke to her brother Jack and his family. Aunt May never owned a car; the interurban trolley cars from Springfield to Westfield, Holyoke, Chicopee, and other towns made a car unnecessary. She always brought some kind of fruit or nuts, and occasionally candy. She remembered everyone's birthday.

Our "maiden aunt" was popular with us and with Uncle Jack's children. Each seemed to think, as I discovered, that he or she was her favorite. She was, however, my godmother. When I had been baptized, she had vowed to care for me, and perhaps for that reason, and because so early in my life I was the "odd one out," she eventually lavished more attention on me than on her other nephews and nieces.

Aunt May read the funnies to us. In addition to Katzenjammer Kids, Gasoline Alley (the Gumps), Happy Hooligan, and Bringing up Father (Maggie and Jiggs), there was an educational cartoon story. I remember saying, "Look! He's building a fire in a bathtub!" Aunt May explained that the man was an Indian and he was burning out the middle of a tree trunk to make a dugout canoe. That was so surprising to me that it sticks with me when the memories of other cartoons in that series have totally disintegrated. It was also my first awareness of American Indians. He had a feather in a headband and no other clothing except a breechclout, details I hadn't noticed at first, the smoke and fire having galvanized my attention. Later my interest in the First American would grow – but not for some years.

The only other visitor that I remember coming to see us was Irene's father. He would have pieces of paper-wrapped candy in various pockets in his jacket and trousers. It was a game for us kids to climb all over him and search his pockets until we found all the candy. Probably Irene's mother came with him, but I do not remember her in this context – perhaps because there was no search for candy with her as the hiding place.

I had a toy wagon, a birthday present, in which I pulled my brother Robert. Phillip, still a toddler, wanted a turn. I helped him into the wagon and began to run, pulling it, as I had with Robert, but when I reached the edge of the lawn at the line of peach trees, I turned too sharply. The wagon tipped over. Phil fell out and began to cry. Irene came out, picked him up and soothed him. He was not hurt but dumping him out of the wagon upset him. "Momma" told me to be more careful.

One might take this scene to be the fairytale stepmother rebuking a child not her own, but that was not how it was. I believe her correction of my reckless manner of giving rides would have been the same had I been her own child. I never felt she favored her own children over me. At the time I did not yet realize I was not her child. I understand now that she was a good woman who indeed loved her husband's other children. My memories of living on Beckwith Street are pleasant memories.

Every summer Dad drove us to Springfield where we picked up Aunt May and then on to Nantasket Beach, over a hundred miles away, for a two-week vacation on the ocean shore. We always stopped somewhere along the way for lunch. On one occasion, there was a bowl of blueberries put on the table for dessert. Before anyone scooped out servings into smaller dishes, I put salt on the berries in the bowl, spoiling everyone's dessert.

I do not remember this, but heard it so often that it is fixed in my memory. I have a photograph that Ruth gave me; in it Aunt May, Dad, Irene, and Irene's mother are sitting on the steps of the cottage we rented. Baby Dorothy is on Irene's lap; the rest of us kids are dispersed among the adults.

In autumn Dad drove us on a Sunday to see the foliage in the Berkshire Hills.

At home we had a Victrola, a polished wooden piece of furniture that played large, flat, black disks set on a peg in the turntable. When we cranked this primitive record player by the handle on the side of the cabinet, the turntable would revolve, and we would delicately place the armature holding the needle so that the needle fit into a groove at the outer edge of the disk, which we called a "record," and marvelous music would fill the air! Beneath the turntable was a little closet to store disks of which we had several, but I remember only one. No doubt because I heard it so often, since Dad said it was his favorite, but when he wasn't present, and even when he was, we must have played the others. I remember only the beginning of the lyrics:

> *It's three o'clock in the morning*
> *We've danced the whole night through.*

In later years, after Dad was dead, I wondered why that song was his favorite. Did it remind him of some occasion that was significant in some way to him? Some songs remind me of my high school prom, others of Pearl Harbor, where for some weeks while the torpedoed ship I was on was being repaired, I spent many hours listening to a ship's band playing while I drank beer with shipmates. Knowing how music heard under certain circumstances will thereafter recall the circumstances whenever that music is heard, I could imagine him dancing late

15

into the night to that song and it subsequently reminding him of his dancing partner. Since he said this was his favorite song, he must have had a favorable opinion of his dancing partner; in fact, for the feeling to have lasted so long, he must have loved her. Who was she? I liked to think it was my mother, but it could have been Irene – though I wonder if her strict mother would have allowed her, still unmarried, to be out so late. And Dad didn't have much time for courting Irene – if he started after my mother died. It could even have been someone else who turned him down, as perhaps beneath her station, before he managed to become a small businessman with a store on Main Street. When he did first marry, it had been "above his station" for an immigrant laborer's son. His bride, my mother, came from a property-owning family, already "older stock" and prosperous to middle class standards.

There are some scenes I probably didn't dwell on when reminiscing in the orphanage. A dispute with a playmate over a toy – whether mine or his I can't now say – ended with me yanking it out of his hands and hitting him on the head with it. His scalp was bleeding and he was taken to the hospital. It was not a serious wound – no concussion – but I was in bad odor for a while.

Whatever images I recalled at the time, the reality remained that I was ousted from home and still in the orphanage with no rescue in sight. Eventually, I decided that God helps them that help themselves, and prepared to run again. The nuns were now watching me more closely. I couldn't use the same strategy again. But the injunction to pray gave me the excuse to go to the chapel. They would not deny me this privilege. Once they were accustomed to seeing me go to the chapel, kneel for a while, and return to the group, I was able to find a time when no one else was there. Instead of going out the main door at the back of the chapel into the main building, I exited by the door to the room where the priest donned his vestments before Mass, and from that room to outside the building.

Having accomplished the journey once, it was easy to repeat. How much time had elapsed since my first escape I cannot say. When I showed up, Dad repeated what he had done before: he called Brightside, told the nuns I was with him, fed me a restaurant meal, took me to the movies, tried to talk sense to me, and took me back to Brightside. I said a strange thing: "If you won't let me live with you, I'll run away and hop freight trains." I cannot now explain how (at age nine, or was I already ten?) I knew about riding freight trains, except that during the Depression many unemployed men took to the freights to move around in search of work, and I must have heard about this. I did not imagine then that before another decade was out I too would ride the rails.

Some weeks went by. I had a kind of notoriety. No one had run away in recent memory. Boys took notice of me, either keeping a wary distance from me, or becoming chummy, and wanting me to tell them about my exploits. Some thought I was crazy to brave the outside world. Some envied the nerve to do it. One boy kept saying, "Will you take me with you the next time you go?" His parents were both dead, but he had a grandmother who lived in Longmeadow, which was a little south of Springfield. I didn't want to be encumbered with another kid. That would only make escape more difficult, but in the end I did take him with me, not because I had given in to his entreaties, but because he happened to be with me when the opportunity occurred.

The problem was finding the moment to move suddenly when I was not being observed. Boys all had a round of chores; the time to wash dishes happened to come for me and this kid at the same time. After the evening meal, the day was essentially over, and everyone was more or less relaxed. When we dawdled so we would finish late, we were able to leave the kitchen after all the others, except for the nun in charge, and she did not follow us out of the kitchen. We ran, with no jackets, just ran. I no longer remember this kid's name; our adventure together was brief. He had lived with his grandmother before being put in Brightside so he knew the way once we got to Longmeadow. His grandmother wailed at the sight of us. She was old and feeble. That was why she had put him in the orphanage. She fed us bread and tea, and called the local police who took us back. Brightside accepted him, but refused to take me in – I was a troublemaker, a bad influence on other boys. So my inadvertent taking the other kid with me accomplished what I wanted: escape from the orphanage. I didn't care that it was by expulsion.

Dad had to take me. He accepted me with more welcome than my behavior deserved. But I was his oldest son; I carried his name with the tag of junior after it. He saw my going to Longmeadow instead of coming to him as a measure of the desperation I had voiced in my threat to hop a freight train. My being with Dad put some burden on him; now he had to put up money for my meals, and he soon found out that he could no longer stay at the rooming house with a kid in tow, so we had to move to a hotel, which was more expensive than the rooming house. But he never complained about that in my hearing.

CHAPTER TWO

HOTEL LIFE

Dad was living in a rooming house, but that soon proved inadequate for the two of us. It was just off State Street, not far from St. Michael's Cathedral, so naturally I was sent to Cathedral school. In mid-afternoon when school was out, I returned to the rooming house to leave my books in Dad's room. The woman who ran the rooming house asked with a growl, "What are you doing here?"

"Dropping my books," I told her, which I did, and headed for the door again.

"You can't come in here at this hour," she shouted at me. "Don't do it again."

She rented to men who left their rooms in the morning to go to work and didn't return until evening after they had had supper in some restaurant, perhaps even had spent some time in a tavern, or gone to a movie, and returned only to sleep, or perhaps to read the newspaper before retiring for the night. She didn't want some noisy kid coming in when it was still daylight and disturbing her. Can't blame her.

I would have joined other kids in the neighborhood, but it wasn't a residential neighborhood and the kids fanned out in various directions from Cathedral school to go home, and I was left in an area of insurance companies and lawyers' offices bereft of anyone to play with. So I went just down the street from Cathedral to the Carnegie Library. Saint-Gauden's statue, "The Puritan" was on the grassy knoll beside it. That it represented a Puritan was obvious on sight; newspapers around Thanksgiving had pictures of men garbed in that fashion, but I didn't know until much later who Saint-Gauden was.

I'm not sure if I had ever read a book not assigned by school before, probably not. Now, with nothing to do, I spent hours in the children's room of the library. I read the recommended children's books: the adventures of Robinson Crusoe, Treasure Island, the Knights of the Round Table, Robin Hood, Richard the Lion-hearted. I went through all without realizing what was historical and what was fictional. Somehow I found myself reading about American Indians: *The Last of the Mohicans* and other Leatherstocking tales. An author named Schultz had a series of novels about Blackfoot Indians on the Great Plains and the foothills of the Rockies.

From then on I read omnivorously, perusing everything in print that came my way. I knew how Robinson Crusoe felt after he had read and reread all the books he had saved from the shipwreck and wanted something new to read. My passion for reading started as a pastime and eventually became a desire for knowledge. As time went on, I sought knowledge of everything, trying to follow up references, but other topics always distracted me before I got through all the references, and I went off in other directions, seldom fully completing a search because I had meanwhile become too committed to a new attraction. There was always a sense of disappointment at letting a pursuit of a topic lapse (meaning to come back to it, but usually not managing to do so), but I consoled myself with the realization that omniscience is impossible. This haphazard way continued into my college years.

Andrew Carnegie, for whatever harm he did to others in acquiring his millions, gained "grace" (in a secular sense) by donating libraries to so many cities. My thanks to him for the Springfield Library on State Street.

In addition to haunting the Carnegie Library, I wandered through the streets, and saw on South Main a storefront with Indian beadwork and other paraphernalia as well as bottles of a brown liquid in the window. Probably there was a sign extolling the bottled stuff. An elderly Abenaki Indian from Canada sat inside waiting for customers to come in and buy his bottled herb medicine. He wore a feather headdress. I didn't then know that this was a Plains Indian headdress and would not have been worn by an Abenaki, but Americans generally didn't know this and no doubt he wore it to establish to his customers his Amerindian identity.

He had no customers at the moment, so when I pestered him with questions, he seemed to welcome the distraction. He answered my questions, however fatuous they must have been, and told me to read *The Indian How Book* by Arthur C. Parker to get information on all the things I had asked about.

The book was not in the children's room. The librarians were by this time familiar with my face as a regular reader, and after I described the nature of the book, one of them took me upstairs and got the librarian there to agree to let me take out *The Indian How Book*. True to the Abenaki's recommendation, Parker's book told me how to make a birch bark canoe, a bow and arrow, deerskin clothing, and lots of other things, none of which I ever did. There was no birch bark available on State Street, nor any deer to hunt with bow and arrows. But it did give a detailed picture of Eastern Woodlands Indian life, and so although Parker was a Seneca Iroquois, his book was reasonably accurate as well for the Abenaki, an Algonquin people. I took the book to show the man who had recommended it, but the store was empty. He had gone.

Parker's Seneca name was Gawasso Wanneh, and I would refer to him and his book by his "authentic" name, not the English name he had acquired, but I learned nothing else about him from this book. I was unaware that he wrote articles for scholarly journals, or that he was an assistant to General Ulysses S. Grant during the Civil War or that subsequently, when Grant was President of the U.S., Parker was made head of the Bureau of Indian Affairs, the first Indian to hold the post; there would not be another till a century later. When I got to Columbia University as a graduate student in anthropology, I surprised some of my professors that I knew the name of Arthur C. Parker.

I never learned the personal name of the Indian who I bothered with my questions; he suggested I call him "Chief." But the name "Abenaki" stuck in my memory, and I would encounter it several times in the future. As a college student I worked as a counselor in a children's camp in Vermont two summers; it was on a lake called Abenaki. At the time I thought the name geographically out of place because I associated it with Canada, whence the herb-oil-selling Abenaki came, but I later learned that the Abenaki once occupied much of northern New England – all of Vermont and New Hampshire, part of southern Maine and a bit of northern Massachusetts. Canada was a refuge during and after the wars of the eighteenth century.

Once, at an anthropological conference on Algonquin Indians, I heard Gordon Day, from a museum in Ottawa, give a paper on an oral tradition he collected from an old Abenaki woman about the Rogers' Rangers' attack on an Abenaki settlement on the mouth of the St. Francis River where it empties into the St. Lawrence. This is probably the place, now a reservation, that the Indian I met came from. And my friend Bruce Trigger of McGill University edited a book published by the Smithsonian Institution that contains about as much information on the Abenaki as is available.

At some time, rather later I think, I saw the movie *Silent Enemy*. The enemy that made no noise was hunger, and whenever the herds of caribou that the Cree Indians of Canada depended on to supply meat were absent, hunger attacked everyone and starved some to death. Grey Owl, a Cree, acted the lead. A shaman wanted the hunter to go in one direction; the hero, drawing on his experience, argued for another direction. A girl, of course, was looking favorably on the hunter but the shaman wanted her. The end was a happy one. I had sometimes stayed in the theater to see a movie a second time, but only once did I stay for three showings – for *Silent Enemy*. I got back so late my father was concerned.

"Where were you?"

"At the movies."

"But all day?"

"I saw it three times. It was about Indians."

His expression showed that he thought I was crazy. At the time I thought he might be right, but later I saw this interest in Indians as a stage in my development as an anthropologist.

The Carnegie Library and my Abenaki friend are in some way connected with the genesis of my aspiration to get out of the city and into the forest, or as we might say – to go camping. Real camping, away from the city, began with my friend Fitz, but this would be at least a couple of years after my urban "camping" on the roof of a shed.

This strange event occurred during the few weeks we lived in the rooming house. I have only fragments of a memory of the occasion. It is associated in my mind with "camping." Where my early idea of "camping" came from is now impossible to recall; my family had never engaged in any activity that could be called "camping." The word somehow connoted living out in the open, sleeping under the sky, or under a tent, at most in a rough cabin in the woods. It was related to American Indians, of whom I had just become aware thanks to my recent acquaintance with the Abenaki herbal-medicine seller. "Camping" had as yet not anything to do with Boy Scouts, an organization I had not yet heard about. Nor did "camping" have any connection in my young mind with the adult practice of going for a vacation at an organized campground, or traveling in a motorized vehicle called a "camper" (sometimes with a canoe on top), both of which, for lack of better alternatives, I later occasionally adopted.

My first instance of sleeping under the sky can only be called "camping" by wild exaggeration. It was in the city, sleeping on a sloping roof of a shed attached to the back of an apartment building. I remember getting onto the roof from a window of an apartment, accompanied by a recently found friend, and the friend's much younger sibling, both of whom lived in that apartment.

This memory is like some snapshots, old photos dredged up from the back of a long-unused cluttered drawer, in which I recognize a younger version of myself, but I can't put a name on the other persons in the picture. One of them, about my age, was a girl. And her sibling was a toddler. How we were ever permitted to be out there is one of the questions I cannot answer. My father, I suppose, agreed nonchalantly that I could spend the night at the house of a friend (did he even know that the friend was a girl?). But where was the girl's mother? All I can say is she's not in the picture.

A second image is of the girl getting out of her blanket, taking a few steps, then squatting with her toes at the edge of the roof, and pissing into the alley. Probably this somewhat lubricious incident is why the otherwise nearly forgotten event persists in my memory: a sense of a guilty secret attaches to it. But that was all there was to it: seeing the back of a clothed girl and hearing the liquid stream splattering the ground below.

Depending on which month this occurred (before or after March), I would have been nine or ten years old. The way I calculate my age at that time is that it was before I had been transferred from Cathedral to Sacred Heart School, a transfer I can date to prior to November 1928, because I was there when the nun let us out of school to see the great Catholic candidate for the presidency of the United States, Al Smith, who was passing through Springfield on his campaign. I was ten years old at the time of that election, having been born in March of 1918, and since this event happened before the election (and before my transfer to Sacred Heart) I couldn't have been older than ten. Since we were sleeping outdoors, it must have been a warm month rather than a cold one; it seems I would have recently passed my tenth birthday.

My attendance at Cathedral school was brief and I never made any friends there.

Dad and I stayed at the rooming house only a few weeks and then moved to the Springfield Hotel, a multi-storied building next to the railroad station. It had once been a rather grand establishment, but had become rather shabby, losing clients to the Worthington Hotel in midtown, though it still had bellhops. The change of address required a change in schools. I was transferred to Sacred Heart grammar school in the North End. However, we did not stay at the Springfield Hotel very long and our next, and final, hotel – The Campion – was not far away and so I continued at Sacred Heart.

SACRED HEART SCHOOL

My sixth grade, like Caesar's Gaul, was divided into three parts: Sacred Heart was the third school I attended that year, starting in Brightside, then Cathedral, now Sacred Heart. All were Catholic schools in the same archdiocese, but the curricula were not identical, or at least, the order in which subjects were covered was not the same. I repeated some lessons I had already gone over in the other schools, and some things I never was taught at all. I was not promoted. I had come to Sacred Heart almost at the end of the school year, so the nun who taught sixth grade had little time to observe me and with certain blank spaces on my exams had little choice but to hold me back.

I repeated sixth grade. I'm not sure it was with the same teacher, but Sister Francis Edward, who taught me for a full year, is the first nun I can remember as a teacher. Every teacher before that is faceless and nameless. The nun who brought me an apple and sympathy that night at Brightside I remember only for the act of kindness at a time of my distress. All of the nuns who preceded Sister Francis Edward as my teachers are blurred together in a silhouette of a nun's black habit with the starched white around the face.

The reason Francis Edward stands out is not particularly to her credit. She was, I grant, a dedicated teacher and pushed rules of grammar which we learned by rote, being called on to stand and rattle off in alphabetical order all the adverbs, or some rule of grammar, such as, *i* before *e* except after *c*. However, what stand out in my recollection are instances that exhibited her narrow bias, or her ignorance. I had to stay after school one day for throwing a spitball. I had to write "I will not throw spitballs in class" one hundred times on the blackboard, then clean the board and clap the erasers against each other, leaning out the window while doing so and making a cloud of chalk dust that settled on the brick wall below. While I was writing, I was aware that she was sorting pictures into two piles. Her custom was to give a pupil a "holy picture" as a prize for a good performance in certain exercises, but I didn't know why she was putting them in two piles. I looked over her shoulder. "Oh, 'ster," I began (we always elided Sister to 'ster), "can I have that one?"

She had been unaware that I was looking over her shoulder; her cowl restricted her peripheral vision, and she was startled by my voice so close to her ear. "Boys!" she expostulated, "always into something they shouldn't." She took the picture I requested and the pile on which she had placed it and tore them into pieces and threw the scraps into her waste paper basket. The picture was a Renaissance painting of a Madonna and Child,

27

but it was unacceptable to her because the artist had shown the Madonna preparing to nurse the infant and part of her breast was uncovered.

The Boys' Club was on Chestnut Street, not far from the school. When I had been going to Cathedral school, the YMCA was nearby and I had attempted to go in, but was turned away because I didn't have money for the fee to join. The Boys' Club welcomed poor boys. I became a regular there. We played basketball. With some other guys from Sacred Heart we formed a team that got the name Crusaders. I'm not sure where the name came from – the boys or the gym coach. And we went swimming in the pool in the basement. We did not have to wear bathing suits; nudity was permitted probably because if bathing suits had been required, many boys would have been excluded for lack of a suit or money to buy one. Sister Francis Edward heard about this pool in the basement. The word "basement" (which was used in the school to refer to the location of the toilets) seemed to set off some virulent reaction in her.

"You must not go down in that dark basement." We were surprised by this.

"But 'ster, it's not dark down there. There's plenty of light."

"Don't argue. I know what you do down there!" Again, we were dumbfounded by what she was saying.

"Promise me you won't go down there any more."

"But 'ster, we just swim."

Some of us went to the priest and told him of Sister's ultimatum. "She thinks we jerk off there. We don't, Father." No one affirmed that this forbidden activity didn't sometimes occur elsewhere. The priest convinced Sister that our going to the Boys' Club and swimming was permissible, and we heard no more about it. I would have gone anyway and I guess many others would have, but getting rid of the nun's injunction made us more relaxed about going there.

A boy in my class with whom I hung around for a while, probably mainly because he was a latchkey kid like me, had no one to go home to. He is the one who told me the amazing news that female bodies are as different from boys' bodies as their clothing styles are different. I expressed my incredulity. According to him, girls didn't have a "dong." "That's right! They just have a hole!"

I laughed at that idea. "If they had a hole," I told him dismissively, "their guts would fall out."

"I'm telling you. I seen it," he claimed. I still wasn't about to believe him. "The man," he went on, enlarging the area of discussion, "sticks his dong in her hole." I guess I laughed or made some disparaging comment about this ridiculous concept. He was determined to convince me. "I seen my mother."

We were sitting in his one-room apartment; his mother was at work. "I'm lying right here," he said (we were sitting on the cot he slept on) "and I seen Uncle fuck momma!"

His mother was a widow, or divorced, separated, or never married -- I don't know which -- but currently she had no husband, but she did have a male friend whom the boy called "Uncle." When Uncle stayed over, which was a couple of nights each week, he slept in the big bed with the mother. There had been an earlier "uncle" who had disappeared before this new one appeared. In this tiny apartment there was little privacy. There was a separate bath and toilet that provided the only seclusion from the rest of the rented area. The kitchen was in a corner, next to the bathroom door. A table where they ate divided the kitchen from the rest of the room, most of which was occupied by the big bed. There wasn't enough space left over even for an upholstered chair. The boy's cot, where we sat, was flush against a wall, parallel to the bed, giving him, as I could see, a clear view of whatever might happen in his mother's bed. "They think I'm asleep," he explained, "but when I hear them, I open my eyes, and I see them fucking!"

I had known the word, but considered it a "swear word." After all, it was used about a chair if it broke when you sat on it, or it referred to other inanimate objects. Used as a verb rather than adjectivally, I suddenly understood the word's principal meaning. This kid must have been about my age, but knew vastly more about human anatomy and the physiology of sex than I had ever dreamed of. In contrast, I had just come out of an orphanage where the only females I saw were nuns, draped in voluminous black "habits" from the top of their heads to their black ankle-high shoes, with only a starched white cowl around their faces. Why would I have imagined an actual fleshly body inside such a disguise? Of course, I knew that boys were different than girls, but precisely wherein that difference resided, other than dress and manners, had remained a mystery.

By word of mouth, I now had knowledge of what adult sex consisted of, but it was some time before that information was verified. The kid who informed me of these basic facts is sketchy in my memory. His mother moved soon after this conversation and he of course went with her and I didn't see him again, but as the revealer of fundamental realities, he persists in my recollections.

THE CAMPION HOTEL

The Campion, located on Main Street, was only a block away from the corner of Congress Street, where in the mid-1880s Dad was born. The Campion was labeled "A Family Hotel." Aside from the family that ran the hotel, Dad and I were the only family I ever saw there. A woman named Hortense ran the hotel; her last name escapes me but she came from Quebec. Hortense was unmarried and had only the help of an uncle who was quite elderly. Unlike the Charles Hotel where travelers came and went, the Campion had a number of men who were there on a regular basis, traveling salesmen who had a route that took them to different cities in the region. They would be at the Campion for a few days, then gone for a couple of weeks, and then back again. There were also a couple of pensioners who lived year round; one I remember was Old Tom. He was as active as any of the rest but got his epithet for his pure white hair and white eyebrows. The building was only three stories, with commercial shops and a restaurant on the ground floor, and a registration desk and lounge at the top of the stairs. The lounge was at the corner of the building so there were windows on two sides. A rack of today's newspapers was placed where it was readily visible, and there was a radio. The owners had a suite at the rear of that floor with kitchen and bedrooms and living room, but there were also a few rooms for transients or regulars on that level. The top floor was entirely rooms to let, and Dad and I had one, the only one with twin beds.

This hotel was not only more congenial but was cheaper. I lived there with my father for six years. Mothers of my friends would cluck and say something like, "You poor boy," but I found it a great place to live.

One of the salesmen had lost both hands and one eye in an explosion. He said he had once been a miner. He had a glass eye and artificial hands that could be strapped on to his lower arms. He was willing to show me how he took them off and put them on, pulling the straps with his teeth. He had the metal and leather prosthetic hands off most of the time around the Hotel. He was a smoker and could get the pack out of his shirt pocket by pushing it upward with the stump of one arm. Then, with the pack held between the two stumps, he'd shake it to pop the tip of a cigarette above the open pack and get the cigarette to his mouth. In a similar operation, he could light the cigarette, holding a box of large wooden matches between his knees and a match between his handless wrists. It was an amazing thing to see. He used a box of the large matches, because the smaller wooden matches burned his arm stumps.

He told me he could do as much without the artificial appendages as with them. The prosthetic fingers didn't move, but were fixed in a position that permitted him to hold a fork in one hand and a knife in another. I saw him eating in the restaurant below the hotel, where I also ate, and he managed fine, if with movements that for someone else would seem awkward. I can still see his face in my mind's eye, but his name has faded. He was one of the most cheerful men I ever met. He used to flirt with Hortense, bringing her peppermints. He presented them with the song:

I always buy a nickel's worth of peppermints
Every time I go to see Hortense.

During school vacations, Hortense had her nephew visit; he was younger than I was and I never got to know him well. Some of the regulars at the hotel thought that the boy was her son and was sent to boarding school, and did not live with her sister, his putative mother. Usually the men didn't say too much about such things when I was present, but I often sat in the lounge with one of the newspapers that were daily put on a rack for roomers to use. With the paper opened wide in front of me, I was almost invisible to someone coming into the lounge and he might say something before someone gave him a signal that I was in the lounge. I did get into the habit of reading the papers, but my ears pricked up to hear what others were saying. Eventually the men, grown accustomed to me being there, were less reticent to say whatever they wanted to say.

A radio in the lounge entertained us in the evenings with Will Rogers' ironic comments on current events, Walter Winchell's gossip, the supposedly Canadian comedians Joe and Baptist, and the *faux* black Amos 'n Andy. The men sometimes gathered around to cheer or boo a sports program. I heard the boxing match when Jack Dempsey was defeated, to the disgust of most of the listeners.

The Greeks who ran the restaurant below the hotel, where I usually ate -- two brothers I believe -- were accustomed to seeing me eating and noticed that I was not spending much money on Saturday lunch. I told them I was saving some money for the movies. They surprised me by giving me a dessert free. It was rice pudding, the cheapest dessert, but it was a generous thing they did. A ticket to the movies cost only ten cents for a child in those days, so it wasn't much that I had to save from my meal money, but ten cents would buy a piece of pie with ice cream. One could get three doughnuts and a cup of coffee for a nickel.

Some time after we arrived, Hortense sold the hotel to an Italo-American couple, Tony and Maria. Again I'm at a loss for their surname. Maria had a baby shortly after they took over the hotel. On Saturday mornings, there being no school and having nothing else demanding my time, I sometimes helped Maria make up beds in the rooms. I even helped change the baby's diapers. Tony taunted me, saying I was infatuated with his wife. He was right; I did think her very pretty and had affection for her. This annoyed Tony. Maria invited me to eat with them on a few occasions, and I learned to like foods I'd never had before, polenta, for example. I even watched her make it. It was different from anything I had previously eaten. Talking to Maria about strange foods brought to her mind a saying her mother used to say: *Mangia questa minestra o si salta dalla finestra* (Eat this soup or jump out the window). It was said when there was no other choice of food, or metaphorically whenever there was a narrow choice in any situation. Years later I realized that Maria's family probably came from northern Italy because polenta is very popular in the north and whenever a southern Italian cooks polenta, they use a different recipe.

Tony usually manned the registration desk at the top of the stairs. Hortense had never rented a room to a couple without luggage, but Tony was not as discriminating. Maria apparently did not object too strenuously to this leniency, but when Tony rented a room to a woman who took men from the street to this room, there was a row. The woman had to depart but not before strident words were hurled back and forth between the two owners of the hotel.

It was a place for an adolescent to get an adult education.

The Campion was in the North End, a section of Springfield where recent immigrants found moderately priced living space. My introduction to human diversity began here. On a side street, only a block away, was a Chinese laundry and a Chinese restaurant. I took my father's shirts to this laundry and was supposed to pick them up because Dad didn't get back till after the laundry closed. I forgot several times to pick them up.

"You can remember that it is 93 million miles to the sun and 23 million to the moon," he said, referring to one of the many times I told him of something I had read, "but you can't remember to pick up my clean shirts. I cannot go to work in a soiled shirt. You must remember. It is the only thing I ask you to do." I did try to remember, but other things distracted my attention from this not-onerous duty. I found it interesting to go into the laundry and see the appearance, odd to me, of an East Asian face and hear the peculiar accent of his speech, but that didn't always serve as a reminder to pick up the shirts before the laundry's closing time.

On the occasion of Chinese New Year the two Chinese businessmen, who were opposite each other, would close their doors and stand on the curb in front of their shop windows and toss stings of firecrackers into the street between them. It was a noisy spectacular celebration that surprised most non-Chinese. People came to see what was causing the Fourth of July-type concatenation, and until then I hadn't realized there was any other calendar.

The other Chinese man who tossed firecrackers into the street ran a restaurant. Uncle Jack for some reason came to Springfield. It must have been on a Sunday because Dad was not at work and I was not in school. We were going to have lunch.

Dad suggested the Chinese restaurant, since it was close by. "No," said Uncle Jack, "they scrape whatever is left on a plate, mix it up and serve it again to someone else. You don't know what you might catch!" So we went elsewhere, but Dad ate at the Chinese restaurant occasionally, and so did I.

On the same street where the Chinese laundry and restaurant were located there were some apartment buildings. In at least one of the buildings there were some Syrian families. They, or at least some of them, were not Muslim but Catholic, so the children went to Sacred Heart School, and since they were only a block away from the hotel, I found myself walking along with them on my way home. In this way a boy in my class became a closer acquaintance and I went with him to his family's apartment. He had a sister who was a year or two older than him and I found her interesting. Soon I was spending more time with her than with her brother. I was there on several different days but one day his mother told me not to come there again. The reason was, it seems, that although the girl was surrounded by Irish girls in class every school day, her mother did not want her to be familiar with an Irish boy. Given our tender ages, such a concern ought to have been premature, but perhaps mothers know best.

There may have been some Negro families in Westfield but I had never seen a black person while I lived there, nor did I encounter one in my brief stay in Holyoke. There were no Afro-American boys at Brightside at the time of my incarceration. Walking to school in Springfield one morning, I saw on the other side of the street a cluster of kids also carrying schoolbooks and heading in the same direction. Two of them were black. I must have made some exclamation of surprise. "They don't go to Sacred Heart," my Syrian friend, who had no amazement at their color, informed me. Of that much I must have already been aware. Sacred Heart was a small school and I had been going there long enough to have seen any pupil as unusual to my experience as these two at whom I couldn't stop staring. They were going to the public school, not far distant from Sacred Heart. I must have made some inquiries about them because I remember that they were a brother and sister and the girl's name was Ruby, as exotic a name as her appearance, but I never spoke to either of them. Shortly after this I decided to walk to school by another route, after the retraction of my welcome at the Syrian family home, and didn't any longer see the public school contingent of the two black children and their white friends.

I made some other friends in school. Bob Meahen was in my class, and -- if I took this alternate route -- we could walk together when we left school. Bob had a younger brother, Joe, who was always in a cheerful mood, with a sunny smile and a gleeful word; everyone around him seemed to be buoyed up just by the sight of him. He also had a pretty sister, Eleanor, already in high school, the belle of the neighborhood. The Meahan family lived in an apartment building just off Main Street, a few blocks north of the Campion. Beside the four-story brick building was a large open lot, not a playground, but where kids played ball anyway. Beyond the lot were one- and two-story wood houses where several children lived. The lot became my hangout. On a rainy day I might be in the Meahan apartment, perhaps playing checkers or some other game. It was probably on such an occasion that Mrs. Meahen, calling her children to supper, told me to sit down at the table with them. She had already set a plate for me.

Other kids who might be visiting knew their supper was getting ready elsewhere and on their own initiative went home. I ate in the "greasy spoon" restaurant under the hotel at any time I felt like it, with money Dad gave me for meals, so I suppose I was tardy in vacating my hosts' apartment; that may have prompted the invitation, but more likely it was the generosity of a kind woman. She had heard from her children what I had told them about living in a hotel with my father, my mother being dead, and she felt pity for a boy in that situation.

This possibility of saving meal money gave me an idea. On Saturdays, I had gone to the afternoon movie with money saved by skimping on lunch. If Mrs. Meahan fed me Saturday lunch I could take Bob to the movies, and we would have enough to buy nickel chocolate bars. He proposed our scheme to his mother and she saw no harm in it. She would have fed me anyway and she had no money to give Bob, or her two other children, so it was a bonanza all around.

Bob and I went to see movies every Saturday until Dad discovered that the restaurant sold meal tickets for ten dollars that would be punched for the amount of a meal, usually less than $1.00. The inducement to buy a ticket is that the amount available for punching was twelve dollars, a two-dollar bonus. This did not completely stop my movie going but did terminate my having Bob as a beneficiary. Dad didn't know he was messing up my scheme and I didn't tell him. His purpose was to get extra food for me by using the meal tickets; I didn't presume to argue against such an economy. Shortly after getting a meal ticket, I found that I could ask for ten cents in change and have it punched on the ticket; that enabled me to go to the movie. This was not a regular practice to get money from the ticket, and probably not a permissible way to use the ticket, considering the bonus involved, but when the Greek brothers learned the ticket was preventing me from seeing my customary Saturday flick, they let me get the price of admission.

Roger lived in the building where the Meahan's lived. He was my age, or perhaps a little older, and did not go to Sacred Heart but to public school. He was more "worldly-wise" than any of the Meahan's. When Eleanor Meahan came walking down the street, Roger chanted to us but out of her hearing, "Titty-boom, titty-boom, titty-boom" to the rhythm of the bounce of her breasts as she stepped along.

He was more focused on sexual things than Bob or I, though we were not unaware of that element, and listened to and laughed at his dirty jokes. One evening Roger and I were walking along Main Street. He was telling me a tale about a girl he said he knew, and just as we came in front of the Campion he said, "Has she got two handfuls? One tit!" I was aware of Old Tom standing beside the hotel entrance, getting a breath of fresh air. I wondered if he heard and what he thought. He was never one to tell risqué stories in the lounge as some other men did. The embarrassment of his almost certain overhearing of Roger's eulogy for the wondrous size of the breast of some girl who probably didn't even exist, or if she did had not been measured in the manner he described, is no doubt the reason this otherwise forgettable remark has stayed so clear in my memory for nearly seven decades.

My education in sexuality at that period was increasing. There were single rooms at the Campion with a single bed, and double rooms with a double bed like the room next to ours, which was not regularly occupied. When that room was taken, it was usually by a man and a woman and not infrequently I could hear sounds that aroused my curiosity. There was a door between our room and this other room; the builder apparently allowed for the possibility of a suite, but since our room was permanently rented to Dad, that never was possible while we lived there. I was sometimes in our room while my father was away. Late one afternoon doing my homework, I became aware of noise from the next room. It was the squeaking of bedsprings. The boy who told me about his mother had mentioned that noise. I got up, put away my schoolbooks, and listened at the door. Then I looked through the keyhole but the view was parallel to the bed and I couldn't see the bed. I had a pocketknife, which in addition to the blade had an augur. I bored a hole, quietly as I could, at the corner of a panel in the door. I could now see the bed, but I was too late; they had finished.

The man was on the bed, but the woman, completely naked, was across the room in front of the sink, with her back to me, apparently washing her crotch. She came back to the bed, lay down beside him, and they talked. I had failed to see what I had bored the hole to see, and I thought -- now I have a problem. I realized that at night if a light was on in one room and not in the other, the hole would blaze brilliantly. And declare what I had done. A little piece of paper, darkened with ink, crumpled up, and carefully plugged into the hole would prevent that. I was about to plug the hole when activity on the other side recommenced. This time I saw a confirmation of my classmate's story of a "dong" going into a "hole." This spectacle didn't present itself very often, but there were other occasions when I spied on lovers, or perhaps a whore and her john. And so far as I was ever aware, no one noticed the bored hole in the door panel.

DAD AND AUNT MAY

It was a good thing I had some friends. Most days I saw little of Dad, who went off to work in the morning as I went off to school. I had the rest of the afternoon and evening free, but Dad seldom got back until after I'd had my supper. He'd read the newspaper and would often comment on some item. My earliest awareness of politics derives from these conversations. He talked to me as a person, not as a child.

It was 1928, and Al Smith, Governor of New York State, was running for the presidency of the United States on the Democratic Party ticket. I wasn't yet interested in politics. Dad told me he voted for Al Smith, not because he was Catholic, but because as governor of New York he had done some things to help poor people. Eventually I also favored the Democrats – at least some of them – for the same reason; their record as a political party, though mixed, was better than that of the Republicans in regard to voting for policies that helped common people. As a one-time owner of a small business, one might have expected that Dad would have leaned toward the Republican Party, which was the party that claimed to promote the interests of industries and businesses in general, but Dad's father and brother Jack were workers, and he himself had been an employee as a young man, and now after bankruptcy was again an employee.

Sometimes on a Sunday we would go to Forest Park and have a picnic lunch, or he might take me to a matinee movie. We developed a comfortable relationship. He was my best friend as well as my father. Dad never lifted his hand to chastise me though I may have deserved it on occasion; he never even raised his voice when he was annoyed, as when I forgot to get his shirts from the Chinese laundry. When I became a father, I looked back and wondered how he could have kept his calm. He was a better father than I managed to be.

Though I was left on my own a great deal of the time – an arrangement that suited me – I did get to know Dad and something of the outline of his life. In the decade prior to my father's birth in 1886, Thomas Edison was experimenting to invent the electric light bulb, but the house on Congress Street in Springfield where Dad grew up still had gaslights. The Great Age of Railroads, that had dominated much of the nineteenth century, was coming to an end, but Dad's father worked twelve-hour shifts in a locomotive as a fireman, shoveling coal into the furnace. Draft horses provided the only public transport in town, but "horseless carriages" — soon shortened to "cars" — appeared when he was still in his teens, and before his business went bankrupt, he owned a Pierce Arrow touring car, but he told me he was never completely comfortable driving it. Airplanes also became familiar in his youth, but he never flew in one. Lindbergh flew across the Atlantic in 1927, the year Dad's business went bankrupt.

The growth of these technologies characterizes the generations of our lives as father and son in time sequences. I never saw gaslights; I took automobiles for granted and owned several at different times; and flying has been indispensable to complete trips on my schedule. Actually the acceleration of technological change seems to have had little direct impact on Dad's life. What was more intrusive was the development of the economy that forced small enterprises to merge or disappear. Chain stores with branches in many towns and cities made nearly impossible the survival of individually owned stores. His lifetime was a time of rapid changes, and after he died the changes would continue and intensify.

Dad's schooling, only eight years, was limited, but he was a reader of newspapers and magazines. I do not remember seeing him with a book in his hands, but perhaps he read a few when he had time. At any rate, his vocabulary sometimes surprised me. He said that a cup of coffee in the morning loosened the *peristaltic* action and thus encouraged a bowel movement. Once after we ate asparagus at a Sunday dinner (one of the few meals we would have together), he pointed out that it was the *aspergilic* acid in the asparagus that caused the greenish color and peculiar odor of our urine, which I had remarked upon. There were other unusual words, not all referring to physiological matters, that he sprang on me. I never looked them up, though I had a dictionary handy, and I remember these two particularly because I never heard them from anyone else.

We were comfortable with each other, unlike some of my friends who were fearful of their fathers' wrath. Nevertheless, I was cautious in what I told him, and did not confide everything that was going on with me. And perhaps for a similar reason I did not probe him about sensitive subjects, so I did not know him as well as I thought I did. This became evident when he died, as I will recount later.

In Springfield, I was close enough to visit Aunt May. She had visited me regularly while I was at Brightside, and now she set a weekly dinner for the two of us. I was to put on clean clothes and come to her shop, upstairs in the Johnston Bookstore Building just before five o'clock, which was closing time. I made my appearance as precise as I could so there would less likely be a customer in the shop. I hated being introduced to some strange woman who felt required to say some inane thing to me, or about me to my aunt. It was less likely to avoid the woman hired to do some of the sewing, under Aunt May's direction, of the hats that my aunt designed specifically for each individual customer. But at least this woman, after a while, was no longer a stranger and mere greetings sufficed.

I was once introduced to Mr. Johnson, the owner of the building, who made little impression on me except that he was the father of the captain of the yacht *Yankee* then sailing in the South Seas and wrote stories published every once in a while in the Sunday Supplement to one of the Springfield newspapers. The *Yankee*'s crew was unpaid, college students who went for the fun of (free) travel. I fantasized that one day I might be one of them. I had already found Joshua Slokum's *Around the World Alone*, and would read many another small boat sailor's account of travels. That idea was destined to remain a fantasy, though I would see some of the Pacific islands from a U.S. Navy ship during World War II, an event still unimaginable to me at the time.

Aunt May might take me to a restaurant. If she did, she would inform me about polite table manners, which fork to use with which course, and so on. If I were invited to a meal in someone's home, she instructed me that if I was offered a second helping, it was permissible to accept "just a morsel," but if a third helping was offered, I was to say, "No, thank you. I have had a sufficiency." She gave me the money to pay the check. "You're the man. It is appropriate you should pay." This sounds old fashioned now, but I paid attention because I was happy to know that she was promoting my chances of succeeding in a difficult world.

More often we would go to her apartment. It was a three-room apartment on Bryar Street, with a window overlooking the section of the Springfield Armory grounds where the Colonel's house stood, just visible atop a hill, but the glory of the view was a magnificent spreading tree that stood grandly in isolation on a wide grass sward. She would buy something on the way. Schirmerhorn's Deli was a favorite place to shop for ingredients for the evening meal. Then in her tiny kitchen she would cook our dinner. We met on Thursdays because that was the evening we could hear "The Little Theater Off Times Square" on the radio. That was the best drama program on the air at that time. We settled into comfortable upholstered chairs as the announcer said, "The first nighters are hurrying down the aisle. The curtain is about to rise." Each week we listened to a new story, the same actors playing the parts. Often Aunt May would send me off with a bag of fruit. Sometimes she would loan me a book; one that I remember was André Maurois' biography of Shelley.

Once when Aunt May went to New York City to buy supplies of hat-making materials for her millinery shop, she took me with her. She had done this with at least one of Uncle Jack's daughters and with my sister Ruth, but I think I was the only one of her nephews to be so privileged. We stayed at the Commodore Hotel near Grand Central station where the train arrived, and that evening I was taken to the theater. Impossible now to tell what the play was, but what remains vivid is the excitement of being in a theater and seeing live actors on the stage. It was enough to eclipse the radio dramas. The following day I traipsed along beside Aunt May as she went to a section with suppliers of ribbons, fabrics, buttons, feathers, and materials of all sorts for making hats. She was well known to her suppliers, to whom I was introduced, and the men or women would take a moment from the business to say something patronizing to the child.

It was Aunt May who enlightened me about my paternal family background. Her father, Patrick MacCaul, was born in Ulster, and came to the U.S. with only four years of schooling, yet in his seventies he was devoted to reading, especially Shakespeare. He read without glasses, but holding the book out at arms' length, indicating, I realized later, that he was far-sighted as am I, and was an inveterate reader as I was then becoming.

Her oldest sibling was Patrick junior, who went off to the Spanish American War and returned, but not to Springfield; he sent greetings to her from Ohio at Christmas. I wondered if something happened to him during the war that prompted him to avoid his home, but got no further information. She was the next born, and then Dad. Patrick junior kept the Scottish spelling of his name, but she, my father, Jack, and Francis had their spelling "corrected" by the nuns when they went to school. Francis was the "baby" of the family. He was an alcoholic, and worked when sober as a dishwasher in restaurants, but sooner or later would lose every job by going on a binge.

Aunt May would give him some money to get himself cleaned up and find another job. She did not want him to come to her shop, so he had to phone her and she would meet him somewhere over a cup of coffee and slip her gift to him, or she would give me an envelope to relay to him. None of my siblings apparently ever saw Uncle Frank, and I saw him only on a few occasions. His obscurity was not because his siblings were ashamed of him as much as his own seeking privacy, probably an expression of his own feeling of shame. Uncle Frank, both Dad and Aunt May said, was the smartest one in the family. They did not criticize Frank for being a "drunk," but I was warned of the dangers of drink.

At a family gathering a few years ago, I told my brothers and sisters that our Grandfather MacCaul was a Presbyterian and that Dad and Aunt May were brought up Catholic because their mother, née Neally, was Catholic. As part of the wedding agreement Grandfather had allowed her, as her church required, to bring up the children in her faith. When I alluded to this, there was an outcry of disbelief. None of them had heard such a story, but I said I had been told that by Aunt May. Why had she not told them? I do not remember when I heard about this mixed marriage, but I suspect it was when I was having doubts about Catholic dogma when I was in junior high school. None of my siblings had ever set eyes on Uncle Frank; they were not privy to as many family secrets.

Grandma Neally MacCaul came from a family that was in America before the Revolutionary War. I had known that Grandpa MacCaul was an immigrant, and counted myself as a third generation American, but that was accurate only in a strictly patrilinear descent system, as an anthropologist would say. At the time, I had no contact with my mother's family, the Sweeney's, but my mother was more than a third generation American. Her grandmother was born on a farm in Easthampton, Massachusetts. And my father's mother was more than third generation.

On her mother's side, Aunt May said, one of our ancestors had come over in colonial times, before the War of Independence, which would put that progenitor at least as early as the eighteenth century, perhaps even earlier. There were some relatives who were not Irish, but English, e.g. Phelps, and some who were perhaps Dutch, or at least a name that I recall because it seemed peculiar to be in our family tree, Van Allen. She also said that one of these ancestors had been a governor of Massachusetts. If the one who was a governor was also the one named Phelps, that would put him in the seventeenth century, and make him the one who, despite opposition by Cotton Mather, put a stop to the Salem executions of "witches." That would be an illustrious ancestor to have, but the connection is very iffy.

Aunt May even told me stories of her own early years. It seemed surprising to me, looking at my elderly aunt, to hear her talk about herself as a girl with another girl joking and laughing on the street, a demeanor not approved of by elders at the time.

Aunt May had a retirement plan. She would buy a small farm in Vermont when she closed her millinery shop, and she suggested that she and I would run it when I graduated from high school. That never happened. The idea came from a book, popular during the depression, called *Five Acres and Independence*. Keeping a mating pair of pigs, a few chickens, some honey bees, and raising some vegetables, it was possible to provide most of the family's food, and basic necessities not obtainable from the five acres could be purchased from the sale of the surplus of what was raised on the farm.

During my time at the orphanage and while I was living in hotels, Aunt May and Dad were the only adult relatives whom I could see on a regular basis, and from whom I received comfort and advice. Aunt May was my godmother; Dad was her favorite brother she once told me, and I was his oldest son, but none of this required her to give me the quantities of time, or bear the expenses she shouldered for things I needed — new clothes, school books, etc. (until dad's income became adequate) — and things I didn't have a physical need for but were in my best interests: affection and instruction in the ways of society as she understood them.

Escaping from Sacred Heart

Sister Francis Edward had called the Boys' Club a "godless institution" because it was not Catholic; it allowed Protestants and Jews to join. She would shortly afterward call the Springfield Public Library a "godless institution." The occasion was another time I had to stay after school and write on the blackboard, this time that I would not talk in class. I had a tendency to whisper comments on a lecture to the student in the seat in front of me. Leaning forward, his ear was not far from my mouth, and I would whisper inanities meant to be amusing to him.

While I was writing, I was telling Sister about something I had read in a book.

I recounted how a people with chariots, called "Aryans," invaded India. "Where did you find that book?" she wanted to know. The answer was: "In the North End Library."

The reason it was a "godless" institution was because it was teaching heresy. The Arian heresy.

"No 'ster," I said. "Not A-R-I-A-N. They were A-R-Y-A-N. They lived in 1500 BC."

This did not satisfy her. "The spelling is not important. You should not be reading about heretics."

Had she not heard? Or catch the date? Or did she so quickly react to the temerity of my contradiction of her, my teacher, that she formed her next statement before I finished talking?

"But 'ster! They could not be heretics. They lived before Christ."

Whatever the case, she sternly repeated, "Do not go to those godless institutions." That she did not know about the Indo-European invaders of India surprised me. In retrospect, one must admit that she did not need to know something that was not on the sixth grade curriculum, but I might have hoped for a teacher with a little curiosity. Why was I telling her anyway? It must be more because I am loquacious than that I thought she'd be interested. She never talked to us about anything except grammar, arithmetic, and catechism.

This incident provided a major motivation for my wish to transfer to the public school. I had become acquainted with some kids who went to Chestnut Street Junior High School, and what I heard from them made me feel that that was the school for me.

When the next school year began, I did not go to the classroom to which I had been assigned, but to Sister Superior's office to ask for transfer papers. "My father wants me to go to Chestnut Street Junior High," I announced. That was a partial truth. I had told Dad I wanted to go there; he asked why, and I said, "I can take Latin and French and they have shop classes, none of which are offered at Sacred Heart."

"You want to take shop?" That surprised him. Dad did not have any tools and rather prided himself on his lack of skills with them. "I'd hit my fingernail, not the metal nail if I had to use a hammer," I had heard him proclaim. I later decided his stance was an aspect of his having "risen" from the working class status of his father and brothers to become a businessman. Without his example, and lacking tools or opportunity, I was as inexperienced in anything mechanical as he was. Why the sudden interest? Actually, there was no interest; shop was one of the things the public school had that this particular parochial school did not, so I added it to the list to make it more substantial. I did want to begin studying languages; that much was real.

"You're getting a good education from the sisters," Dad parried. I didn't tell him of my doubts on that subject. Aside from Sister Francis Edward's confusion of Aryan with Arian, I didn't know how I would be able to substantiate a counter argument.

"Irene would not approve your going to a public school." This statement told me two things: one, he did not object, and two, he would prefer to avoid any protest from Irene. I hadn't thought of my stepmother in connection with my decision to switch from a Catholic school to a "godless institution." I had seen her only a few times since we all left Westfield. While in Holyoke and in Brightside I had not had a visit from her, which is understandable (she had her hands full with other responsibilities), and in the year and some months I'd been living in Springfield, she had become to me a distant relative who lived in another town. She had invited Dad and me to dinner at her mother's house on Thanksgiving, Christmas, and Easter, but it wasn't her house -- it was her mother's, and that woman was old and sometimes grumpy, and I'm convinced she didn't like Dad, blaming him, rather than the economy, for his bankruptcy. In short, I had forgotten about Irene as having anything essential to do with me. That she didn't want me to go to the school I wanted struck me as an irrelevancy. But if Dad was concerned, perhaps I needed some support. I asked Aunt May the next Thursday when we were having dinner what she thought of my going to Chestnut Street public school and studying Latin and French.

"Marvelous!" She approved of learning languages, and gave me her encouragement. Catholic versus public was never mentioned, nor was shop or Irene. I told Dad that Aunt May thought my idea was a good one. Dad took Aunt May's opinions seriously, but I knew he still was concerned with what Irene would say. When I told Sister Superior my father wanted me to go to Chestnut Street Junior High, I believed it was qualifiedly correct.

"Tell your father to come and see me. Now go to your class."

That evening I said nothing about the request for him to see the Sister Superior. I knew she would try to talk him out of letting me transfer, and was afraid she might convince him. Next morning, I again confronted Sister Superior. "My father is busy this week. He said," I prevaricated, "to give me my transfer now. He'll come to see you next week."

"That is fine. Go to your class and we'll talk about your best interest when your father comes to see me."

I walked out of her office, knowing she would not give me transfer papers unless my father asked for them, and if he did come to ask, she would probably give him a hard time and he might not stand up to her. So I continued right out of the school, hurried a few blocks north on Chestnut Street and entered the public junior high school. I was far from sure that this was going to work. I half expected I'd be sent back to Sacred Heart — after all, I had no transfer paper. Never having been in the building before, I did not know where to go but saw a door with a glass window with PRINCIPAL'S OFFICE lettered on it. I opened it and saw a woman behind a counter.

"My father wants me to come to this school but Sister Superior at Sacred Heart won't give me my transfer."

"What is that?" the woman asked.

I repeated word for word what I had said. I had been going over those words all the way from Sacred Heart to the public school building.

"Just a moment. I will get the principal." She knocked and went through another door. After a few minutes, during which I sweated, the door opened and a man came out and stood across from me on the other side of the counter. It happened that he was standing directly under a light in the ceiling and it shone on his bald pate and rimless eyeglasses. He seemed inordinately tall and his face looked stern. "What is it you said to my secretary?"

For the third time I said aloud my refrain.

"Go to Room 37 and tell Miss Chase you are a new pupil. I will get your transfer." He hadn't smiled but he no longer seemed stern. That was the last I heard of a need for transfer papers. I never had occasion to speak to the principal again. Mr. Cannon always looked stern, but I knew he was good-hearted.

I looked through the glass in the upper half of the door to Room 37 and saw that a class was in session. I hesitated, wondering if I should intrude, but Mr. Cannon must have known that a class was in progress when he directed me to come up here, so I barged in, saying, "Excuse me. The principal told me to tell you I'm your new pupil."

Miss Chase, a tall red-haired woman in her late thirties, interrupted what she was saying to the class, and turned to me.

"What is your name?" she inquired, in a pleasant welcoming tone.

I told her.

"Take a seat, Daniel. We will work out your schedule later."

There were three or four empty places; I sat in one. The class resumed, but not for long. A bell in the hallway rang loudly indicating that the class was over. All of the students except me grabbed their books and papers, got up, all talking at once in relief at the end of the period, and left the room to go to their next class. This was different from Sacred Heart where a nun simply shifted from one subject to another while the children remained seated in the same room.

"Now, Daniel," said Miss Chase, "let us begin to find out what you will be studying. You must take English, Math, History, and General Science, which meet three times a week, plus Civics, Art, and Music, which each meet only once a week. Then there are electives from which you can choose as many as the remaining time will allow. Different kinds of shop and several languages are available."

I had known about electives from what I had heard from kids in the neighborhood who went to public school; it was basic to the reason I was determined to transfer to public school, but I was uncertain about the options. "I want to take languages," I blurted out.

"General Language is a requirement for other language courses. We can put you in that class now. Next year you can choose Latin, French, or German."

Children were coming into the room and taking their seats.

"I have to take a shop class," I added quickly to get that in before the next music class began. The "have to" for shop was in contrast to the "want" in regard to languages. I thought I "had to" because I had told my father that it was one of the offerings in public school of which I wanted to take advantage. Miss Chase explained that there were three shop classes: metal working; woodworking; and auto mechanics. "I will get one of the shop teachers to take you around so you can see something of each before you make your choice. You didn't really hear much at the end of the last hour, so you may as well stay here for now." Then she rose to begin the new class.

I watched her use a hand-held device that held several pieces of chalk to draw parallel lines all at once on the blackboard. She pulled the chalk across most of the length of the blackboard and then again a second set of rows a little below the first set of lines. Then she drew a design at the left end of the upper set of lines and explained, "This is the treble clef." Next she began putting notes of different kinds on the lines or the spaces between them, explaining the concepts as she went. I was fascinated by the clever little chalk holder that drew equally spaced lines all with one movement of the hand (I had never seen one before), but I have to confess I never mastered reading music. As soon as she had a tune on the blackboard, she led us in singing it, indicating with a pointer the notes as we sang.

As I would find out on other days, we might listen to recorded music after introductory remarks about composers and their musical styles, and there would be subsequent comments and questions from the teacher after the piece was finished. Music class was enjoyable, and may have had some effect on my preferences in listening: classical in preference to popular, but my education in music never went much beyond what I absorbed in seventh grade.

At the end of the hour, Miss Chase told me the number of the room where I would find the General Language class. This was an introductory course that gave us the fundamentals of linguistics (though as far as my memory goes that term was never mentioned). It was the right way to start out and I have always been glad that Springfield public schools in 1929 already had this in the system. Actually the overview was limited to Indo-European languages, and basically to Latin, Romance and Germanic languages, along with some mention of classical Greek.

My first day at public school, and I was already engaged in the pursuit of becoming a polyglot. It was a happy day. I was delighted with the success of my scheme to escape from Sacred Heart and become a student at Chestnut Street Public Junior High School.

"Polyglot" was an exaggeration. I'm not sure I even knew the word at that time, but I already had the concept and held to it as a goal. Actually, I was on my way to becoming bilingual. What I learned of Latin was important as a background for other words (e.g. inter*rogate*), but French is the only other language I eventually felt at ease in speaking despite playing around with several other languages. While I imagined myself ultimately speaking several languages, I had no model for a polyglot.

The first polyglot I ever observed was Boris Goldofsky, years later, when I was an undergraduate at Boston University, an occasional usher at his New England Opera Theater, and once even a "spear carrier" on stage when the story called for a crowd. Backstage I watched opera goers come to congratulate

Goldofsky on the success of a newly translated opera for the N.E.O.T. He answered in English, Yiddish, Russian, and I think other tongues too, switching from one to another as the crowd around him surged in to speak to him. Count Vinigi Grottanelli, who decades later became a friend, was an anthropologist and a curator in the Pigorini Museum in Rome. He invited me to the opening of an exhibit and I watched as people came to speak to him. He was completely fluent in Spanish, French, German, English, and of course Italian. He and his brother, he told me, had had tutors in one language after another until they were competent in these five. "But didn't you gradually forget a language you didn't have an occasion to speak?" I was imagining a childhood more confined to a single lingual environment. "Oh," he said, "we had relatives in these other countries and we visited them and they visited us, so we were called on from time to time to converse in the other languages, and of course we read the European literature recommended to us." Aristocratic families, being a relatively small number in the national population, often arranged international marriages with individuals from aristocratic families in other countries, and maintained connection with relatives at longer degrees than ordinary persons are likely to do.

That elite system provided an easy way to become a polyglot; but my family had no international connection and, other than French, I bumped into other national forms of speech not as a child but as an adult, without a family-provided tutor. I struggled on by my own efforts to try to find comprehension in a muddle of sounds. For anyone with connections in foreign lands, learning a language spoken there was an *entrée* into that other society, whereas for a poor kid who lived in a mid-sized town in New England there was little to be gained by acquiring fluency in another language. There were, it is true, persons in Springfield who spoke other languages, but they were recent immigrants who if they were numerous enough, clustered in a selected neighborhood and might be unfriendly to outsiders. The South End of the city was dominated by Italians, and the boys on those streets often liked to pick fights with boys from other sections of the city. Boys from the North End, where I lived, tended to avoid the South End. Thus, neither locally nor internationally was learning to speak a foreign language an advantage.

One reason I found languages an attraction was wondering what information was concealed from me in the strange words. For me the linguistic challenge was just a hurdle to be overcome in order to get at the semantic content of the document or literary form. My brother Robert told me that when he became a Catholic priest, he spent a year at the Vatican where priests from various language backgrounds, who might not speak Italian, could converse with each other in Latin. Aside from that year, his career was wholly in the United States, so he generally had no need of that conversational ability in a supposedly "dead" language, but I find it interesting that he was able to utilize Latin as a vehicle of communication and not solely as a set of ritual responses to be said in church during the celebration of Mass.

The only other member of my family who became bilingual was my youngest sister, Barbara, who studied French at Our Lady of the Elms College, in Chicopee, Massachusetts, and later spent a year in France teaching American soldiers, stationed there after World War II, to understand and speak the local language.

My own chaotic experience with language was to struggle with whatever language I confronted wherever I found myself. These were consecutively Yiddish, Russian, Japanese (briefly), Spanish, German, Twi and Dagarti (in Africa), Moroccan Arabic, Italian, Greek, Flemish (reading only) and minimally Turkish. With English that makes a baker's dozen; some were more successful than others. Several were temporary efforts and didn't get far, but coping with different languages was a continuous part of my life. Linguistics, as a discipline, became one of my tools in dealing with the problem of comprehending peculiar ways of speaking. A measure of progress in this effort: I reviewed books in German and Italian as well as in French. On a walking trip with my daughter in northern Spain, I read the newspaper *El Pais*, which she could not do. But she could speak with people we met less haltingly than I in a language she had never studied but had picked up in New Orleans from people she hired to work in her ceramic studio making Mardi Gras masks.

CHAPTER THREE

CHESTNUT STREET
JUNIOR HIGH SCHOOL

Parochial schools gave me a foundation in grammar and arithmetic, but they had not stimulated in me an eagerness to acquire knowledge. My schooling -- in the sense of accumulation of information -- began first in the public library and then in the public junior high school. Every teacher I had at Chestnut Street remains in my memories. The reason is because each one aroused an eager excitement as I was led into new realms of learning.

There was some continuity from the earlier schools I had attended. After all, school was school. I had always had an inclination to direct *sotto voce* comments on the lecture to the pupil in front of me. At Sacred Heart I had had to write one hundred times on the blackboard "I will not talk in class unless called on." But that hadn't cured me. The difference now was that a girl, instead of a boy, was sitting in front of me. Whatever I said is now long forgotten, but what the teacher said when she noticed me in the act is still vivid in my memory: "Daniel! Tell the class what you whispered in Katherine's pretty pink ear." I sat back in my seat, red-faced and silent. This embarrassment broke me of the habit of talking when I shouldn't have been.

Katherine remains only a name engraved in my memory because of that event.

I had told Miss Chase that I wanted to study languages, and that I "had" to take a shop class. I chose woodworking and made something, I have no idea now what, and remember it mainly because I took it to show Dad, validating my alleged interest in shop courses. I think it was a birdhouse: what would we do with a birdhouse in the hotel? I remember proudly showing it to Dad. It satisfied what I considered a sort of promise I'd made to him, who didn't, I'm now convinced, care if I took shop or not.

In later years, I realized I should have taken automobile mechanics; that might have helped me when my second-hand car broke down in the "bush" far from a town in West Africa. But I looked into the auto shop and was not attracted to what I saw, whereas I felt comfortable with wood. This feeling for wood remained dormant for decades, but was reawakened in Africa as I watched a sculptor hack away chunks from a log with an adze to create a wondrous figure. I asked the carver if I could buy an adze from him. "Not from me! What would I do without it? I couldn't earn a living." I should have asked a blacksmith, but didn't get around to buying an adze, being involved in pursuit of my research. Some years after that I did do some wood carving: imitation African masks, and imitation Reimenschneider, a late Gothic, South German wood sculptor, whose works I saw in a Munich museum.

What I really wanted to study was languages. Latin had been thrown at me while at Sacred Heart: I had been designated to report to the curate who would teach me the responses an altar boy gives to the priest during certain stages in the celebration of the Mass, but that experience was frustrating because the priest did not want to bother to explain the meaning of the phrases I was supposed to memorize. *Introibo ad altare Dei,* one phrase began, and it was so easy to translate that I guessed it meant, "I enter to the altar of God." Other phrases were more opaque. I told the priest I would not make any effort to remember gibberish words and that if he wouldn't teach me the meanings of the Latin, I would not become an altar boy. I never did become an altar boy. This particular priest's refusal helped spur me to find a real Latin class.

Mrs. Tenant, my Latin teacher, was on the verge of retirement, and I suppose the burden of years had taken a toll. If she ever had a sense of humor, there was little of it left. She was sad rather than stern in appearance. When in second year Latin we read Julius Caesar's *Commentarii de Bello Gallico,* I was as interested in understanding the story as in translating it. When Caesar said he made his army move for a certain number of days at "forced march" and our edition had a note giving the number of miles per day covered at normal march and how many at forced, I calculated how many miles he had gained and plotted on a map where he reached, and where he would have been otherwise. The difference seemed impressive to me, and substantiated the reported surprise of the Gauls. I tried to tell Mrs. Tenant of my findings, but she chided me for wasting the class's time with inessential talk. Grammar and vocabulary was the focus; she had no time for the historical or literary content of the text.

Perhaps she viewed me as a student who was frivolous. In first year Latin, our book began each chapter with a vocabulary list of new words that would be used in this chapter; next was an exercise in grammar, introducing another grammatical feature.

Once one had gone over these, it was easy to read what followed. Sometimes it might be necessary to look back to earlier chapters, but not often if one had internalized the previous lessons.

My method of doing the assignment was to look at the new vocabulary and go over the designated pages for the sense of the text. If it was interesting, I would go further, but I never bothered to write the English interlineally as many students did; in fact, that was standard practice. With several classes to prepare for, it is not surprising that when classroom recitation came, I didn't always have all the vocabulary down pat and having no "trot" in front of me, I would have to improvise. When someone was called on to give the interpretation of a paragraph, he or she would read their handwritten English. When I was called on, I had to sight translate the Latin, relying on whatever vocabulary was securely in my memory and the sense I'd made of the passage prior to class. Once I came to the phrase *rex rogat*. The context indicated that the king was angry, but I wasn't quite able to recall the meaning of *rogat,* so I tried, "the king roared." The roaring, though more restrained than the king's in my version, came from the class that erupted in laughter. Everyone knew from his or her written trots that the king had merely "asked." I never after failed to recognize this root in inter*rogate* or *rogatory.* I got good marks in Latin, but I think my teacher's perception of me was founded on incidents like this.

Mlle. Roy, on the other hand, was younger and enthusiastic and was happy to supplement the French language with details of French culture. She spent her summers traveling in France and came back with posters of various localities that she put up on the walls of her classroom. We read silly little stories, *Mère*

Barbarin and *Tartarin de Tarescon*, etc., but in our second year we read some Victor Hugo, for whom, as I later learned in my travels, a street in virtually every town in France is named. Mlle. Roy told us -- in English with an interlarding of French expressions -- stories about France that developed in me a desire to see the country. This introduction to French things made me feel that France was my second home. That feeling has remained for life and I have spent more time in France than in any other European country. Mlle. Roy's enthusiasm was contagious, for me at least, but I took to languages with an enthusiasm of my own, and French class helped me get through Latin where the teacher was not so inspiring.

I recognized from first impression that Miss Chase, my homeroom teacher, was a kindhearted woman. I saw her every morning when attendance was taken, but otherwise only once a week in music class. Teacher would call on someone to pass out the books. One day, she called on me to do this task. I took the armful of books with paper covers, handed one to each pupil and, when I came to the empty seat I had just vacated, put the book then on the top of the pile on my chair, one with a torn cover. Miss Chase noticed and called the class's attention to my having treated myself without favor. "Other pupils shift through the books to give themselves one of the newer ones, but Daniel accepted the old tattered one." I recognized this as praise but was surprised because the condition of the cover was unimportant. I did not as yet own any books, but I had handled many in the public library and read quite a few. What was important was the content, not the cover. My personal library, now that I have one, has always had some second-hand paperbacks that are in bad shape, but I don't throw them out because I treasure the information they contain.

I saw more of other teachers because most courses met three days a week. Yet I remember Miss Chase with affection, in part because I did eventually see her outside school. She and another unmarried teacher shared a house; the other teacher was Miss Steele, the science teacher, and she was the one who invited me.

What Miss Steele taught was not entirely, but largely, the naturalist's view of our environment. She had a number of wire cages, glass walled terrariums, and fish bowls. "Who would like to feed the squirrel?" was the first thing I remember her saying. A mother squirrel had been run over by an automobile and the baby squirrel needed to grow before it could survive on its own. Some boy had been feeding it but had been bitten. The baby squirrel had sharp teeth. I raised my hand. It was the only one in the air. No one seemed eager to volunteer. A tiny *squirrel* was a dangerous animal! Every day thereafter I went to the science classroom and fed the hungry beast. I did get bitten a few times but learned to be careful.

There was an empty terrarium. On a weekend, I went out in some woods and found a snake slithering along. I was prepared with a forked stick, and thrust the two prongs into the earth on either side of the snake's head. It was then safe to pick it up just behind the head and put it in a bag. This was a technique I learned, not from the *The Indian How Book,* but from Ernest Thompson Seton, a naturalist and prolific author of books for young readers. I found his works in the library. It would have been fairly safe to pick up that snake without the forked stick because it was not a poisonous variety. On Monday I brought the bagged snake to school and it was put in the terrarium.

I now used the North End Library, not as large as the Carnegie Library on State Street, but it must have covered a range of subjects since this is where I read about the Aryans -- the topic that upset Sister Francis Edwards -- and in addition to Thompson Seton's books, I found Hendrik van Loon's self-illustrated books, H.G. Wells' *Outline History of Mankind*, and a series on all the sciences, presenting a current state of the fields in anticipation of the Century of Progress World Fair to be held in Chicago in 1933. I didn't understand everything in the science books but persisted to the end of each volume anyway. I never gave up reading fiction, but I began to have a heavy emphasis on non-fiction.

The series of books on the sciences served me well. One day Miss Steele drew a hexagon on the blackboard and then wrote some letters that did not form words at the corners of the hexagon; the letters represented chemical elements. "Does anyone know what this represents?" she asked the class. My hand was the only one to go up. She called on me, and I said, "Amino acid."

"And what is an amino acid?" she continued.

"The substance from which the protein in our bodies is made," I answered.

There were two consequences to this exchange. One was that Miss Steele took note of me and arranged for me to have an I.Q. test. The other consequence was that a boy in the class who fooled around with chemicals in experiments in his cellar wondered how someone in his class knew something about chemicals he hadn't known. This was John E. Fitzgerald. I was unaware of his reaction to my answer to the teacher's question; it would take another event, which I will relate in due course, before we became friends. Then we soon became inseparable.

As it happened the house Miss Chase and Miss Steele shared was on the outskirts of the city and there were woods behind the house. There were squirrels, chipmunks, rabbits, and birds that they delighted to watch. Because of my participation in discussions in Miss Steele's science class, she invited me to visit on a Saturday and explore the woods near her house. With binoculars one could identify birds too distant to make out clearly with the naked eye. I was also told how to recognize the songs of various birds. One said its name, "Bob White, Bob White." Another had two notes repeated three times, and I was encouraged to hear this as "Look up! Treetop! See me!" Living in the city, I didn't see or hear these birds again for a long time. Not having binoculars, even when I was in a wooded place, I could seldom see the bird that was singing. I often afterwards, when I could no longer recall the markings of the bird that made a particular song, thought of that day. I never became a bird-watcher, but I am grateful for the kindness of these dedicated teachers who introduced me to the pleasure.

Something that did stick with me: I was shown how to identify a number of trees by their leaves or by the type of bark and conifers by their needles. The main purpose of the visit to the teachers, however, was to stay till dark so Miss Steele could identify for me constellations of stars in the nighttime sky. I had asked why they had names of characters in Greek stories, such as Cassiopeia, which I had read balanced the Big Dipper, and when the latter was not visible, could be used to locate the North Star. Later when I was in college and had a summer job as a counselor in a camp for children, one of the things I did was take a bunch of kids on walks in the woods and have them feel the different kinds of bark on the trees and show them the variety of leaves; also on an evening I'd have a cluster of children around me lying on blankets on the grass while with a flashlight's beam I pointed out constellations and told stories of why the ancient Greeks gave them the names we know them by. That Saturday, the two teachers fed me lunch and dinner. This was the first but not the last time teachers gave me, outside class time, extra instruction.

FIRST DOUBTS

One day leaving school I was walking with Joseph Burns, who was called "Fat" Burns. He was not fat, solid rather, but chunky enough to make the epithet not too ridiculous. Someone had tagged him with it, apparently for the double entendre, and everyone called him that. "Do you accept what Miss Steele said about Darwin and evolution?" Burns asked in reference to the day's lesson.

"Yeah. Sounds plausible."

"Do you believe in Adam and Eve?"

"Of course."

"You fool! You can't believe in both!"

I think I must have stopped in my tracks. I was stunned. I had long since just accepted uncritically the oft-told story of "our first parents." Somehow the biblical account never came to mind when I listened to the theory propounded by Charles Darwin. That may not be so surprising. Catholics -- those days anyway -- were not encouraged to read the Bible as Protestants usually were; we got our scripture from the mouths of priests and (if you were a child) from nuns. Now I realized there was a conflict. This must be why the nuns called public schools a "godless institution." I would have to put one of these explanations of human origin in relation to the other, which meant choose one and reject the other. But it was not that extreme. I went to confession and after reciting my sins, told the priest my confusion about evolution and the Bible. He gave me a pamphlet by Rev. Daniel J. Lord, put out by the Paulist Press, which stated one could, if one wished, accept the idea of evolution if one added to Darwin's theory the reasonable step that made us truly God's children, namely that God breathed a soul into human beings but not into animals. This satisfied me for a time.

I went to 8 o'clock mass on Sundays, the children's mass (some parents or others also attended) as I had before leaving Sacred Heart and would see kids I knew. They all sat together and I had to find a seat away from the parochial school rows. It was clear that I was now a pariah; Sister Francis Edward enforced a ban on talking to me after mass -- at least in her sight. In an effort to prove that I "kept the faith" despite the warning by Sister Superior that I would lose my religion and end in hell if I went to public school, I also made the novena that I would have made had I still been at Sacred Heart.

In March, the Sacred Heart students were required to attend 7 o'clock mass each morning for nine days, a novena, and each class filled designated pews. The Sister who taught the class sat next to the aisle in the last row of pews occupied by her class, so she could survey them all and kept them quiet and attentive. If they were not, she might get up and tap with her clapper (a wooden instrument that made a clicking noise when pressed, used to call attention when there was any disruption) on the head of the offending child.

During my first year in public school, I attested, by my presence throughout the daily masses for the novena in the early mornings, that I was still a good Catholic. The pews down front were filled with Sacred Heart pupils; the other pews had few adults, mostly elderly women, and hardly any children, so my presence was easily noted. Whether I did the same in the second year I am not sure, but by the time I finished junior high I was in effect no longer a practicing Catholic, although to avoid arguments with adults I didn't proclaim this. Dad had always been still asleep on Sunday mornings, the only day he could sleep late, when I had gone off to the 8 o'clock mass, so he didn't observe that I no longer did so.

Some have told me that it was presumptuous of me, at my age and inexperience, to reject dogma that many brilliant persons had examined and found they were able to support. Not denying that it was presumptuous, it is also not surprising: religious conversions, studies by sociologists have found, often occur in adolescence. The reason is that at this time of life, on the verge of adulthood, one makes certain choices of direction for the kind of life one hopes to have, and religions have in their scope attitudes and practices that determine the manner of living. So also does the secular attitude.

It was not the public school as much as the public library that was a contributing cause of my rejection of the Church. There was no sustained pressure in any class on anyone's religious beliefs. Aside from the one class when evolution was discussed, there was little, so far as I can recall, that impinged on religion. But the library had resources to be explored and, if one was interested, there were books on religious as well as scientific topics. As I review the situation from this long after-moment, it seems to me that there was no restriction in my choice of reading. I was now a bit older, and not confined to children's books, or maybe the North End library was more lax in supervision of young borrowers. I am reminded of a title, *The War Between Science and Religion*. It seemed to me to be up-to-date, but I later learned it was published in the nineteenth century when the controversy over Darwin was raging. That didn't matter since my mental state was more or less that of the nineteenth century.

And somewhere I came across the statement: "Doubt is the beginning of wisdom." Taking things on faith does not enlighten one, but questioning may lead to eventual understanding.

POETS, MUSICIANS, AND ATHLETES

Mrs. Frazier, the English teacher, encouraged us to *memorize* poetry. Most students in the class were not even accustomed to *reading* a poem. She recited, without reading, a few poems for us, identifying the poets not only by name but by styles and placed them in time and locality and in the history of American and British literature.

A few snatches of poems were in my head from the early recitations of Aunt May, but now we were required, each of us, to select a poem and "learn it by heart." That may sound to some as the same as learning by rote, but the idiom of having it *in your heart* -- the poem you selected for yourself -- has a connotation of something quite different from mechanical memorization. The poem is more than the useful but unlovable multiplication table. "Heart" is conventionally the locus of love.

If you selected a particular poem and learned it by heart, you must have certain affection for it.

Poetry had not been completely lacking at Sacred Heart. Sister had the class recite with her, one might say chant, the stanzas of a poem. The one that sticks in my head (perhaps it was the only one) is Longfellow's "Evangeline." Keeping pace with Sister, we declaimed in singsong fashion:

> *This is -- the for-est -- pri-me-val,*
> *The mur-mur-ing -- pines and -- the hem-locks...*

Mrs. Frazier preferred to have individual recitation, and coached our presentation to give an emphasis proper to the ideas. She was a small woman and there were some big boys, the "jocks" as they would be called nowadays, in the class, but she got them as well as the scholarly types to recite poems from memory.

For Mrs. Frazier's class I learned Shakespeare's twenty-ninth sonnet. The reason it appealed to me, I didn't realize then but do in retrospect, is that it begins in despair and ends in joy:

> *When in disgrace with fortune and men's eyes,*
> *I all alone beweep my outcaste state*
> *And trouble deaf heaven with my bootless cries,*
> *And look upon myself and curse my fate*

But, then (after a few lines needed for the sonnet's form):

> *Haply I think on thee, and then my state,*
> *Like to the lark at break of day arising*
> *From sullen earth, sings hymns at heaven's gate;*

And, finally:

> *I scorn to change my state with kings.*

I felt that sense of release from despair when I got out of Brightside. That the twentieth-ninth sonnet was a love poem ("for thy sweet love remember'd such wealth brings") I was vaguely aware, but that element did not yet mean much to me; it was the transformation from the depths to the heights that I perceived in it.

Thus began a great number of poems that I took to my heart. But learning poems was not the end of Mrs. Frazier's injunction to us; she asked us to write poetry. The class broke out in groans coming mainly from the "tough" boys in the back of the room. "Do you think poems are for sissies?" she asked. Laughter and sniggers told her that they did. Then she recounted the story of Christopher Marlowe, one of the greatest poets and playwrights of the Elizabethan Age when great poets were plentiful. Marlowe was also a spy for Walsingham, Elizabeth's spymaster, and was killed in a brawl.

"Tough enough for you?"

Then there was Sir Walter Raleigh, swordsman, soldier, sea captain, privateer, explorer, courtier, and *poet*. Did all this have any effect on the targeted boys? Hard to say, but probably not.

Under this benevolent guidance I essayed to compose sonnets, triolets, and other forms of verse. At the time I was pleased with my efforts, and continued blithely into high school still fitting thoughts into measured strophes, but by graduation from high school I had decided that prose was my natural medium.

But long after leaving Chestnut Street Junior High I continued to commit poetry to memory. My tastes changed, matured perhaps, and the music of the sounds of words and the rhythm of phrasing (Poe's "tintinnabulations of the bells, bells, bells") became less a criterion for selection than the sometimes brutal truths (Edna St. Vincent Millay's "I loved you Tuesday; What is that to me? I do not love you Wednesday; That much you can see."), or just the recognition of a familiar feeling (Joaquin Miller's "There is something in October that is native to my blood."). Even today, poetry is likely to bring up in my mind's eye the image of Mrs. Frazier.

My willing participation in poetry exercises, science class, and learning additional languages found its contrast in algebra. I had no trouble with geometry. It is easy to visualize the forms, but algebra was more opaque and my algebra homework was always relegated to after the preparations for other subjects were done, and often enough didn't get completed. I was sent to the narrow cloakroom and sitting there with everyone's coats hanging around me, I had to do last night's homework, and while doing it missed today's lesson. When final exams came, I couldn't do some of the work -- I had missed too much. It was the only subject I didn't pass and my resistance to doing the homework caused me difficulty later when I had to improve my mathematical skill in certain college courses.

One of the few disappointments, perhaps really the only one, came early in my time at Chestnut Street. An announcement notified students who might be interested in joining the band to report after school to the auditorium. Why not? I thought. So I showed up at the appointed time at the designated place and found a small number of students, some with their own instruments. Some of them were juniors or seniors and already members of the band. Those of us who were not members and were not toting instrument cases were asked to raise a hand if we had any experience with an instrument. My hand had to remain limp. Some students claimed to have had some lessons on a string or a wind instrument. One was given a clarinet that was the property of the school to practice on. Others were given other instruments. Finally my turn came. All that was left was a French horn. "I guess it will have to be the French horn," the bandmaster said. "Do you want it?" Of course I did. I didn't know one horn from another anyway.

A little instruction was given me, and I was sent home with the horn and a music book to follow as I practiced. In my room at the hotel, I was out of sight, but not beyond the hearing of others. There must have been complaints. Hortense told me she was sorry but I could not practice the horn in the hotel. I can't blame her or anybody; it must have been awful. That was the end of my musical career, finished before it began.

Never before had I been at a school where there was a gym. Sacred Heart had a playground on each side of the school, for boys on one side, girls on the other, but even if both had been combined there would not have been space adequate for a ball game. We played basketball at Chestnut Street. I was already familiar with the game from the Boys' Club, and did well enough to be asked to be on my class team. We played the two other classes in intramural games, and played our class equivalents at other schools.

My team had a black player. Although I knew him only in school activities, I remember his name for two reasons. One, I thought it a peculiar name because it seemed descriptive: Gentle Walker. If Mr. and Mrs. Walker had picked a different first name for him, one wouldn't think of "walker" as an activity, but with a first name that could be an adverb, it was hard for me, with my literal mind, not to imagine him as ambling leisurely along.

The other reason I remember Gentle Walker is that when we played Forest Park School in their gym, a kid on their team asked in a derisive tone, "How can you have a nigger on your team? How can you stand the smell?" There was a moment of shocked silence. Then I said, with a sniff in his direction, "Look who's talking about smell!" He came at me with fists flailing. There was soon a free-for-all, most of each team joining in support for the one from their team. The two coaches had to break it up.

Our regular gym classes were mainly devoted to tumbling on mats and using parallel bars and the "horse." We also climbed knotted ropes suspended from the high ceiling. The gym teachers also taught us to dance. The girls' gym teacher danced with the boys' gym teacher to demonstrate the steps. Then the boys, lined up along the wall on one side of the gym, were told to cross over to the other side, where the girls were lined up, and ask one of them to dance. This didn't do me much good; it didn't happen often enough for me to really learn. The result was just an awkward few moments. The boys' coach told us to practice with a sister, but I didn't have a sister handy -- my sisters were in another town.

In addition to our coach, we had a college student from Springfield College, where physical education was a specialization, who came as part of his training to help out coaching in a public school. The student coach who came to Chestnut Street when I was there chose to teach us to wrestle. College rules, he informed us, were different from professional wrestling that some of the class might have seen. The latter was a commercial entertainment, he insisted, and a lot of fake torture was put on for the public. What he taught was a sport with regulations that forbade some of the things seen in professional rings.

Responsibility

In my third and final year at Chestnut, my homeroom teacher was one from whom I never took a course. I cannot say what subject she taught, and I fail to dredge up her name, but I can see her face with crow's feet at the eyes and gray hair. She kept me after school. I didn't have to write anything on the blackboard, but I got a talking-to, a gentle consultation. "You have been late too many times," she began. It was true that I had not been in my seat when my name was called as she ran down the alphabetical list to confirm attendance, but I had always been there before the bell rang and everyone scattered to whatever room where the first hour course might be. So she could always report to the office whether I was in school or not. "But that is not the point; you have been late, not once or twice, which I could tolerate, but by being tardy too many times, you show disregard for the rules of the school."

I said nothing. What could I say?

"Do you understand that even though you are a good student as far as your work is concerned, you will impress people as a slacker when it comes to your duties? It is one of your responsibilities as a pupil in this school to follow the rules, and if you do not, you will get a reputation for unreliability that will hurt your chances in life."

I understood her point. I didn't want a reputation that would do me harm, but she seemed to be exaggerating the significance of my fault, not really serious as I saw it. I must have said something like, "it's only a few minutes."

She countered: If every student came in only a few minutes late, there would be chaos. Classes couldn't begin on time. Mr.

Cannon would never be able to say for certain whether or not a particular student was in the school.

Her argument carried the day. She asked me to make a vigorous effort to cultivate the habit of promptness. I would be glad later if I did.

I agreed to try (Aunt May had urged the same thing when I came to meet her at her shop on Thursdays), and I was never late to her class again. This incident is the only memory I have of this teacher.

Despite my great satisfaction with Chestnut Street public school, I wrote an essay that did not win approval by my teachers. Students in each subject were told that Osaka, Japan, was a "sister city" to Springfield, Massachusetts, and the students there had produced a book with essays describing their city, their school, their families, and so on, and sent it to us. It was at the mayor's office, I suppose. I do not remember seeing it. In consequence of this gift, we were encouraged to respond with essays, or drawings, to send to the school children of Osaka.

For my topic I chose the public library. The public library, I asserted, was the primary educational institution in our city. It is true that we have schools and they facilitate learning, but schools have their limitations, because courses are introductory and classes progress slowly due to the number of pupils, whereas in libraries one can choose for one's self and not be restrained, and expand one's learning in any direction.

My essay was not included in the book sent to Osaka. No teacher ever said anything to me about it. I've wondered since what they thought about it. The committee making the selections included most of the teachers who taught me. I hope that they did not see it as denigration of their efforts, but I suppose that is how it must have been perceived. I wasn't mature enough to give as much credit to the excellent system of the Springfield schools as they deserved before going on to laud the virtues of libraries. Probably, also, my demotion of schools to a lesser status than libraries was a lingering feeling about my experience at Sacred Heart.

CHAPTER FOUR

FITZ

It was at Chestnut Street Junior High that John E. Fitzgerald and I became friends. He had been in Sister Francis Edward's class when I was at Sacred Heart, but he went north to his home when he left school and I went west to the hotel, so we never bumped into each other out of school. The difference in our homeward orientation from the public school was the same as at the parochial school, and we were still unacquainted though we knew about each other.

Our friendship came about because of an event outside of school. It was bicycles that brought Fitz and me together. Someone told me about a banged-up bicycle that could be had for nothing. A kid had an accident and didn't want to ride anymore, but the bike, he thought, could be fixed with little expense. A *little* expense might be manageable. I ate in a "greasy spoon" restaurant; if I scrimped on a meal, I could get a little cash, but anything major would be impossible. How much damage had been done to the bike? I couldn't find out until I saw it.

My friend took me to the house of the kid who owned the bike. I didn't know him; it was the father who was there. The kid was in the hospital. The father showed me the bike. It was lying on its side on the lawn outside a garage. From the crumpled way it laid there, it looked badly broken. The front wheel was bent so that it couldn't be rolled along; if I took it I would have to carry it away. It didn't seem something I could get fixed. I thought the front wheel needed replacement and I had no idea how much a wheel would cost, and though much cheaper than a complete bicycle, I knew I didn't have the money.

My friend said, "I know someone who I bet can straighten out that wheel. Let's take it to John Fitz! He'll fix it."

"Who?" I asked.

"John Fitzgerald. He's always fixing things."

Since it was free and the man was happy to get rid of it, we carried the bike several blocks to 44 Lexington, where the Fitzgerald's lived. We found Fitz in his back yard with a tool in his hand tinkering with something. He put aside what he had been doing to look at the mangled bike. "I can fix the wheel. All you need is a few spokes. But the fork is sprung. I can't do anything about that."

Spokes were a matter of a few cents. I managed to buy the spokes with some change that I got from the restaurant by having a few holes punched in my meal ticket and not eating anything, taking the cash instead. The wheel, that I would have described as destroyed, was anything but when it had some new spokes. Fitz tightened one a bit and then another, selecting the one to tighten next based on the remaining twist. Gradually he brought the rim of the wheel back into a perfect circle.

When the wheel was repaired, it would not rotate through the fork without scraping against one side, and Fitz could not straighten out the fork. The fork of a bicycle is the bifurcated metal brace that holds the front wheel and connects that wheel to the rest of the bicycle: an indispensable part of the bike. A new fork was a big problem. It seemed I might have carried the busted bike for several blocks for nothing. Now I'd have to carry it to the dump.

"Might be able to find a fork at the dump," Fitz suggested. We went to the dump. It was a long way but in those impecunious days we were all used to walking a lot, and being young we didn't mind doing so as long as we had a good reason as an incentive. Our hope was that a bike that had been discarded because of some broken part might have an undamaged fork. We were not lucky.

We went to a bike shop and found out how much a fork would cost. Any amount over a quarter seemed enormous to me. Yet it didn't seem an unattainable amount -- if Dad would agree that it was a small price for the whole bike. I had never asked him for money before, and as far as memory serves I never did again, but this was a special occasion. I presented the situation to Dad as a piece of information, not actually asking him for money to buy a fork, but the implication was there. I described in glowing terms the miraculous resurrection of the mangled wheel, and noted that it would be a pity now not to complete the renovation of the bicycle. I would not have been surprised if Dad hadn't come through with an offer because money was really scarce, and I never knew how much Dad earned. Fortunately, Dad had by this time been hired by Thom McAn Shoe Store and had a regular income, somewhat bigger than the uncertain amount earned by door-to-door peddling.

Dad gave me the cost of a new fork. Actually, he was glad to give me what I needed for a fork, for he approved of me having a bicycle. He told me that when he was a boy he envied his older brother, Patrick MacCaul, Jr., who had a bicycle. He described it as something I had never seen, and still have seen only in old pictures: it had a very large front wheel and a small back wheel. It put the rider much higher than the ordinary bikes of more recent times. Do I remember correctly that he said there were no brakes? Dad rode Pat's bike on a few occasions. Once he was going down a hill when he hit a stone. The jolt threw him off balance and he fell off the high seat of the contraption into a briar patch. Why anyone conceived of the idea of a bicycle with an enormous front wheel and a tiny rear wheel is hard to comprehend. Dad advised me to be careful in riding. "Remember that you have this bicycle because some boy had a serious accident." I agreed and meant it -- at the moment.

I had a bicycle! I had not been yearning for a bike previously. Suddenly, however, it put me in a new category. Not that being a property owner then meant anything to me. Nor was quicker transport or ease of mobility something I sought. As a boy who took a walk from Brightside to Springfield in his stride, I didn't ever mind walking. What I loved was the exhilarating sensation of coasting down a hill with the still air rushing past my face as if it were a wind. That was more than worth the effort of pumping the bike up the hill.

There was still a problem: the kid who had owned the bike had been hit by a car; the bike had been tipped over on one side and the pedal on that side was broken off. A new pedal would not have solved the problem because the pedal, in being torn out of the rod that held it, had cracked open the perforation in which it fit and another pedal therefore could not be securely inserted into the rod. The rod was a part of the sprocket, which propelled the chain that turned the rear wheel, making the whole bike go forward. A whole new sprocket would be needed. I never even considered asking Dad to cough up for this part.

This was the one unrepaired damage to my bike. However, I could ride my new bike. I would pedal the left pedal and when the right pedal-less rod came upright, I could bring my foot down on it and push it down. It was hard on shoe leather, and my pedaling was rather jerky, but it was less of a handicap than one might imagine. The left foot had to do most of the pumping. My right foot dangled intermittently until it could catch the pedal-less rod as it came perpendicular and push it downward, contributing a little to the power needed to propel me, and the bike, forward. There were two consequences: one, it wore a hole in the sole of my right shoe long before the left was worn out, and two, all bikes had coaster brakes then (hand brakes didn't come on the market until decades later) so bringing the bike to an abrupt stop was not as easy as it ought to be.

One thing neither Dad nor I had thought about was that we had no place to keep the bike. We were not allowed to keep it in the hotel and if we left it outside, it would be stolen. The solution was soon found: I would leave it at Fitz's, next to his bike.

This was my first bike – the first of three. Each bike was significant in a different period of my life. This one in my youth, which I rode around Springfield and vicinity; the next in maturity, with which I explored New England, took to Old England, Wales, rode across France from Paris to Marseilles, and finally sold in West Africa; the third in post-retirement years, which has never been off the island of Martha's Vineyard. My three bikes symbolize the Shakespearean "Ages of Man." First one gets around a little, then long trips are possible, and finally one is back more or less to the scope of childhood.

When it was finally all together, the first thing we did was go for a ride and test my new acquisition. Fitz had a bike and so did his neighbor, also named John, so both avoided the mutual cognomen. He was dubbed Beg, an abbreviation of his last name. Beg had been there watching the final repair of the bike. Then the three of us started off from Lexington Street. I had never been on a bike before, so balancing took a little getting used to, and it was hard to keep up with Fitz and Beg, whose bikes of course had two pedals.

We were soon in Van Horn Park on gravel paths. Beg led us to a decline where short lengths of logs were set into the slope to make graded steps for pedestrians. I didn't see the two bikes ahead of me negotiate this descent, and didn't realize they had swerved slightly to one side and gone down smoothly while I bumped over each step, arriving at the bottom a bit shook up. Beg laughed at my discomfiture.

Thus began a conflicted threesome. Fitz and Beg had been friends for a long time. Fitz's backyard abutted Beg's backyard; no fence separated the two properties, just a bush at the corners to mark the property line. They had grown up together. I was an intruder.

Beg lived with his sister; their parents were dead or at least never to my observation in the picture. The sister was married to a man who worked at Spaulding Sporting Goods Manufacturing Co. The husband's brother also lived with them -- not a typical family when the United States still had traditional families. What effect this may have had on him is hard to say, but he was more "grown-up" than either Fitz or I. He acquired adult ideas and attitudes about such things as smoking, drinking, and fooling around with girls sooner than we did. He told jokes that had sexual connotations. Where he heard them I never at the time thought to wonder. Typical was the one he told at the time Edward VIII married Mrs. Simpson: "Edward asked Wally, 'Have you still got your cherry?' 'No,' she answered, 'but I've got the box it came in.' When she proved she still had it, she exclaimed, 'Oh, Eddie! You're so BIG!' His Royal Highness replied, 'Didn't you know that every ruler has 12 inches?'"

Beg even knew about homosexuality when it was not talked about openly as it is now. I didn't quite know what to make of the story he told of the preacher with a facial tick. "The congregation was concerned about their minister because they knew he was pious but he had this uncontrollable facial tick. He would say in a sermon, 'Thou shalt not commit adultery.'" At this point Beg's right eye winked in imitation of the preacher's tick. "So they took up a collection to send him to a doctor who could cure the tick. The doctor was in Paris. The minister arrived in Paris and said to a taxi driver, 'Take me to a hotel.'" Again Beg winked. "The driver took him to a brothel. The madam showed him to a room. 'Do you want me to send up a girl?' The preacher said, 'No.'" Beg winked. "The madam called out, 'Oh, Pierre! Come up here.'"

Our jokes, when we had any, were innocent and innocuous: "What is the sharpest thing in the world?"

"A sword?"

"No."

"A razor?"

"No."

"What, then?"

"A fart! It can go through your pants without making a hole."

Beg was the one who was most assertive in trying to "make out" with girls. We were all still inexperienced in sex, but he was bold in his attempts to "feel up" a girl. He was also something of a daredevil. He dove from the twenty-foot-high diving board at Lake Lorraine when the twelve-foot-high board scared us. Eventually he would be the first to drive a car (his sister's). Wearing a fedora he led us into a bar (where we wouldn't have ventured on our own), ordered a beer, and was served – though the barkeep refused to serve us. "Do you mind," Beg asked, "if the kids wait while I drink this?" Fitz was a couple of months older than Beg, and I was six months older than Fitz, but in the circumstance, Beg was the elder.

By the time Beg was borrowing his sister's car and hanging out in bars, Fitz had inserted a little distance between himself and Beg. But until Fitz went to college the rupture never occurred. Then it was a geographical separation that gradually became an end to association. So there were a half dozen years while we were in junior high and high school that Beg was a presence in our lives. As far as I was concerned, I only saw him when he was in Fitz's company.

What drew Fitz and me together was our interest in ideas. We were both readers. I never saw Beg with a book. Fitz and I would be talking about something we (one or the other or sometimes both) had read and Beg would come on the scene, perhaps listen for a while, but soon say let's get on our bikes and go to some place he'd suggest, or let's do something – he'd always have a specific suggestion. In my view, he interrupted good conversations. In his view, no doubt, he considered me a drag on fun activities.

The bicycle provided the chance to get acquainted with Fitz, and we had hit it off from the first day. From then on until we finished high school Fitz and I were well nigh inseparable in after-school hours. In later years we kept in touch and saw each other whenever we could. Having someone to ride my bicycle with was a kind of bond, but would not have been the basis of a life-long friendship. Our connection was our curiosity, stimulated by what we found in books, and needing to talk about things and ideas. I found someone who was glad to listen to me repeat what I had read, and he had many things to tell me about how things worked.

Fitz astounded me by making a crystal set radio. It was just a piece of board with a couple of small attachments and a few wires, but it captured sounds out of the air enabling us to hear music, voices, and a lot of static. Fitz read widely, but included how-to books and manuals, a genre I had ignored and generally continued to ignore. He was always trying out some experiment.

If it had been only Fitz's mechanical skills, the friendship probably wouldn't have been as strong. He recognized that I was interested in things he was interested in but previously he had had no one to talk to about what he was thinking. My situation was similar except that I told anyone and everyone around me what I was learning, whether they were interested or not. I scrounged the library and funneled information outward. It was as if when I learned something that was interesting, and so much was interesting to me, that I had to tell someone – or everyone. How could they go on not knowing?

Without knowing it, I was strengthening my memory. When one reads about something, it is recorded in the brain cells, but forgetfulness almost immediately starts to nibble at it. Every time one tells someone of the substance of the reading, the memory is renewed.

Fitz and I were the intellectuals of our class. There were other intelligent boys, but they were not, for whatever reason, insatiably pursuing facts, ideas, concepts, interrelationships, hypotheses, or theories. Their energies might be directed to sports, amusements, prestige, or other goals. We wouldn't have claimed the accolade of "intellectual" then because we were not yet familiar with the term, and later we might have been leery of it after hearing Dalton Trumbo's couplet:

The epitome of the ineffectual
Is that anomaly the intellectual.

Intellectuals famously argue small points, thereby delaying making decisions, but that may, in some instances at least, prevent a hasty decision that leads not to the intended goal but to disaster.

I owed my possession of the bike to the man who gave me the wreck, to Fitz who fixed it, to Dad for giving me the money for a new fork, all of whom I'm sure I thanked. But there was also the boy who told me about the availability of the busted bike, took me to the house of the unknown kid, and brought me to Fitz's house (I had not known where he lived, or that he could fix the bike). I probably thanked him too, but oddly, I cannot remember who this important person was! I have an image of the man whom I saw only the one time when he gave me the bike. His face is blurred, but I see his white shirt with sleeves rolled up and straps of suspenders dark against the shirt, but the boy alongside me is not visible to me in this memory. Why would that part of memory fade? I suspect it is because I felt guilty: he was the kid I chummed with until then and afterward abandoned to be with Fitz. It was probably "Fat" Burns, but it might have been Bob Meahan. Whoever it was did himself out of a companion.

While I forsook my earlier sidekick, Fitz would not have been able to give up Beg, a neighbor whose back yard abutted the Fitzgerald back yard. The two boys had been companions for years, and Beg also had a bike. The three of us often rode together. Summers we would ride seven miles to Lake Lorraine to go swimming. Sometimes we would catch on to the tailboard of a truck to save having to pedal. My bike, with one pedal, was inevitably slower than the other two. Each of them would take one side of the tailboard. I had to grab the middle when I caught up with them. That meant riding blind because I couldn't see in front of the truck. They would warn me when a red light ahead would require the truck to stop. I would have to overcome the momentum of the fast ride, first by using the coaster brakes with the one inadequate pedal, and then by pressing with my hand on the tailboard to keep from crashing into it. It was a risky thing, but in the attitude of invulnerability of adolescence I never worried about it.

I was at Fitz's house so regularly Ma Fitz began to take me as if I were one of her own and would tell me to sit down at the table and eat when the rest of the family had supper. Fitz had three older sisters and an older brother. Mary, the eldest, was almost old enough to have been Fitz's mother, but she was married and only at Lexington Street for visits. Tom had had a career in business before the depression and was then working as timekeeper on a W.P.A. project. Betty was a nurse at Mercy Hospital, and Rosalie, when I first became a regular visitor, was still in high school. Later she was a secretary. Fitz also had a younger sister Helen and a kid brother George. His father was a steam fitter, a well-paid job when there was one, but he hadn't worked at that trade for some years. Before the depression, Pa Fitz had been promoted to foreman, and when the men went out on strike, he went out with his men, which was seen as defection by management. Subsequently he was blackballed from further employment in that field. When I knew him he was the policeman at the Jefferson Cinema, that is he wore the uniform as a special policeman, but he was not a member of the city police force. Before the children began working and contributing to the family finances, they must have needed the rental income from the upstairs apartment in the home Pa Fitz had bought when he was earning an ample salary.

Maybe it was the disappointment of his comedown in employment, or the mood of the economic depression the whole country was going through, or maybe it was just his deteriorating health, but Pa Fitz always seemed a saddened man. He almost always had a pipe hanging out of his mouth that seemed to emphasize its down-turned direction. Fitz used his father's tools and sometimes didn't put them back precisely where they had been, and his father would get angry. The two were not on friendly terms as I was with my father, but that didn't seem to bother Fitz.

Actually, there was a way in which they interacted favorably. The father had put up a blackboard on one of the kitchen walls, and he would put a math problem on it and challenge all of the children to solve it. Tom had once been the star at this game, but currently he was drinking too much and was out of his father's good graces. Some of the children ignored the task, but Fitz enjoyed finding the answer and usually did.

Mrs. Fitz, like her husband, was born in Ireland. She arrived in the U.S. and found a position as a maid on Beacon Hill in Boston, which gave her room and board, so she saved virtually all her earnings. She brought over her brother with her savings. He worked as a plumber. Between them they brought over the rest of their siblings. When this uncle and his wife and kids visited, he would call the moves in an Irish dance while Tom played his violin and Mary, if she were there, would play the piano. Such a big family! I felt rather isolated in comparison.

Mary said she had known my mother. I accepted this without question. Now I wonder how Mary, in Springfield, would have known my mother, who lived in West Springfield before her marriage and after that for at least four years before her death in Westfield. There were so many queries I might have made and didn't. I suppose it may have been in some Catholic solidarity, a women's organization associated with church parishes; Sacred Heart in Springfield and Immaculate Conception in West Springfield were not far apart and may have had some interchanges.

The extent to which I became integrated into the Fitzgerald family, even sleeping over with Fitz in his room in the attic, made the designation "orphan," that had been tagged on me, essentially inappropriate. Ma Fitz was like a mother to me, even more so than Mrs. Meahan. Aunt May, my godmother, was always looking out for me, as well as my stepmother Irene who invited me to Sunday dinners now and again. Far from motherless, I had more "mothers" than anyone I knew.

One day I was sitting in the Fitzgerald home waiting for Fitz to finish doing something before we were going to go out. I had picked up a dictionary and was looking through it. What I was doing was checking the Greek words from which certain English words derived. The sources were given in the Greek alphabet and by comparing the English to perceive the sound and attach that to the Greek letters, I was teaching myself the shapes of the Greek letters of the alphabet and their associated sounds. My efforts did not tell me the order of the letters in the Greek alphabet, but I was getting familiar with the shapes and could recognize most when encountering them again. Also I was learning a bit of etymology (itself a Greek-derived term: "word, study of"). Many Greek words came to English via Latin and sometimes also via French; the transformations of the shape of the word as it crossed language boundaries were interesting. Plus I was discovering a new "beasterie." I had just added "nosehorn," otherwise known as rhinoceroses (Gk. rhino "nose" + keros "horn") to the earlier discovered "riverhorse" (Gk. hippo "horse" + potomos "river").

Fitz's sister Rosalie happened to come upon me with my nose in the book and exclaimed, "For goodness sake, don't *read* the dictionary!" The implication was that it was fine to look up words when needed but not to browse in a dictionary for pleasure. I attempted to explain what I was doing. Her eyes went up to the ceiling and she shook her head. "What would you want to do that for?" It was a good question; what use did I have for the Greek alphabet? None immediately, but I was already studying Latin, and one might ask, what use was that to me. Eventually what I learned of both Latin and Greek were useful to my interest in linguistics, though at that time I was barely aware of the word "linguistics" or of the discipline it designated.

Rosalie was the beauty of the family, and I, sensitive to her beauty, always enjoyed talking to her. I believe I spoke with her more than to any of Fitz's other sisters. She was not *too* much older than I was, and there was a nice frisson in having her attention. She told me I was wrong in my assessment of Sister Francis Edward, who had taught girls' sixth grade before being assigned to be the boys' teacher. "We all loved her," Rosalie said, "we called her Franny Eddie – though not to her face." That may have been the nun's natural place, dealing with girls, but Rosalie's opinion did not change my feelings about her as a teacher. Rosalie liked listening to Perry Como. I had never paid any attention to him previously, but took notice of him after that. Rosalie's disapproval of my grubbing in the dictionary saddened me.

THE LONG TRAIL

There were some activities in which Beg did not join Fitz and me – one was hiking over the Long Trail. Someone had told us about this Long Trail, which ultimately became the New England section of the Appalachian Trail, which stretches from Georgia to Maine. It ran north/south about 50 miles west of us through the Berkshire Hills. We could hitchhike on Route 20 to where the Trail crossed the road and start north into Vermont's Green Mountains, cross a bridge over the Connecticut River and get to New Hampshire's White Mountains. We never ventured as far as Mt. Katahdin in Maine but we covered much of the rest a few times.

We had to carry food with us, but it would have been ridiculous to take cans since that meant carrying a lot of water and the weight of the metal. Also, cans in a backpack would press uncomfortably into our backs. We put a number of dry things into cloth bags with drawstrings to close them: flour already mixed with baking powder to make biscuits, dehydrated milk and eggs, beans, rice, oatmeal, prunes, raisons, nuts. Fresh meat might spoil in the summer heat, but "hot dogs" would be safe if well cooked and eaten within a few days. Sliced bacon wrapped in wax paper (to keep other things ungreased) would last longer.

These bags, divided into two more or less equal groups, were wrapped in the blanket roll each of us carried. The trick of supplying ourselves in this manner may have been known to us from my reading of E. T. Seton. The blanket that each of us took from home (in my case, from Fitz's home because I couldn't take one from the hotel) served, while hiking, as a pack for our sacks of food and our extra clothing, and at night, as bedding. In order to make it so versatile we needed some very large safety pins. Where we got them I can no longer say, but we called them "horse pins." Perhaps they were designed to be used in stables? They enabled us to turn the blanket into a sleeping bag, and they supplemented the rope we used to tie the pack together.

We also had an Army canteen that attached to the belt around our waists that held up our pants. This makes me think we must have had some input from Mike Kerry, Fitz's brother-in-law, husband to Mary, Fitz's oldest sister. He worked at the Springfield Armory, and would know about surplus Army supplies. Mike was always trying to get us to do something active and "manly" instead of sitting and reading. He was the one who later, when we were in high school, encouraged us to spend a couple of summers with the Citizens Military Training Corps (more on that later).

In addition, we had a special hiker's lightweight frying pan with a handle that was attached with a screw nut permitting it to turn and go over a metal dish that fitted upside down in the frying pan. Inside the pan and the inverted dish a saucepan was stored, and inside it was a cup, all made of aluminum. This all went into a strong cloth sack with a shoulder strap. This was a gift from Mike to Fitz and we had only the one for all our cooking and eating. Eventually, though not on our first hiking trip, we had a short-handled hatchet that had a leather case over the metal axe-head that attached to the belt around our waists. We took turns carrying its additional weight. The expense of this essential piece of equipment makes me wonder about its provenance: did it also come from Mike? Or from Fitz's doting older sisters? Certainly our stuff (one cook-kit, one canteen, one hatchet) emerged from the Fitzgerald family side. The distaff side of the family must have sewn the bags we carried our dried foods in. However, I could buy some of the food supplies, diverting money from my restaurant meals. Dad gave me cash for the trip instead of buying me another meal ticket at the restaurant on the street floor of the hotel. Nevertheless, without my connection to the Fitzgerald family, I probably would not have become a hiker on the Long Trail.

With things hanging from our belts, and blanket roll over one shoulder, we hit the road and hitched rides west into the forested hills to the junction of the Long Trail, and then we walked north. In the next few years we became quite familiar with the southern New England parts of the trail. In those years we ate a lot of beans, soaked overnight in brook water and cooked the next morning. We reversed breakfast and dinner, having beans in the morning and oatmeal in the evening because the latter did not have to be soaked for hours before being cooked. We munched nuts or raisons as we walked. We had certain favorite cabins and lean-tos. A cabin on Bromley Mountain had an oven in which we could bake our biscuits instead of having to improvise a "Dutch oven" by putting biscuit dough in our dry covered saucepan and putting that on the fire.

The only scary incident in all the times we were in the mountains happened on an evening just after we had arrived at a lean-to where we were going to spend the night. I went out in the dusk to gather dead wood for a fire to cook our supper. This was before we had the hatchet. I was simply going to pick up fallen twigs and branches of appropriate size. Thus I had no weapon of any kind when I found myself face to face with a lynx. Its face was long and wide in proportion to the body and seemed even larger with the stiff hairs extending upward from the tips of the erect ears. We both, the lynx and I, stopped and surveyed each other. After a moment the cat moved off to one side. As long as the animal stood there, I was frozen, wondering what to do. I didn't want to turn my back to it, and I didn't want to walk backwards and perhaps stumble over some log or boulder that might be in my way. As soon as the lynx moved away, I turned around, shaken, and went back to the lean-to empty handed. After a while, Fitz and I went out together – safety in numbers – and picked up enough wood for cooking.

There was probably no danger in the animal, but as a city boy, I had no experience with animals that had not been domesticated, nor with many that were, but I knew from books that the lynx was a carnivore, and as such "red in tooth and claw." A lynx, not as large as a cougar, locally called a catamount, was nonetheless strong enough to be more than a boy wanted to grapple with. For a moment it had been a scary encounter; for the rest of the evening, in the open lean-to, the nearby presence of the animal was a cause of a little anxiety, but afterward it was a valued story even if it was a very small adventure. By the 1930s the woods of Vermont were pretty well cleared out of dangerous animals.

CAMPING IN EASTHAMPTON

Fitz and I joined Troop 14 of the Boy Scouts. We had our meetings in the gym at Chestnut Street School. Mr. Hanson was the scoutmaster of the troop. He was a young man and enjoyed getting out of the city, so he encouraged the troop to go for a week or more in the summer, or for a weekend in the spring and autumn, at the camp leased to the troop. The camp consisted of a cabin built on a hillside in the woodlot of a farmer in Easthampton. For a token of one dollar a year, the farmer allowed the troop to use the cabin, fish in his pond, and wander in his woods. He sold us milk, eggs, apples, and cider, reducing somewhat the loads of food we needed to tote in and earning him more than the nominal fee he charged for the lease of the camp.

I never had a scout uniform. Few of the boys in the North End of Springfield in those years could have afforded to join the Boy Scouts if uniforms were required. We did have to buy a neckerchief with the colors and design of our troop. With that inexpensive identification we were considered adequately accoutered for any official appearance. The only merit badges

I earned were for fire building without matches and cooking. These were the pragmatic skills needed for camping, and easy after our experience on the Long Trail. But I wasn't deeply into the scouting movement; it was camping that drew me to join the troop. Fitz and I never missed a chance to go to the camp – it was the main reason we had joined the troop.

We went with the troop a few times and experienced the cabin filled with a dozen or more boys, but the way I remember it is with just the two of us, Fitz and me, having the cabin and the woods to ourselves. Our young scoutmaster, Mr. Hanson, decided to get married and, with his energies directed elsewhere, gave up his post, which for as long as we were associated with the troop was not taken up by a replacement. The farmer knew us and so Fitz and I could go to him, get the key, and move in to the cabin.

We would wear our neckerchiefs when we went to the farmer's house to get the key to the cabin and to buy eggs, milk, apples, cider, and sometimes bread. In this way we could go to the camp even when the scoutmaster was not with us. Except for one time this was always in warm weather; the exception was one year between Christmas and New Year's. We wore long-john underwear, sweaters and warm jackets. The cabin was not winterized; one could see daylight between some of the boards of the walls. We were so cold at night that we put a spare mattress over our blankets. In the morning we found that eggs were frozen in their shells, soup was solid in the can, and the cider had ice in it – we called the liquid that remained "applejack" and thought it amusing that we had what we considered an adult alcoholic drink.

During the days we were active and didn't mind too much the low temperature or the wind, but the nights when we were huddled fully dressed in our blankets, we'd say, "We should go home tomorrow." In the daylight we felt better about everything and hated the idea of going back before we said we would and having people say, "We knew you wouldn't be able to stand it!" We stayed the five nights we had planned to stay and when we returned to the city and into a heated house, our skins turned red as the blood, which had retreated to deeper parts of our bodies, came again closer to the surface.

We tried walking through the woods without making a sound as Indians, according to James Fennimore Cooper, were able to do, but we never managed. Years would go by before I realized that we were not in "the forest primeval" but in second growth woods that had much more "undergrowth," whereas with the large well-established trees of former times spreading their branches out and robbing the plants below of sunlight, the forest floor was much more clear of the bushes that crackled as we pushed through them.

Before Mr. Hanson resigned as scoutmaster, he announced that he was going to build a sailboat. Would anyone like to volunteer to help him? It would be a chance to learn how a sailboat could be constructed. I volunteered. Fitz said the scoutmaster just wanted some free labor. Perhaps so, but I was curious to see the boat take shape and be a part of the process. Mr. Hanson didn't work on Saturdays and on some of those days during that winter he worked in his garage on his project and on some of those Saturdays I helped by doing whatever he told me to do. He had built the ribs, and connected them with struts, before he called me to join him. He needed to bend several thin boards over the ribs and to do that the boards had to be steamed to make them more flexible. We achieved this by soaking rags in very hot water and wrapping them around a board. When it could bend without danger of cracking, he would screw one end of the board to the stern and I would hold the board in its position at the bow while he put screws through the bent board securing it to the ribs. My hands were almost cooked with handling the steaming rags, and my arms were tired from keeping one board after another in its bent position fighting against its inclination to return to a straight line. For my help I was rewarded with a few days of sailing with Mr. Hanson the following summer.

During the succeeding winter, the boat was stored not in Mr. Hanson's garage but at a marina. In the spring, he was unable to pay what he owed for storage and lost his boat, and I lost my right to further days of sailing. The reason Mr. Hanson defaulted on his bill at the marina is that he had been courting and spending more on his fiancée than he had planned. Moreover, there were the expenses of setting up housekeeping when he married.

Mike Kerry, the husband of Fitz's sister, was transferred to the armory at Albany, N.Y., which is near Watervliet where I had an uncle. In fact, Harry Moore, married to my stepmother's sister, was my favorite uncle, which was partly because he treated me, a teenager, as an adult, but largely because he was a well-read man with a large library. He had a gruff humor, telling great stories and laughing more at them than did his listeners. Fitz and I hitchhiked west on Route 20 to Albany. He stayed with his sister Mary and her husband Mike while I stayed with Uncle Harry and his family. Uncle Harry had eight children, some older than me, and one just about my age. It was he who told us about Lake George. There was an area at the lake where camping was permitted.

"Do you have a map of New York?" Uncle Harry asked.

"No, only of Massachusetts."

"Go down to the gas station," Harry said to one of his sons, "and tell Joe I want a road map of New York State." The boy ran off as he was instructed. Harry ran his family as a general ran an army. Perhaps with so many children that was the way that was needed to avoid chaos, but there may have been another factor: Harry was an admirer of Napoleon. He owned every book in English on Bonaparte that he had ever heard of and he read and reread them.

Road maps were given out free in those days to motorists, but a kid coming in to ask for one wouldn't get one. Harry, however, was a traveling salesman for a casket company and started out each Monday morning to visit funeral parlors to take orders to replace coffins that had been sold, and he filled his gas tank at this neighborhood gas station so he knew Joe would give his son a map.

Harry gave me the map, marking the location of the camping area at Lake George, and discussed the best route for hitchhiking there. We had come without camping gear, but I took the map with me when we returned home, and before long Fitz and I were back in Albany and Watervliet again, visiting our relatives and using the visit as a jumping-off place to get to Lake George.

By this time we had a pup tent, available from the Army and Navy Surplus Store. It came in two parts and was fastened at the peak when in use, but the convenience of it was that it slept two and each occupant could carry one of the halves. We wrapped the waterproof canvas of the tent half around our blanket rolls, which was an improvement over our earlier system that exposed our bedding to dirt and wet. However, the backpack now was heavier, not so much from the canvas, but from the collapsible poles and metal stakes, and guy ropes (again divided in two groups) required to hold the tent up and not blow away. On the Long Trail we went from one constructed shelter to the next and did not need a tent. At the Boy Scout camp in Easthampton we stayed every night in the cabin and a tent would have been superfluous. At Lake George campgrounds a tent was essential.

Did we get it for the trip to Lake George? As usual, it must have come from Fitzgerald resources. By now Tom, the oldest son, had got into politics, and probably was already working for the city's mayor, and Betty, as mentioned, was working at Mercy Hospital, but both were still living at home. There was a bit more disposable income in the family, and there was a degree of recognition that brother John was the golden boy of the family. I was merely a beneficiary.

I remember the beauty of Lake George, but not much else. Almost as soon as we arrived and got the pup tent set up, I began to run a fever. I got into my sleeping bag and tried to sleep, but without success. A man camping nearby gave Fitz a bottle with a little whiskey in it for me. "This will make him sleep!" he said. I did have a sound sleep. Fitz said the next morning that I snored loudly all night. I felt better, no fever, but was drained of energy, so we decided to leave. It was the shortest camping trip we ever had. What I remember most of the trip was the visit to Fort Ticonderoga on the way there.

We used the pup tent at another lake, closer to home, in Brimfield, Massachusetts. It also was a less-than-happy experience. Rain fell all the time we were there. In spite of having trenched the tent with deep gullies around the edges to encourage water running down the tent to flow away and not seep into the tiny area we hoped to keep dry, our blankets got wet with the droplets we carried in with us on our clothes.

Aside from the memory of being drenched, one event stands out: a bright streak of lightening came down, almost in a straight line, from the darkened sky and hit the surface of the water. We talked about it for a long time. Why did the lightening not strike something higher than the lake? Lightening, we had been told, hit high objects. Was there metallic rock under the lake that attracted the lightening? Would we have been electrocuted if we had been in the water at that time? Water, after all, is a conductor of electricity. Later, after we'd had a physics course, we would have known the answers to some of these questions, but at the moment we were awed with the mysteries of the universe.

Eventually we walked into town, found a place to buy a hamburger, and sat long after finishing it in order to dry out. We walked back, crawled into our tent and hoped the next day would be better. It wasn't.

There is yet another locus of camping memories: Camp Robinson was available to Boy Scouts of whatever troop. Unless for some special gathering, we would not have gone there so long as we had the Troop 14 camp in Easthampton available. I guess no one paid the farmer his annual fee of a dollar, and he assumed the troop was no longer interested – or even in existence – and so rescinded the privilege to a couple of rag-tag boys with neckerchiefs. At any rate, one summer Fitz and I spent so much time at Camp Robinson without spending enough time in town to get a haircut that our hair was down to our shoulders. We thought of it as in the style of Johnny Weissmuller, who had appeared in a film, *Tarzan of the Apes*. We were sitting around our campfire one evening when a group from some other troop arrived, toting their gear past our pup tent when one of the arriving boys, seeing the silhouette against the firelight, called out, "Jeez! Look it! GIRLS!"

SEMINARIANS

Two young men dressed in dark suits, an unusual appearance on a weekday in the summer, came to give their greetings to Mrs. Fitzgerald. They were seminarians, one of whom had been a classmate of Tom's at Sacred Heart, back in the neighborhood for a vacation from their studies. Ma Fitz beamed at them. Such fine young men, she said when they left. There was also something to the effect that we didn't match up to their standard. She didn't go so far as to suggest that we ought to aim at becoming priests; perhaps she already had suspicions that "the faith" was not strong in us.

Tom, when he came home, said they have to go everywhere in pairs. One invites a friend to his home for the vacation; next time they both go to the other's home. That's so one can chaperone the other. All the girls swoon at the sight of them, so they have to be protected from the temptation and "occasions of sin." He took a dimmer view of them than did his mother.

Tom's comment made us feel better. Boys in Catholic families, when they were "on their best behavior," as advised to do while relatives were visiting, were always being told as a kind of compliment, "Sure and you'll grow up to be a priest." Well, neither Fitz nor I had any such ambition. Quite the opposite.

We were both backsliding from belief in the doctrines of the Church. At some point, probably later than the seminarians' visit, Fitz was going to go somewhere on a Saturday afternoon. "First, you've got to go to confession," his mother told him. Not wanting to disobey, but not wanting to take too much time, he jumped on his bike and rode as fast as he could to the church. While he was inside, someone stole his bike. He was angry. "I'll never go to church again," he said to me, but he didn't repeat that to his family, and he did go to church whenever he was accompanied by either of his parents. His father would have been furious if he had heard what Fitz told me. After the father died, Mrs. Fitz became aware of Fitz's unbelief and she was to his surprise not really upset about it.

Ever since the day the conflict between evolution and the Bible had been made suddenly and starkly clear to me, I had read everything I came across on the relation between religion and science. A British astronomer, Sir James Jeans, was asked -- newspapers reported -- on the occasion of a new and more powerful telescope being installed, if he expected to be able to see God or the happy souls in heaven. Perhaps the query was meant to be ironic. The astronomer, however, replied that God was spirit; even with the greatest amplification of any telescope he could see only material things. Souls also are spirits, but human bodies are not, and while souls, it is agreed, generally leave deceased bodies to be buried, there is one exception, according to what we were taught. Mary, the mother of Jesus, did not die, but was "assumed" to heaven. This doctrine of the Feast of the Assumption of the Virgin Mary (August 15), if true, meant there would be one material human body somewhere up there. In the vast space, trying to locate a material human body about five feet in height would be like looking for a needle in a haystack, so it would prove nothing if she were not visible. It was only juvenile naïveté that had led me to think there could be some relevance in astronomy to my problem with the credibility of religion. My interest in astronomy decreased. There was more than enough on earth to keep my attention occupied.

Of course Jeans was probably not Catholic and might not have held to the story of the "assumption" (the technical term used by the Church instead of "ascension"). Still, I wondered, did he believe in a divinity, or was his answer – to avoid controversy -- a cop-out? Some scientists talked about a First Cause to get the universe operating. But wasn't this just a creator deity in non-anthropomorphic guise? There were a lot of unanswered, perhaps unanswerable, questions, but I adhered to my preference to doubt rather that retain unquestioning faith.

The year of Jeans' statement may be a bit later than I'm putting it here, but the point is that while in junior high I renounced, not publicly but in my own mind, the existence of a soul, a heaven where disembodied souls resided, and of God, as defined by Catholic dogma or in any other form. It was the problem with miracles. Clarence Darrow and others argued that some so-called miracles could be scientifically explained, and others were made-up stories to enhance the power of the supposed deity. That sounded reasonable to me. I decided I preferred a scientific explanation to the claimed miraculous nature of so-called miraculous events, or reports of such alleged events.

THE NORTH END

The North End of Springfield was like the League of Nations, I'd heard it said more than once. The second floor of the Fitzgerald's house was rented out to a family from the Soviet Union. They were acceptable because they were not Communists but Catholics. Ma Fitz called them "Roosians," but as the daughter told me, they were not Russian but Ukrainian. "Same thing," Ma Fitz insisted. Ukraine was just a part of Russia, as Massachusetts was a part of the United States. "Yeah," I said, "it is now, but it was independent originally and later it was ruled for a while by Poland, which explains why some Ukrainians are Catholic and not Orthodox like the Russians." The Public Library rather than school was behind this spouting of my erudition. "Hmm," was Ma Fitz's only comment.

Next to Fitz there was a Jewish family, with three girls who were *zaftig,* as the Yiddish word described them, curvaceous, literally "juicy." Across the street was a French Canadian family with a son, Gerard, younger than us, whose mother would come to the door at dinner time and call him in from play, "Giddo, venci!" which I recognized from my French lessons as *vien ici,* "come here." In my class was an Armenian boy. I had to look in an atlas to find Armenia, which I had never heard of before. And there was Mr. Hanson, our Norwegian scoutmaster. The North End was in contrast to the South End that was largely Italian. Hungry Hill, as it was dubbed, was largely Irish, and Forest Hill was mainly Yankee, that is families with generations in America, as distinguished from all us come-lately immigrants in the rest of the city.

Raymond Hagerty, Irish, Ray Gendron, French Canadian, and Abe Hoffman, Jewish, were friends from the neighborhood that Fitz and I hung around with. At Abe's house I learned to like borscht, knedlik, blintzes, latkes and other Yiddish specialties. What I ate at Fitz's seemed the usual American fare. What

French Canadian cuisine might be, I can't say, having never eaten at Ray's house, but once on a summer day when we, Fitz and I, waited for him to have breakfast, I watched in amazement while he ate a stack of pieces of buttered toast, half a loaf at least, while we waited for him to come out with us. It seems that after the Meahen's, I was invited to the table only by the Fitzgerald's and the Hoffman's.

With a mixed population with shallow roots in this country, and many unemployed, and with the economy in a crisis and perhaps on the verge of collapse, the North End was ripe for street-corner speakers proposing radical solutions. We boys would stand on the edge of the crowd listening to a member of the Communist Party telling everyone there was no other remedy but ending capitalism and substituting collective ownership of the means of production. Sometimes a collapsible table would be set up with pamphlets spread out. "Get yer litertur here!" another communist would entreat, but most people were reluctant to be seen taking subversive propaganda. As the speaker finished and the crowd dispersed, we would go up and look at the pamphlets. Prices on them were usually 25 cents. We didn't have any money, but stood there reading the titles. The seller, having no further sales, would more often than not give us any pamphlet we wanted. "Take it home, give it to your father."

One evening, as we walked away from a street corner orator, one of my friends said he did not ask for any pamphlets because he couldn't take any "Red rag" home and read it. His mother would take it and throw it into the stove and burn it. He was Catholic and Communists were condemned from the pulpit. Another friend said he didn't have to worry about that; his mother respected anything in print and would never destroy it.

He was Jewish and his mother was as anti-Communist as our Catholic friend's mother, but there was a difference in attitude toward ideas and published arguments. I did not have to be concerned with parental supervision: I could read undisturbed in my hotel room while my father was at work. I disposed of the pamphlets without showing them to him. Dad didn't want any truck with Communists. He voted the Democratic ticket and was a fervent supporter of Franklin Delano Roosevelt who approved of his efforts to save capitalism.

I read the Marxist pamphlets. Some of it made sense to me; some was dubious. My library reading offered a different version of reform, Fabian socialism. This British movement was largely literary. H.G. Wells, Bernard Shaw, and other writers hoped to "educate" the capitalist ruling class to give up power because they would come to see that socialism was better for everyone, including the wealthy. This was naive but the goal was to be achieved without a bloody revolution. Communists seemed to be more or less similar in that revolution was seldom mentioned. The claim of inevitability of Marx's "dialectical materialism" and "scientific socialism" was not convincing, but the vision of an egalitarian society and an absence of class conflicts – no multi-millionaires while masses were going hungry – was attractive.

I went with a friend to some meetings of the Young Communist League. There were not very many other attendees. A man held a sort of seminar on "surplus value" and such topics. Fitz was leery of the whole thing and wouldn't go. Once on a Saturday, we had an YCL picnic. It might have been YMCA plus YWCA as far as the activities were concerned: baseball, hot dogs, soda pop, boys and girls, speeches. The Young Communists I met were just ordinary kids who for the most part seemed to be only mildly interested in the ideology, but some adult Communists struck me as too intense. Having just extracted myself from Catholicism, I didn't want to submit myself to a comparable dogmatism.

At the time, with the limitations of reliable information we had available, it was easy to accept the Communist line that held that the horrible things said about Joe Stalin were capitalist propaganda. Looking back, it seems to me that if the Soviet Union had not existed, the issues in domestic politics that the left chose to be active in would have gone further, that is, there would have been more progress in dealing with social problems if there had been no possibility of shouting the label "communist" and thereby alleging a foreign power seeking to subvert American power. The issues might have been discussed in a more rational manner. But probably some other label would have been manufactured to create the same effect of distraction from the real problem.

The leader of the YCL told me, that as a guy with an Irish name, I could have great opportunities in politics in Massachusetts, for the Irish were prominent in politics. I would be able, he said, to push the Communist cause. I had no ambition to be a politician, and if I had, I wouldn't have expected that as a Communist I would have had much success. Politics did interest me and I followed what the newspapers printed on the activities of local and national politicians, but I couldn't imagine myself involved in any activity except voting. The speechifying, the shaking of an endless line of hands, and all the folderol of campaigning seemed very unattractive to me, and a demand on time that left less time for other activities that were more satisfying.

CHAPTER FIVE

REUNION

When I was looking forward to being graduated from Chestnut Street, I expected that I would go to Classical High. Fitz and I had been in the same classes for the most part, but we were planning to go to different high schools. Springfield had three public high schools: Technical, Commercial, and Classical. They were all within a stone's throw of each other, two on State Street, near the juncture of Chestnut and State Streets, and "Tech" just off State Street. The Catholic High School, St. Michael's, was also in that neighborhood cluster of high schools. All had in common some basic courses, but each emphasized some special interest not found in the others. If we had followed the course the Sisters of Sacred Heart had recommended, Fitz and I would have ended up at St. Michael's, putting the finishing touches on catechism. Commercial, which neither of us considered, was strong on accounting, typing and stenography, but we did not see our future in business. Fitz chose, and he thought I should too, Tech, which offered more math, science, and mechanics. My determination to go to Classical High was based on the courses offered there: languages and literature, history and social studies.

Our different choices foreshadowed the division of our ways – Fitz to science, and me to the humanities. When C.P. Snow came out some years later with his essay on the "Two Cultures," we recognized the reality of that dichotomy in our lives. Fortunately for us, our friendship persisted, and Fitz provided me with more input of some concepts and data of science than I would have otherwise received, and my prattling about my studies supplemented his own extensive reading outside his chosen field of the sciences. Both Technical and Classical High Schools were "college preparatory," but neither of us could count on going to college. Only about one out of ten high school graduates managed to go to college in those days. The problem was financial, and neither of us seemed to be in a favorable situation in that respect, but we had hopes that somehow opportunity would open up and we would be ready. Ultimately, we were lucky.

As it turned out, I never did go to Classical High because Dad and I moved out of the City of Springfield and I was no longer eligible to attend that school. We moved just across the Connecticut River to the town of West Springfield and joined the rest of the family that I had missed so much seven years earlier when we had been separated. By now I had almost forgotten them, for I had grown and changed in the meantime. The Hotel and Chestnut Street Junior High School were two of the factors in my divergence from the rest of the family. I had lived in a secular environment. No one at the hotel, not even my father, ever mentioned church or religion, and public schools had pupils of various religions and avoided anything that might be disputatious. The family I was about to rejoin went to the Catholic Church every Sunday and sometimes oftener, and my siblings attended parochial school. This difference would become a problem, but at the moment that was not seen by me as inevitable.

Much of the joy I found in Springfield was in continuous learning. In public school I learned an organized set of knowledge in the curriculum; from the public library I acquired an eclectic variety of facts and ideas, and at the hotel and elsewhere in the city I observed adult actualities of life, at least as lived in Springfield. I felt I was bursting with knowledge, but was already acutely aware of how much more I was ignorant. At some point I read in the newspaper a report of a study of how much school children remembered after the lapse of a year of what they had known as indicated by their year-old exams. It was said to be a mere 18 per cent!

That raised the question whether it was worth the effort to learn anything. But then I realized that this figure was an average. Some kids remembered much more, some virtually nothing. Lumping kids who would skip school along with eager learners could not represent the amount of memory a dedicated scholar would retain. Still, forgetfulness was an inescapable handicap. Sometimes when I went to bed and waited for sleep to come I went over in my mind the things I learned that day and tagged the things that were especially significant to me in my fund of knowledge. By significant, I meant things that somehow connected with other things. Isolated facts were interesting, but clusters of interrelated facts were more meaningful.

I had been quite happy living in the hotel. Part of my reluctance to move was giving up Classical High, but part of my misgivings came from my occasional Sunday visits, as I realized that I was different from anyone in that household. Certainly I was not in the mold of Grandma Sheehan, who had been born in Ireland

and came to New England as a grown girl, and had worked in a factory next to another young woman to whom she never spoke. "Why not?" I asked. "She was Protestant." I was supposed to know that was sufficient reason. Grandma Sheehan never used her electric iron if it was raining. Lightening was electricity, and during a storm extra electricity might come out of the socket and kill or at least shock her.

Irene was more sensible, but she was as strict a Catholic as her mother, and I, in my adolescent self-confidence, had decided that not only Catholicism but the dogmas of all religions were simply superstitions. Obviously, I was not about to tell Irene what I believed and did not believe. I hadn't even revealed my position to Dad or to Aunt May. There was likely to be trouble ahead for me in West Springfield.

My sister Ruth graduated from West Springfield High the same spring I graduated from Chestnut Street, and she was hired by the West Springfield Tax Office (Uncle Ray Sweeney was the Tax Collector). Now that she would be paying room and board to Irene, she had some clout when she said she wanted the family to move from a ramshackle house in a run-down district to a better house in a better area. Also, in that summer Dad decided that finally his income was sufficiently adequate and secure (he was still working for Thom McAn) to bring the family together again. Dad had been giving some money each payday to Irene, but with the family reunited what he had been paying for the room at the Campion and what was spent on restaurant meals could go toward the family finances.

I may have had something to do with Dad's decision to rejoin his fractured family. A fragment of conversation sticks with me. Dad asks, "Is that what you want?" And I reply,

"Yeah," but with a feeling of not quite certain agreement. The question was about moving to West Springfield and living with my sisters and brothers. The idea of being part of a family seemed attractive, but the reservation was due to wondering if I was being manipulated. Irene worked at S.S. Kresge's and Dad at Thom McAn, both on Main Street in Springfield. On lunch break or after work she could find him, and I knew there had been some discussion of the situation. The Sunday previous I had been to dinner at Irene's and she had sent Dad a message by me concerning the prospective move. Now that Ruth would be earning a salary, this was a propitious time for him and me to move into the new home they were about to establish. Was Dad reluctant for a familial reunion? He never said that to me, but why had I been given the message by Irene for him? If my response tipped the balance in Dad's decision, I was to come to regret it. But there were two years of amity before the crisis broke.

Ruth picked the house. It was on Park Street facing the park and was right across from the Town Hall, where she worked. It was a large house with a wrap-around porch (Dad called it a veranda), then owned by the bank, but once owned by a member of one branch of the Smith family founded by Horace Moses Smith, the gun manufacturer. An elderly Mrs. Smith, a widow, lived alone on the second floor. We had the first floor. There was a large carriage house in the rear that we called a barn. In it were old magazines. Some of the magazines were no longer publishing, and those that were still appearing contained illustrations with quite different styles of clothing, automobiles, and most anything. Robert, Phillip and I, and our friends from school, would look at the pictures in the magazines, seeking something that struck us as ridiculous. "Hey! Look at this!" someone would shout and fling the magazine across to someone, who would look, howl with laughter, and fling it to someone else. These publications were already antiques, and someone could have profited from putting them on the market, but after we tossed them around, they were too damaged to be of much value. We did not know their value. We were intruders from the low-rent area into a middle-class section of town.

The house next door was occupied by an elderly woman who was better off financially than Mrs. Smith. She had servants to care for her and her house. When she went out, she drove an electric automobile. Its shape was totally unlike other cars on the road. It was box-like, and the lower part flared out fore and aft, with fenders over the wheels. She sat upright in her black dress and black veiled lace hat in the box, which was largely glass on all sides, and steered not using a wheel but employing a stick that could be turned right or left as needed. It ran silently on a large battery under the seat, and it crawled along at about 15 miles per hour. It was a menace to other cars that had to slow down or pass it. Whenever we saw the odd vehicle going out the driveway, we stopped and stood and stared.

On the other side of our house was the American Legion. We used to play ball on the broad space between our house and the Legion. Dad found the location convenient; he was not a member, but used to go in and play cards and have a drink or two. (Irene did not like him to keep "booze" in the house.) Legionnaires had taken over the once-proud home of a well-to-do family. This essentially public use of the house and our renting part of the Smith house marked the decline of the neighborhood. Park Street had been co-opted as the street on which national Route 20 ran through the town, which probably had something to do with the former owners of the Legion house selling it and moving to a more secluded area. A few years after the war, I drove down Park Street and saw that all three of these fine old houses had been torn down and brick buildings of no architectural distinction put in their places -- less elegant, but more rentable space squeezed onto the lots.

Almost immediately after we moved to Park Street, Irene became pregnant, and in due course a baby girl was born and named Barbara. Twenty-one years younger than Ruth, Dad's oldest child, she was essentially a different generation from me. She would still be a toddler when I left home a few months after graduation from high school.

There are a few scenes that stick in my memory of our family life on Park Street. One is Saturday night bath time. In the kitchen next to the stove stood a tall hot water tank. The gas heater under it was usually turned off. Small amounts of hot water were heated on the stove. Only baths required quantities of water sufficient to need the tank to be heated. There was an order in which members of the family took their baths. Ruth took hers early, and often went out on a date afterward. Then baby Barbara would be bathed by her mother and put to bed. Dorothy, Phillip, Robert, and I followed. I picture Irene standing by the water tank controlling the production of hot water, but it is unlikely she stayed there all evening. But she did designate the turn of each to go into the bathroom, dispensing towels as we went in.

Another memory is doing homework around the kitchen table. When meal times were over, the table was pushed against a wall. Robert and Phillip faced each other across the table, each of them near the wall. I sat facing the wall, between the two of them. We each had space on the table to do our work. Dorothy must have had another area for her homework for she is not seated there with us in my memory. Phillip had made a double promotion thereby becoming only a year behind Robert. Then he had made another double promotion, and was in Robert's class, so they had the same homework.

Phillip would finish his homework and put his head down on the table and doze off. Robert would still be working on his math problems. Sometimes he would say, "Phil! What did you get on number five?" Phillip might need to be prodded awake, but he would raise his head and give the answer and explain how he got it. Having seen this I was surprised, and annoyed, when Robert got higher marks than Phillip. "We reward effort," the nun explained to Irene. "Robert is attentive and tries hard. Phillip's attention sometimes wanders and his efforts are slovenly." Ruth said Phillip was the smartest one in the family.

Phil's falling asleep after finishing his homework was not the only time he dozed off when others were active around him. When we played baseball in the space next to our house, if his team was not in the field and if he was not at bat or running bases, he would lie down on the grass, and likely as not fall asleep, and have to be awakened when his team had to take their places on the field again. It was suspected he had diabetes and he was tested but found not to be in need of insulin. I recalled this early suspicion of diabetes years later when Phil in his fifties joined Alcoholics Anonymous. The body's assimilating of sugar and alcohol is interrelated. Fortunately, Phil overcame both problems. Once he decided to stop drinking, he remained sober – so far as I know. His physiological malfunction must have been minor for if he had a "touch" of diabetes, he would not have reached more than 80 years of age, for four decades is more or less the length of survival after diabetes is diagnosed.

Why Phillip is more prominent than Robert in my recollections of the period is hard to say, but I do not remember Robert playing ball though he probably did, and for that matter, I didn't hang around the area of the house very often. Aside from the homework scene at the table, I cannot dredge up a picture of Robert during that time.

These cameo scenes that persist vividly in my memory may suggest a repetition day after day and week after week, but there would have been many gaps because I so often went to Lexington Street in Springfield after school to see Fitz and returned after the family had gone to bed.

THE SPORTING LIFE

At West Springfield High, I expected to go on with the two sports I had done in junior high: basketball and wrestling. But there was no basketball team. Being a small school, there were not enough boys to fill teams for all the team sports, and football was given preference. Coach asked me to go out for track since I had long legs. I did and stayed with it for the first year, running and jumping, but didn't care much for that. I joined the wrestling team my freshman year, in the 145 pound class, and continued each of the remaining years, a little heavier, in the appropriate weight class.

I had been fairly good at basketball, playing center, because I was taller than most of my classmates, but I was only so-so as a wrestler. I won some matches and lost some, but the one that I cannot forget is one of the earliest after I made the team.

121

My opponent was my weight, 145 pounds, but short, broad shouldered, muscular, and barrel-chested. He quickly got me in a lock I couldn't break and the match was over almost before it began. It was the shortest match on the school's record.

An embarrassing way to start at a new school, but I wasn't going to let that one match bother me. I knew I would do better on other occasions. I was not a jock. I liked to be active and enjoyed the activity in the sports in which I chose to participate, but I didn't hang around with guys on the team. For that matter I did not hang around with anyone from West Springfield High during my first two years there. Most of my classmates had been together in earlier years; I had no old acquaintances among them. I returned to my friends in the town I had left, but it was not merely the absence of local attraction. It was the bond that Fitz and I had built between us in the previous years.

I walked across the North End Bridge most every day after school to go to Springfield. I still used the Springfield public libraries, not mentioning my change of address. And I continued to go up to Lexington Street to Fitz's house. It was miles instead of blocks to Fitz's from where I now lived, but my presence there did not diminish by much. We now had high school courses giving us some things to talk about. Fitz had a slide rule and showed me how to use it. No one I saw at WSHS had a slide rule, but then if I had gone to Classical High I probably wouldn't have seen slide rules there either. He was taking chemistry, and so was I, but his class seemed more advanced than mine. I took a science each year – chemistry, biology and physics -- and had the same teacher, Mr. Piper, all three times. Fitz had a different science teacher for each science. He always knew more science than I, and much of what I know I learned from him. But one teacher I had was at least a match for any in his field at Tech. This was an English teacher with a Ph.D. from Yale, who would ordinarily have been teaching in a college, but with academic positions scarce during the depression, he had taken a job in our high school.

Often enough I had dinner at the Fitzgerald's and did not return home till everyone was asleep. I'd let myself in the back door and quietly go to bed. In the winter, this could be very late, midnight or after, because we'd go ice skating on Van Horn Pond. A fire would be kept going on the shore; anyone feeling too cold could come over to the fire and warm up, and then go back to skating. The result of losing sleep in order to continue skating was that I sometimes fell asleep in class the next day.

Even in warmer weather, it was often well past dark when I would be making my way back to West Springfield. Sometimes Fitz would say, "I'll walk you part way." This was usually because we were talking about something that we couldn't seem to finish, something from one or another of our school courses or something one or the other of us had read in a library book. It was not necessarily non-fiction. We were both overwhelmed by the spectacular story of pre-war Europe in *Europa* by Robert Briffault, son of a British diplomat who had grown up seriatim in various European capitals. Although he was writing about events and characters in his own lifetime, it was already in the 1930s an historical novel about a time before Fitz or I was born. This was followed by *Europa in Limbo,* a novel of the social turmoil during the Great War, and eventually by *Fandango*, about the Spanish civil war. The locations were all Trans-Atlantic, but we were beginning to realize that what happened "over there" impacted the United States and would affect the circumstances of our future lives. In addition to the social and geopolitical dramas, one of the elements that fascinated me was the larding of conversations with – according to the speakers – French, Italian, German, Spanish, and Russian phrases and sentences. Briffault was the first polyglot writer I had encountered, and even his English was richer than most novelists. His seriousness was indicated by his book of essays, *Psyche's Lamp*, and his non-fiction tomes (three volumes), *The Mothers*, a historical search for evidence of a once-upon-a-time matriarchal society. *Studs Lonegan* by James Farrell, set in Chicago, and other novels and novelists gave us an American counterpoint to Briffault's weighty oeuvre. Fitz and I were always kicking around ideas obtained from novels, school, or the daily news, and there always seemed to be another aspect to discuss.

Fitz was never as much of a walker as I was, so when he felt he was getting too far away from home, he'd stop. We'd stand there for a while to finish what we were saying, and then part and go our opposite ways, but sometimes we couldn't let the topic go, and after standing still for a time, I'd say to him, "I'll walk you part way back." And off we'd go in the direction from which we had come. In this way, we went back and forth a few times before we would finally part.

Our wandering in the night usually attracted no notice, but one night a police cruiser stopped beside us, and one of the officers got out of the car, and asked what we were doing. I explained that I lived in West Springfield, and had been visiting with my friend, and he was walking me part way home. However, the police had seen us going back and forth and wondered why we were acting so strangely. We had been engrossed in our discussion and had paid no attention to any cars, police patrols, or whatever, going by us on the road. They suspected that we were looking for a darkened house to break into.

When the officer said, "Let's see some identification," I knew I had none on me but made a performance looking through all of my pockets. Finally, I brought out a folded dollar bill, opened it out, peered closely at it, and then put it away, saying, "No, that's not me. That's George Washington."

"Oh! A couple of wise guys, eh? Get in the car." We got in the back of the cruiser.

"Shall we take 'em down to the station?" the driver asked the other officer as he got back in the front seat, separated from us by a metal grill. "Yeah, it'll do 'em good. Maybe learn to have a civil tongue."

"What'll we charge them with?" the driver asked.

"Vagrancy."

"But they got homes, haven't they?"

"OK," the officer who had interrogated us said, "Get out and go home. And don't let us catch you wandering around in the middle of the night again."

We got out and the cruiser drove off.

"Why'd you make that remark about Washington?" Fitz, annoyed, wanted to know. I had no answer. It had been a momentary impulse I should have ignored. But I felt they had no right to tell us not to be out "in the middle of the night." It wasn't all that late, anyway, only about 11 o'clock. We parted this time for good.

I never asked permission from anyone to absent myself so many evenings from my newly reunited family. I just did as I would have done had I still been living in the hotel – moving about as I pleased. No one in the family ever challenged my right to spend so much time across the river. It was taken more or less for granted that I was a kind of outsider to the family, a semi-stranger who had taken up residence with them.

This independence of movement was exemplified at its zenith when I told Irene that I was going to hitchhike to New York City and be in Times Square at midnight on New Years to see the lighted ball drop. I don't remember that there was any protest! The idea came from Beg, but Fitz and I were immediately agreeable to the venture. What Beg had in mind was not the observance of the turning of the year on the calendar – it was that New York City had certain attractions that Springfield did not. Specifically, it had burlesque theaters.

Three is hardly ideal for hitching a ride, but we got to the Big City in good time. It was still daylight. Beg had come equipped with information about the names and locations of the "strip-joints" and navigated us to the one of his choice. "There it is," I said *sotto voce*. "Why are you whispering?" asked Beg. "They're legal here." I knew that, but it seemed to me that it should be secretive: no one is my family or in Fitz's would even mention a burlesque theater.

Beg bought all the tickets; we each gave him our money to do so. We were afraid we would have seemed too young, but he was the one with the self-assurance needed for the situation. We went to three shows at different theaters, including Minsky's in Harlem, before it was time to see the ceremonial drop of the ball at midnight. Over sandwiches and coffee in an automat we evaluated the performers and agreed that "Exotic Paula," the big bosomed redhead, stole the show.

The crowd was shoulder to shoulder in Times Square, and it seemed the ball would never drop. When it finally did, the shouts of the crowd welcomed it and people quickly began to disperse. We went to Grand Central Station where there were benches for passengers who were waiting for trains and stretched out to try to sleep. The benches were hard and the place was drafty and cold. We did sleep a bit until wakened by a policeman's billy tapping the soles of our feet. Anyone without a ticket for the train was ushered out. We walked around the block, came in by a different door, checked that the policeman was no longer there, and found another bench. The next day we hitched back to Springfield feeling quite adult.

GETTING EDUCATED

Geometry was interesting but it came at the time in the late morning when the inadequacy of sleep the night before, especially during ice skating season, began to overwhelm me. It was usually in geometry class that I fell asleep. But when winter was over, I somehow caught up and managed to just barely pass the course. Ruth's record of high marks was held up to me. Teachers would say, "Why can't you do as well as your sister?" Teachers' comparison of my work with that of my sister Ruth's was the first I knew that she had gone to public school. Dad's concern that Irene would disapprove of my going to public school had made me assume that all the children with Irene, including Ruth, went to parochial school.

If Ruth could go to public school, why had I had so much trouble extracting myself from Sacred Heart? I never asked anyone at the time about Ruth's exemption from parochial school. Now that I look back, I suppose that Aunt Gertrude may have had something to do with it, since she played a role with Ruth similar to Aunt May's continual looking out for my needs. Some of the Sweeney's, despite being practicing Catholics, may have felt that West Springfield public high school education excelled that provided by the nuns.

Mrs. Burke was the history teacher at West Springfield High School. We used a text by David Saville Muzzey. On the Spanish American War, Muzzey wrote, "Admiral Dewey in the battle of Manila Bay showed the courage of his old commander Farragut at New Orleans."

"How could Dewey show courage when all he had to do was enter the bay with his steel battleships, approach the Spanish fleet, mostly wooden ships, sink most of them, and tell his crew 'Well done. Go below and have breakfast.'"

She accused me of exaggerating, but it was on the basis of something I had read. It was clear that the teacher had not read widely on the war. A teacher cannot be expected to research every facet of her/his subject, but a bigger contest was to come in my senior year. (My final year was a culmination of many things.) In senior year history, every student was required to give an oral report on a topic. There was no time limit, only a minimum of three minutes, and none of the reports of my classmates lasted longer than ten minutes.

Mexico and U.S. relations was my chosen topic. In gathering material I never considered how long it would take to present my report. In the event, it took the whole class period. That was the day I realized that I would like to be a teacher. Collecting and sharing information was already a habit, but previously my audience had been friends. That day when I had a classroom of pupils, I discovered my didactic passion. I recounted the nineteenth-century U.S. war with Mexico, the creation of Texas by settlers from the U.S. who subsequently rebelled against Mexico, the eventual annexation of the Republic of Texas, the aggrandizement of U.S. territory by acquisition of southwestern areas including California, and the twentieth-century unsuccessful invasion by a U.S. army under General Pershing in pursuit of Pancho Villa. In the course of this overview I characterized Mexican society as stratified with a ruling caste of European descent, a middle caste of *mestizo* (that is, mixed Indian and European) descent, and a depressed lower caste of American Indian descent. And I described the religious establishment of the Catholic Church and its conflict with the then-current Revolutionary government.

My report took the whole 55-minute hour partly because Mrs. Burke interrupted on a couple of occasions to dispute my presentation. She thought my description of the Catholic Church (her Church) in Mexico was too severe. I had said that Pentecostal and other Protestant missionaries were making some headway because the Catholic priests served mainly the European-descent families, and in many rural areas a priest visited only once a year, marrying those who had begun to live together since his last visit, baptizing recently-born children, saying mass for as many days as he stayed, and then leaving to briefly visit another *mestizo* community. The Indian population, I reported, perpetuated some of their traditional religion either openly or in Christianized form. Mrs. Burke argued that travel was difficult in some parts of the country, the number of priests was limited, and that they did the best they could under the circumstances. Though she defended the Mexican religious establishment, she did not defend Mexican territorial claims. United States expansion had been, in her view, not imperialist but legal and legitimate.

Forty years later, having not seen my classmates in the interim, I attended a class reunion, and the reminiscences brought up to me by several others were of this "debate" with Mrs. Burke.

English was the domain of Miss Bosworth, affectionately known as Bossy to those students who enjoyed British and American literature. She was also the advisor to the student editors of the school magazine that appeared a couple of times a year. I did not pay much attention to the magazine during my first two years, but in 1937, my senior year, the Connecticut River flooded the low-lying parts of the town. I wrote a poem about the flood:

> *Once when the rapid river rushed*
> *Over its banks into the town*
> *Then people fled with faces flushed*
> *To escape the waters coming down.*
>
> *What a scene of devastation!*
> *Muddied mattresses, broken dishes*
> *What a cause of consternation!*
> *Blessed homes defiled by fishes.*

There was more, all doggerel as I later realized, but at the time I was proud of it and submitted it to the magazine editors. Not only was it published, but I was invited to join the staff of the magazine, which I did, and made the first close friends that I had in town. One was Miriam Collins, student editor of the magazine, to whom I wrote my next poem:

> *On her head is a crown*
> *Of ringlet curls of chestnut brown*
> (and so on)

Mim and I went on bike trips in search of items for a mineral collection, a project for Mr. Piper's physics class. The banks on the sides of gravel roads cut by the road construction crews were good places to look for garnet, amethyst, quartz, etc. We took the makings of a lunch, and once after a rain I attempted to show my woodsman's skill by building a fire – and failed. I had done it previously at Boy Scout camp (with dry wood), but when I wanted to show off and could only find wet wood, the most I got was puffs of smoke. But we ended up with the best mineral collection in the school. She was my first girlfriend.

Lower Main Street, where the family used to live, was badly flooded. Our house on Park Street only had water in the basement, but we were evacuated. The flood caused the same division in the family that had happened when Dad's business went bankrupt. Ruth and I went to Aunt Katherine's (our mother's youngest sister), and the rest of the family went elsewhere, where exactly I can no longer say.

I had seen Aunt Katherine only at Christmases the previous two years. The Sweeney Christmas celebrations were hosted by Uncle Ray, the only adult male in the family. There was the usual dinner with turkey and all the fixings, and a decorated tree with mounds of presents under it. Ruth had been invited ever since she had been living in West Springfield, and once I lived there, I was dragged along by Ruth. There was a present for me, so I knew I was expected. My first Christmas I was introduced to each of the Sweeney's, and then I did not see any of them until the next Christmas. As far as I can remember I said very little, and my mother's family remained essentially strangers to me.

Now I became acquainted with Aunt Katherine and found that she was a friendly, jolly person. We were only there for a few days, and the one who made the biggest impression on me was a pretty Polish servant girl. She was only a little older than I was, and I said virtually nothing to her, but was always aware of her blond presence. I hadn't known anyone who was Polish before, and I found out that there were many Polish families in the Connecticut River Valley around Springfield working on the farms that produced onions or tobacco. In some of the smaller towns nearby, polkas and "peevo" (beer) were the Saturday night entertainment.

After the flood, I was asked to babysit for Katherine's two children, Andrew (junior) and Barbara, whenever the parents went out in the evening. Uncle Andrew would pick me up and drive me up to Mittineague Hill where they lived, and would drive me home afterwards. In addition to being paid, Aunt Katherine always made a plate of dates stuffed with almonds and covered with confectionery sugar. There were never any left when the evening was over.

In my senior year, I was not in Miss Bosworth's class. A man with a doctorate from Yale University had joined the teaching staff of West Springfield High School; it was doubly unusual for a male Ph.D. to be teaching English in a high school. A master's degree was the goal of most teachers; doctorates were virtually unheard of. Moreover, it was rare for a man to be teaching English (except for the coach, the science teacher had been the only male teacher in the school, and science was *unofficially* considered a "masculine" subject whereas English was, in that unspecified categorization, a "feminine" subject).

I enrolled in his class. What he covered in class is no longer recoverable, but I can see his slim figure of medium height, his youthful face, and light brown hair. He invited students, a few at a time, to afternoon tea at his house, a practice no other teacher engaged in. His wife served the tea and he initiated the conversation. This was a different kind of after-school activity. The conversation, when I was one of the invitees, happened to verge – no doubt on the teacher's direction -- on the processes of history. History was a favorite interest of mine, and I took part in the discussion. When I was leaving, I was offered a loan of Oswald Spengler's *Decline of the West,* recently translated from *Die Untergang des Abenlandes.* Thereafter, I read a chapter a week and discussed it with him at his house after school on an afternoon different from his teas. Essentially, this is what graduate students in universities call a "directed study." It was an amazing piece of luck that I had one in high school, and a small school in a small town at that!

Madame Tirrell taught French. My two years of junior high French counted as one year of high school French, so in my first year of high school I was able to begin French II. We read some Dumas, *père et fils,* Victor Hugo, and still had grammar exercises. The only club I joined that year was the Le Cercle Français. We met once a month in the evenings.

In my senior year, there were only two other students qualified for French IV since they had to have started taking French in eighth grade. With one teacher and three pupils, it was possible to have conversations. We could talk about anything we wanted to talk about, Mme. Tirrell told us, as long as we said it in French.

One Monday, one of the two other students asked me what I had done Saturday. I could have replied that I went to the movies, but I wanted to respond with more than a simple declarative sentence. I started out by saying a friend came to suggest a movie. He found me mowing the lawn. This beginning turned out to be, I quickly realized, a trap because I had never had an occasion to encounter the French word for "lawn mower." So I said he found me pushing *la chose avec quoi je puis couper les herbes* (the thing with which I cut the grass). Mme. supplied the appropriate French term: *la tondeuse*. I incorporated the offered term in my amended statement and went on with what I had been saying. The word did not stick for very long; it was seldom I had occasion to use it, and now I could not recall it. I had to look it up in my *Concise Oxford French Dictionary* (1934), which I still have.

It was not the first time I had got around my ignorance of a word by describing the object, action, or elements of the concept. Mme. Tirrell extolled my persistence in spite of occasional inadequacy of vocabulary. Students usually came to a stop when they lacked a needed word and opened the dictionary, interrupting the conversation. "Daniel," she told us, "would make a good interpreter." She then recounted a story about a student she had had years earlier who was not a dedicated student, but had the knack of finding a way to express himself. He had become an interpreter for American troops in France during the Great War.

KEEPING THE FAITH – OR NOT

My senior year I found another friend, or rather he found me. George Corcoran had been in a private school but became ill and had been at home recuperating. His parents did not want him to be away again until they were sure he had totally recovered. He joined us in West Springfield High just after the senior year began. He needed to "catch up." George asked me to come to his house and study together. "We can go over our notes from class, compare what we each got." I told him I seldom took notes, but that did not deter him. Years later he told me he was dyslexic and had trouble taking notes. George had a basement room that was his "den," where he had a typewriter and a telephone as well as tools and materials to adjust or repair his short-wave radio. We went there some afternoons and went over what had been presented in our various classes.

Although he was born in West Springfield, George was a stranger to the other pupils because he had been away at the private school. His father was a medical doctor who made house calls as doctors still did in those days, but he had a chauffeur drive him. His mother had her own car, but when she wasn't using it, she allowed George to drive it. He would drive up the road toward Holyoke to Brookside Farms where we would get a delicious frappe; it was his way of compensating me for my time tutoring him after school. We also drove up to the top of a hill where he could listen for calls on the five-meter radio that he had installed in the car. Once he heard a call from Australia. Usually the persons he could talk to were somewhere in the U.S. or Canada, and he had a few radio contacts that he talked to more or less regularly.

George and I talked about various things besides classroom topics. The Corcoran's were Catholic. He supposed I was also. My family went to the Immaculate Conception Church; my siblings went to the parochial school. I told him I couldn't believe the Catholic dogmas. He was surprised, but not shocked, that I was an atheist.

"You believe there is no god, that we have no souls, and there is no heaven?"

"That *is* what I said."

"You may be right," he said, "but if you're wrong, it's Hell to pay."

"Hell is a myth."

Years later I read a statement by physicist P. Bridgman. Concepts like spirit, soul, or god, are not "operational," that is, one can not measure, weigh, or otherwise examine such entities, the existence of which he could neither affirm nor deny. They are not problems in physics. He didn't disallow a non-material sphere within which these alleged entities flourished; he simply put the problem outside his special competence. It was a stance that avoided arguments, and was probably formulated as a shield against attacks from pulpits. Some scientists I would eventually read distanced themselves from any particular religion, but claimed to believe there was a First Cause, some power that set the universe in operation. That seemed to me just another term for a non-anthropomorphic deity. The complexity of the universe was more than I could understand but I saw no point in backing into what was essentially an allowance for the rightness of religions. But I wanted something decisive one way or the other. I couldn't convince myself that any of the various religions had a claim to a cosmology that was scientifically respectable, so I began to consider myself an atheist. Some years later, I realized that one cannot prove a negative, so one is on vulnerable ground claiming what one cannot substantiate. I revised my label to agnostic (Greek: "not knowing"), but I did not grant each possibility an equal chance of being correct, so in effect, my relation to organized religion didn't change despite the difference in how I described myself.

While still in high school, living with a devout family, hell would have been right here on earth if my stepmother knew what I had revealed to George. And that was soon to happen.

Throughout high school I worked Saturdays at the Rood and Woodbury Grocery Store. At first I just took cans or bottles or cartons out of boxes or crates and put the items on the proper shelves after stamping the price on each. This was tedious but I earned a little money. Later I was promoted to the vegetable department, and found that with a little practice I could put nearly exactly the amount of spinach, or beans, or any loose stuff, into a bag and have the requested weight when I set the bag on the scale. Also I could now talk to customers. It was a more interesting job.

I gave some of what I earned on my Saturday job to Irene toward the expenses of my room and board, and saved some. My first expenditure was to buy a sprocket for my bike so I could have two pedals. Next, perhaps a year later, I bought a Corona portable typewriter and taught myself to type.

Eventually my job at Rood and Woodbury changed again. R&W had a delivery truck and groceries were delivered, for a fee, to the homes of customers. On Saturdays the driver had a helper. I got a chance to be the helper and jumped at the opportunity to be out of doors, away from the store. We loaded the truck with boxes containing the orders of the customers, arranging the boxes according to a route the driver would select as convenient. We would carry as many boxes as made up an order to the house or apartment, collapse the boxes, and put them flat on the floor of the truck so we could get at the boxes further back in the truck at the next stop. It was enjoyable to me.

The driver was friendly; the exercise was not excessive. When the weather was good, everything was lovely.

Then one Saturday just before a holiday, the number of deliveries was suddenly more numerous than ever before, and we kept on delivering well after midnight. Many customers were angry at the lateness of the arrival of their purchases. Some had gone to bed. In apartment buildings we left the packages at the doors if no one responded to our knocks. At houses we also left things at the doors, but these were outside doors, and I wondered how many dogs there might be out in the neighborhood. I was sure that R&W would get a lot of complaints. The truck finally was parked in back of the store, the driver and I parted, and I walked home – across the North End Bridge to West Springfield. It was 2 a.m. when I got there. The house was dark. I let myself in and went to bed.

In the morning, Irene came in to wake me for eight o'clock mass. I didn't want to get up. I told her how late I had worked. You can go to a later mass, she conceded. An hour later someone else came in to get me up. I refused to go to the nine o'clock and the ten o'clock mass. Finally my father came in and asked me to go to the eleven o'clock mass, the last mass. By this time I was so annoyed at being awakened every hour by one or another sibling that I told Dad I wasn't going to go to church that day. I suppose I must have realized what the consequences would be, but I was stubborn and defied everyone.

"I will not have an atheist under my roof," Irene declared.

"He is my son," Dad proclaimed.

There was a frigid atmosphere around the house for a few days. Unbeknownst to me, an arrangement was worked out. George Corcoran later explained it to me. Ruth had told Aunt

Gertrude. Aunt Gertrude was a friend of Mrs. Corcoran. Mrs. Corcoran had a brother who was a Dominican monk in a monastery in West Springfield. If I would go to the monastery once a week on an afternoon after school and talk to a monk about my beliefs, there would be no demand that I go to church on Sundays.

That was an excellent arrangement. I was relieved of the boredom of attending a meaningless ritual every Sunday, and the equivalent time I would spend at the monastery was at least intellectually stimulating. And this permitted me to finish school without constant harassment at home. I was turned me over to Brother Jerome, who gave me a course in Catholic apologetics. Each week he gave me something to read and when I came back he would ask me my reaction. He was never satisfied with my response and we bantered back and forth. My adopted motto was "Doubt is the beginning of wisdom." His purpose was to get me to accept faith. We talked past each other on different levels. I learned more about Catholic doctrine than I had acquired from Sacred Heart catechism, but I didn't believe any of it.

An American Socialism

Ruth went on her summer vacation to a beach resort in Asbury, New Jersey. There she met Edward Gaven, a junior executive at Standard Oil of New Jersey.

When she returned home, he drove up to West Springfield to see her. Obviously, he was a new beau. He drove a big car. Her previous beau used to take her out in a pick-up truck. No one was surprised that she preferred a car to a truck, but I liked the guy who drove the pick-up – he was an ordinary friendly person. Her new beau dressed in business suits, and was too hoity-toity for me.

During his weekend visit, at Sunday dinner, I got into an argument with him over the expropriation of oil fields in Mexico by the Mexican government. The recent takeover of oil production in Mexico came up in the conversation, not brought up by me, but when it had been mentioned, my research for my history report on Mexico rendered me prepared to intervene. Ed, as he wanted the family to call him, deplored the illegality of the revolutionary government taking possession of the oil fields that had been developed by American oil companies, particularly Standard Oil, for which Ed worked.

I maintained that the oil beneath the soil belonged to the people of the country, if it belonged to anyone, and the government represented the people and had the right to control the resource. Ed was good-natured and held up his side of the argument, and when it was clear he had not convinced me, he said, "If you do not have some socialist sympathies before you are thirty, you have no heart, but if you still have them after thirty, you have no head." My position was the folly of youth, he and the family agreed; they expected me eventually to change and agree with Ed. Now I'm more than half a century older than thirty, and I still have, essentially, a socialist's outlook on the problems of the world.

True, my view has modified following decades of observing world events, reading further, and thinking. Then, my opinion was formed by Fabian arguments and the pamphlets given out by the Marxist "rabble-rousers" on a street corner. But there have always been other avenues to a more equitable society. Eugene Debs, candidate of the American Socialist Party, ran for the presidency four times beginning in 1900, and did better than most previous third party candidates. This was before my birth and before the emergence of the Soviet Union and the "Red Scare" in the U.S. The concept of Socialism in this country has been essentially moribund since the 1920s. Any utterance of socialist ideas has been shouted down by conservative spokesmen evoking "Moscow gold" as behind the idea.

Nonetheless, it is common sense that everyone should have a right to work. The reverse is also true; everyone has an obligation to work. If one gets food, shelter, clothing and other necessities, then one should contribute to the society's production of useful things and services. Capitalism, however, decreed that work is a commodity to be bought by capitalists. The possessors of unused work, i.e., workers left without employment, can be left to starve, or at least relegated to a breadline for a handout of scraps of food.

There are many tasks that would be good for society that are not done under the capitalist system because there is no profit to be made from doing them; a democratic socialist system would get them done and in doing so would maintain full employment. Who would pay for this "unremunerative" work? Franklin D. Roosevelt gave an answer. The Works Progress Administration and the Civilian Conservation Corps put people to work when capitalists had no "need" for them. This was called "made work," that is, work for which the market does not provide the means because there is no pecuniary profit. But the "made work" in President F.D.R 's semi-socialist New Deal saved capitalism from revolution (as capitalist Joseph Kennedy believed) by allaying the worst effects of the great Depression.

Fabian socialists believed that they could educate the public to push for laws to reform the system and that they could persuade capitalists to give up power. (H.G. Wells's last book shows that he died a disillusioned man.) Fabians did not count on the disposable money capitalists can devote to "propaganda" via all the media that "educate" (or mis-educate) the public in the opposite direction. Some argue, therefore, that only revolution can get us out of the grip of the capitalists. Let us hope that is not true; revolutions are bloody, and release ugly passions that often backfire on the revolutionaries themselves. A constitutional means – in this the Fabians were right - is the better means. That requires a political movement and none is now in sight (I may end as disillusioned as Wells). We have to hope that events will stimulate public realization that socio-economic reorganization is necessary.

Egalitarianism does not require all to be treated in exactly the same fashion. A Picasso, an Einstein, a Grace Kelly, a Babe Ruth, a Marian Anderson, or a James Joyce need not be squeezed into the same lifestyle. While I believe that many industries, particularly public transport services, post office, and electronic communications should be communally owned (as they are in some European countries), and cooperatives in production as well as consumption may have a place, I admit there's a role for an individual entrepreneur; there must be an opening for useful innovations. But a stringent graduated tax should prevent CEOs, baseball players, movie stars, etc., from disposing of incomes so outrageously greater than the average in the society. They would have to be satisfied with a moderate extra, and the sense of a good job well done. This may seem unimaginable to persons brought up in our greed-is-good society, but if brought up in a society that favored cooperation more than competition, such an attitude could flourish.

The Soviet system, some socialists argue, was not socialist, and its demise proves nothing in regard to socialism. A few years later, one of my friends would describe the Soviets as "state capitalists" – that is the Politburo were the capitalists. This is too simplistic, but denying that the totalitarian system was really socialism is essential to the truth of the matter. The theories from which the Soviets started may have been socialistic, but authoritarianism combined with socialism is a disaster; in essence socialism is democratic economically as well as politically.

At a later period the Un-American Activities Committee in Congress interrogated citizens who admitted - or were suspected of - being communists, and a phrase used by some who denied the accusations became famous: "I am not now and never have been a communist." I could have made such a declaration; I never paid any dues but I attended a few meetings of the Young Communist League, and also a couple of free classes in Marxism in a "school" in a commercial building in Springfield. I was what was called a "fellow traveler." I felt that the domestic policies of the Communist Party were pretty much in line with my own attitudes. Their international policies, in so far as they were anti-Fascist, I could also agree with.

The small number of actual "card-carrying" Communists that I met at that time seemed to me to be well-meaning persons, but some of them were inclined to be too zealous and unable to see any other point of view. Zealots scare me. Zealotry in politics is the reason leftist and rightist politicians are sometimes said to have made a religion of politics: religion is the usual home for zealots. Years later, in college, I met some who were communists who were able to discuss political issues without rancor; they tolerated their fellow party members who were less tolerant. But I couldn't find rapport with anyone who never had any doubt in regard to large issues.

There is one other element that has more recently developed in my political philosophy; it derives from the discussion decades ago under the rubric of "technocracy." As presented, it argues that experts should run the world. But experts can be, and usually are, subject to all the motivations to corruption and tyranny as any other human being. Democratic restraints on any bureaucracy are needed. However, in the technologically complex world that has developed since World War II, scientists are more significant than they used to be, but science has been largely co-opted by corporations and the military, which is not a good situation. We ought to have more scientists serving in our legislatures.

C.M.T.C.

Two of the summers during high school, Fitz and I went to the Citizens Military Training Corps. The Citizens Military Training Corps was a summer program for teenage boys to spend a number of weeks at a U.S. Army base. It had some attraction in the Depression to city boys whose fathers were out of work. The boys could be built up with daily exercise in the open air, be fed simple but adequately nourishing food, be given regular hours of sleep, and at the same time – more important from the Army's point of view -- be taught some military skills. Neither Fitz nor I had any empathy for militarism and would never on our own have thought of going. Fitz's brother-in-law, Mike Kerry, told us that if we wanted to learn to ride horses, there was a CMTC program for cavalry at Fort Ethan Allen near Burlington, Vermont. We immediately became interested.

The catch was that one had to start with the infantry, and so we went to Fort Devens, in eastern Massachusetts, in order to be able to go to the cavalry camp the next year. I don't remember much about our summer in the infantry, but the cavalry summer stays with me. There are, however, a few things about that first year that I recall. I earned a sharpshooter ribbon that summer, and never again in my life shot a gun, except once to shoot a rabbit, and the rabbit almost killed me with the disease, tularemia, that I got from it.

Fitz did well when shooting from a prone position, but we also had to sit on our haunches on the ground and brace an elbow on a knee to steady our aim; Fitz did not do well in that position because of some constriction in his body that made the posture hard for him to assume and uncomfortable to hold. This, and frequent constipation, were early indications of his health problems; in later years he suffered from terrible bouts of migraine and various internal problems, resulting, among other things, in two operations to remove parts of his colon. His father had similar ailments and had an operation to have gall stones removed. His mother was never bothered with any illness and lived into her nineties. Not long before he died, Fitz told me, "I inherited my father's genes. Why couldn't it have been my mother's?"

We were eight boys to a large square tent on a wooden platform. We were allowed some time midday free from marching or other drills or instruction, and after lunch mostly we'd hang around in the tent. One guy in our tent always went to sleep on his cot. Another tent-mate played a trick on him one day. He got a container of warm water and put one of the sleeper's hands in the water. "It will make him piss his pants and wet his bed!" It might have worked if the other guys had kept quiet, but despite the trickster's whispering "Quiet!" the shuffling of shoes as each spectator tried to get a good view and the gabbing and giggling woke up the intended victim.

Almost stereotypically I peeled mountains of potatoes on K.P. Marching I hated; it was one of the reasons that years later when I received my draft notice, I went to the Coast Guard recruiting office and joined up even though it meant a period of service twice as long as the stint in the Army to which I was being called.

The next summer Fort Ethan Allen put us in the same big square eight-person tents that we had at Devens, but everything else was different. Every morning we groomed our horses, saddled them, and rode at a walk, a canter, a gallop, and a run. Sergeants at Devens now are nameless and faceless, but Sergeant Scanzelli, who was our drill sergeant at Ethan Allen, is unforgettable. Scanzelli never tired of telling us how useless we were. We spoiled trained horses – after a summer of CMTC use, the horses had to be trained all over again.

We were supposed to know how to break down a rifle and then put it together again, but many had forgotten since the previous year's infantry training. "You're so stupid," Scanzelli told one guy, "You couldn't pour piss out of a boot if the directions were printed on the heel!" Most everyone except the reddened recipient of the verbal abuse laughed. Scanzelli then glared at the rest of us. "You think you could do it? You wouldn't even know to look on the heel for the directions." The laughter stopped. "Don't be too ready to laugh at someone else.

You may soon be the one laughed at." Under the circumstances, that was good advice.

First, we had to learn to ride. The horses were well broken in, but our group of would-be riders had never been atop a horse before. We were led from the stables to a large field, and following the soldier in the lead, all of us recruits walked our horses around in a circle. No problem, but each increment of speed was a problem. Between walking a horse and making it run there are two distinct paces: canter and gallop. We had to master each of these paces in single file in the circle on that field before we were formed into the parade dress of two by two. When we were competent at that we would be taken from the practice field and ride into the countryside. Days and days of exercise in the circle preceded any excursion away from the practice field.

Sgt. Scanzelli, when not on a horse, was very close to the ground. I do not know what his height was in feet and inches, but he was quite a bit shorter than I was. We wondered if there wasn't a minimum height required for acceptance in the army.

"Could he really qualify?" Fitz asked.

"Maybe," I suggested, "in the cavalry height doesn't count."

In his polished brown boots and flaring jodhpurs, starched khaki shirt and neatly-tied tie of the same hue, broad-brimmed cavalry hat, standing in front of youngsters all of whom towered over him, he seemed almost ridiculous, like a miniaturized toy, but that was not the reality. He was a soldier toughened by years of service on horseback. The view I had one day of Scanzelli was a perspective not everyone could claim to have seen. He at that moment was as gigantic as Goliath.

That day, early in our riding exercises, I kept sliding to one side, and would pull myself up, only to find myself soon sliding again. Later I understood that I was not gripping the flanks of the horse with my knees tightly enough. The troop was at a run in a large circle, round and round, and at some point I fell off. Scanzelli gave the order for everyone to rein in their mounts and stop. I was on my back on the ground, the wind knocked out of me, and I looked up from ground level and there was Sgt. Scanzelli in the saddle, up against the sky, looking down on me. "You hurt?"

"I don't think so."

"Get up and get on that horse."

One of the soldiers serving under Scanzelli had brought my horse up before I was on my feet. I mounted. The circle began to rotate again and somehow I stayed atop the running animal. When we were back in our tent, one of my tent mates said, "What a heartless S.O.B. Scanzelli is!"

"Probably a good idea," Fitz told him. "If he gave someone who was thrown from a horse time to think about whether or not he wanted to ride again, that guy might never want to get on a goddamn horse again." That seemed reasonable to me, but I felt it was not my case – I liked riding.

As the end of the month was coming near, we went on a four-day three-night ride through a wooded area of rolling hills, bivouacking each night. This was more fun than our learning exercises on the level ground at the base. We rode down steep gullies and up over ridges, always maintaining as much as possible a close double line despite the uneven terrain. In a roll attached to the cantle of the saddle we had a sleeping bag, change of uniform, ditty bag with tooth brush and whatever other small items one chose, all wrapped in half a pup tent. Fitz and I, putting our halves together, shared a tent.

Each evening we found a new spot to set up tents. Details were assigned to a number of tasks: clearing the area, getting wood for fires, and setting up the picket line, which was a line of rope to which to tether the horses. During the night we took turns standing watch around the tent area and especially over the horses – as if we were in enemy territory.

That was the highlight of the summer. We got what we came for, but it didn't engender any love for the military. Not long after this, at Bowling Green College, I was student director of a production of Irwin Shaw's anti-war play *Bury The Dead*. Its sentiments agreed with mine, but a year after that I was in uniform again, this time a sailor's. Of course there's a difference between fighting defensively and being an aggressor, but I was not convinced, when I signed up, that the U.S.A. was about to be attacked. The idea that the Nazis in control of Dakar in West Africa would transport an army across the South Atlantic, overpower Brazil and move north quickly and invade us from Mexico, as was seriously discussed, struck me as ridiculous. When I received a notice from the draft board to report for induction, I considered declaring myself a conscientious objector, but didn't. Hitler was a monster.

Cavalry had no part in World War II. No one had expected that it would. In the Great War of 1914-18, cavalry had shown itself obsolete in the epoch of machine guns, tanks and other technology of war. The Army, I suppose, had retained a few cavalry units between the wars out of nostalgia. I'm glad they did, and I'm glad Mike urged Fitz and me to go to CMTC.

In addition to being the first time on a horse, that summer at Fort Ethan Allen was the first time I flew in an airplane. Planes rather than horses would later become a common means of transportation for me, but commercial airlines never provided the sense of great adventure that the first ride, which was in an open cockpit of a two-winged plane, did.

The government gave us money for our fares to and from the army base, but Fitz and I hitchhiked and saved the money. We spent some of it on the airplane ride. With the two of us strapped in on the seat of one of the cockpits, the pilot in the other, we ascended and flew over the city of Burlington. We looked down on housetops and cars and people in the streets. Then we were taken out over Lake Champlain and we looked down at the dark blue of the water. "Want to do a loop?" the pilot shouted to us. We looked at each other and knew immediately the other's answer was YES! In a moment we were looking *up* at the lake and *down* at the sky! It was eerie and thrilling. We got much more for our travel money than a ride on a bus.

To Bowling Green and Back

The summer before our last year in high school, Fitz and I hitchhiked to Bowling Green, Ohio. Our purpose was to look at Bowling Green University. We had discovered its existence in a pamphlet entitled "The Cost of Higher Education in the United States," published by the U.S. Government Printing Office. We may have learned about this from Fitz's older brother Tom, who worked as a timekeeper on a WPA project but spent his leisure in a tavern frequented by local politicians. He picked up information there about government options. Or perhaps we heard it from Mike Kerry, the brother-in-law who worked at the Springfield Armory and seemed to know what was available from Washington. One of them had a list of publications from the Government Printer available on request from the public. On the list was a report from the Education Department on the cost of higher education in the United States. Tuition, room and board, books, and lab fees were specified and an estimated average cost per annum totaled in the right hand column.

Going down the right hand column, we located the four cheapest colleges. There were several colleges supported by various states and some were tuition free to citizens of the state but usually had a fee for out-of-state applicants. One of the best in this regard was Bowling Green College in Ohio: all that was required was a fifty-dollar registration fee. No out-of-state fee.

The four on our selected list were one that was in the Philippine Islands, still at that time a U.S. possession, but out of consideration because of the cost of travel. Another was in the state of Washington, a long hitchhike to get to. A third was in Fort Hayes, Kansas, and the fourth was Bowling Green, Ohio, the closest to Springfield. We were not aware of any advantages one way or the other between Fort Hayes and Bowling Green, and decided that if we found we didn't like what we saw at Bowling Green, we'd go on and look at Fort Hayes. In the end we did not go to check out Fort Hayes.

We walked around the campus, looking at the buildings, checking the library, talking to summer session students, and returned home pleased with what we had learned. Fitz had three older sisters, two of whom were working, and one was married to a husband with a good salary. Each of the three was happy to contribute a portion of their earnings to brother John's expenses to become the first member of the family to go to college. Fitz was scheduled to go to Bowling Green as soon as he finished high school.

My situation was different, but not hopeless. All I needed to begin at Bowling Green was the $50 registration fee. If I could earn some money to pay the small registration fee and have a little in reserve for room and board for a few months, and manage to get a part-time job, I would be able to join Fitz at Bowling Green.

It was probably at this time that Dad and I had a conversation about college. My memory of the talk is clear. Dad sympathized with my desire to go to college, and was sorry he could not afford to pay my way. His father, he told me, had four years of schooling in Ireland; he had eight years in Springfield schools. I would soon have twelve years. There was a generational progression. No doubt, Dad prophesized, my son would add four years of college to this lineage. I nodded an acceptance to this apparent inevitability, but the suggestion did not make me feel any better about the implied unavailability of college for me.

CAR CRASH

Rood and Woodbury decided to offer delivery of purchases only on Saturdays. The number of deliveries other days was insufficient to make the service economically sustainable. The driver, who was married, needed a fulltime job to support his family, and he quit when this decision to cut back was announced. As the driver's Saturday helper (he hadn't needed one other days), I knew the routes and the regular customers. The manager asked me if I could drive. I affirmed that I could, but admitted I didn't have a license. I said I had a friend (Fitz), who had a license who would drive for me the first Saturday, and I'd get a license by the next week. Fitz drove and I told him where to go, and we delivered the groceries the week the driver quit. By the next week, I hoped I'd have my driver's license, but as it turned out I did not.

Fitz had been taught to drive by his older brother Tom, who recently got a job that enabled him to get a car. Fitz had a weekend job in a parking garage taking cars at the entrance, parking them, and retrieving them for customers when they wanted them again. Friday evening I went to the garage and Fitz put me in a car and explained the movements of the shift stick, and I practiced going through the motions. Then I drove a car slowly around in the garage.

One of the cars regularly kept in the garage was owned by the man who ran the local (illegal) numbers lottery. He did more or less what the state government now does, but then he was a "racketeer" performing an act against the law every time he took a bet from a bettor. This criminal told Fitz that he, Fitz, could use the car if he wanted to except when the guy used it himself. "We can take this out on the streets," Fitz said, "he won't care, and the police know the car and won't bother it because they are on the take, so he told me." So we drove out into the night and I drove around the area and back into the garage; we didn't want to be away too long in case some customer might come in looking for the attendant, i.e., Fitz.

All went well in my brief grooming as a driver, and also in my written exam on the rules and regulations concerning driving a vehicle on public roads, but it did not go so well on my road test with the officer of the Registry of Motor Vehicles. Fitz drove me to the Registry in Tom's car. He got in the back and the burly-chested officer, in his blue police uniform, got in the front passenger seat. He indicated to me to start the car. I turned the key, revved the motor, put it in gear and moved away from the curb. Halfway down that first street, a car was nosing out of a driveway; I swerved around it before it was fully into the street. The officer made some outcry. He said I should have stopped and let the car go ahead of us. The level of his hostility, as I felt it, made me think I had probably already flunked, but we went on. Distracted by my worry about the officer's attitude, I turned the car and drove to face the edge of the curb, when he told me to turn around, then instead of shifting into reverse, as I had been doing under Fitz's tutelage, I found myself driving the car up over the curb. "Oops!" I stopped quickly, shifted into reverse and backed to the other curb, and then, ridiculous as it may sound, made the same error again and went up the other curb as well. That was the end of the test. I failed and had to wait to take the exam again.

The manager was surprised when Fitz showed up again with me to make the grocery deliveries. I made some kind of explanation of why I had not obtained my license, a matter merely of a delay.

Ironically, it was in West Springfield that the accident happened. A car came out of a street at too great a speed and could not stop fast enough to avoid hitting the R&W truck. The car hit the door on the passenger side where I was sitting and the impact caused me to go out the open window and land on the hood of the still moving car. I slid off and got to my feet, unhurt except for a bump on my scalp from the upper side of the window frame as I flew through. The superficial cut bled profusely, the blood running down my face and giving me the appearance of being badly injured. Someone called an ambulance and I was taken to a hospital, examined, bandaged, and released. Neither the car driver, nor Fitz, were any more than shaken up.

R&W took the case to court demanding not only damages for the truck, but for the interruption of its delivery business. (R&W never again made deliveries.) I did not have a lawyer of my own but the company's lawyer took my case along with the company's. Nothing had been decided by the time I left town to go west, and I never learned until a year later that I had been awarded a certain amount of money for my "trauma."

My father, Daniel F. McCall, Sr.

My mother, Marguerite Sweeney

The family at Nantasket, c. 1920. Surrounding me at center are (counterclockwise from the right) my sister Ruth, Aunt May, my father, my stepmother Irene, Irene's sister Ella, Irene's mother (Grandma Sheehan) and an unidentified woman.

As a toddler in Westfield, c. 1921

*As a seventh grader at Chestnut Street Junior High School,
Springfield, 1932*

My high school graduation picture, 1937

My friend John E. Fitzgerald (Fitz) and me, 1937

Ma Fitz (John Fitzgerald's mother)

In uniform during World War II

The troop transport, U.S.S. Callaway,
where I served as a medic

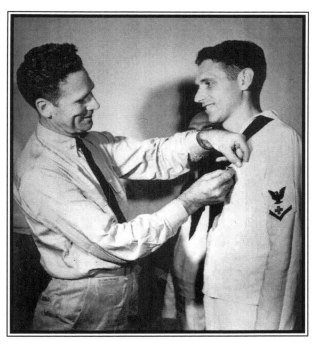

I receive a commendation ribbon on the recommendation of
the doctor for whom I served 72 continuous hours at Saipan

On leave with my siblings (from left) Robert, Barbara (in front), Dorothy and Phillip

CHAPTER SIX

WORKING MAN

The summer of 1937 was a bad time for a new graduate from high school to look for a job. The economy had been in a severe depression for nearly a decade. The prospect of getting work was not encouraging, except perhaps with the Works Progress Administration (WPA) or the Civilian Conservation Corps (CCC), both federal relief agencies. The CCC would have been my choice since it meant working outdoors, living in the woods, and doing something worthwhile, conserving the forests. H. G. Wells, the British novelist, science-writer and Fabian Socialist, hailed the CCC as an institution that should be continued even when there was no depression. He saw these non-military brigades of young men doing public service as a possible replacement of armies and cited William James' essay on "a moral equivalence of war." Wells's opinion had little impact in this country.

Fortunately for me, Dad had a connection. We lived next door to the American Legion Post and Dad, despite not being a veteran, used to go over there and play cards. One of his cronies at the card table was the Personnel Manager at Gilbert & Barker, a subsidiary of Standard Oil of New Jersey and probably the biggest industry in West Springfield. The factory made gasoline pumps for gas stations and gas heaters for homes.

I began work the week after graduation, on the three to eleven p.m. shift. Of course I had no skills. My job was to pull a low, wheeled contraption that could slide under certain metal boxes. It could be backed in under one of these boxes that stood on stilts under the two long sides. The contraption could then be cranked up to raise the metal box off the floor, enabling me to move the box and its contents. I patrolled the rows between machines dragging my tow behind me until a machinist called me. He would give me a slip of paper on which he had written the parts he needed. I would take his empty box to the storeroom where the man in charge of stores would fill the box with the requested parts and I would drag it back to the machinist. A boring job, but I was earning a paycheck, and that was an unusual thing among my former classmates.

Machinists do the same task over and over again. No one built a thing completely. Each processed a part that went into the finished product. Though requiring more skill than my job called for, the machinists got bored too. One way to alleviate the boredom was to play tricks on one another. A new employee was a natural subject for a bit of fun. One of the machinists called me over, but he did not need a new supply of parts to be brought from the storeroom. "Wanna see some French postcards?" he asked me, "you know - naked girls, 'n' guys fucking 'em. Ever see a dog fucking a woman?"

"No," I said to the last question. I had never imagined such a happening, but indicated "yes" I would look at his pictures.

"Can't let the supervisor see us," he said. "Bend down and look under the bench."

I leaned over to look. There was nothing under the bench, but as soon as my head was lowered it was hit with a leather truncheon by the man who had lured me to his workstation. A loud cry went up from the surrounding machinists who were apprised of what was in the offing. I was the butt of the joke and went silently away, with a headache, dragging my tow behind me.

We got twenty minutes at seven o'clock, half way through our shift, to eat a lunch we brought from home. Those who had been working for some time carried a lunch pail. I took a sandwich and a piece of fruit in a paper bag, and I also put in a book so I could read a few pages while I ate. The book I was currently reading was Thomas Wolfe's *Look Homeward Angel*. A well-meaning worker advised me not to read during my lunchtime. "They don't like it!" -- the "they" being management. Why, I inquired, did it matter what I did on my lunch break so long as I didn't cause any disruption or littering? He shrugged and repeated, "They don't like it."

In fact very little fit into my schedule. I was working evenings when others were getting together for one or another kind of entertainment, "shooting the breeze" if nothing else. I was almost completely cut off from my friends. At eleven o'clock at night, when I got off work, my friends were going to bed or were out somewhere. So I'd go to bed, and when I'd get up, others would be going out to work or to look for work. I did a lot of reading, but I lacked someone to talk to about my reading.

I hoped that after a while I might get on to a day shift, and even that I might be able to learn one of the machinist's skills and earn a better wage. My entry-level job was low pay and after turning over most of it to Irene for room and board, I did not have much to save for college. However, if I could observe and learn something about the various jobs of production, I might be able to apply to be selected as a replacement for a machinist who left for retirement or another reason. Then, after a year of working, I would go to Bowling Green, our pre-selected bargain-rate college.

Instead of that happening, I was laid off. In one way, it was a relief. I hadn't liked the job or the company, which was anti-union. One night as I was coming out the factory gate, a man with an armful of flyers was passing circulars to the men leaving work. He was promoting the organization of a union. I took a flyer from him. A few steps away from the union man, one of the men leaving the plant said to me, "Be careful! If the bosses find out you are interested in that stuff, you could loose your job." This company had always been restrictive in who it hired. I was told that years earlier there had been a sign up saying No Irish Catholics Should Apply, or something to that effect.

The three to eleven shift was nearly eliminated, and my job was gone with the cutback. The so-called "Roosevelt recession" was the reason. The National Association of Manufacturers did not like some of President Roosevelt's policies and in protest slowed down production, expanding the unemployment rate, and blaming the president for the consequences.

News of War in Europe

I made the rounds looking for work. I also was reading the newspapers. War was raging in Europe. The war in Spain, often called a civil war, was plainly an international and an ideological war, the extreme right against the extreme left. General Franco, stationed in Spanish Morocco, had brought his army into Spain in rebellion against the elected government. Nazi Germany and Mussolini's Italy sent troops to support Franco. At the time Salazar was at the head of the government in Portugal, and Dollfus in Austria made western and central Europe look essentially a fascist region. France with large Socialist and Communist Parties was an exception, but even there a Croix de Fer movement had strong support. England had Mosley leading a small but vociferous fascist group that had some support among the ruling class. If Franco's army took Spain into the fascist camp, Europe would be almost entirely ruled by fascists. Anti-fascist volunteers from several countries that still had democratic governments, England and France in particular, went to the assistance of the Spanish government, but they could only bring themselves – the Axis Powers sent tanks and artillery as well as men. Franco was winning battle after battle.

It was during my short period of being unemployed that one of my friends in Springfield, a member of the Young Communist League, suggested to me that we should join the Abraham Lincoln Brigade, composed of American volunteers, and go to Spain to fight the fascists. That was the time, I would learn later, that Eric Blair, an English volunteer, was doing just that. When, eventually, I read *Homage to Catalonia*, written under Blair's pen name, George Orwell, it strengthened my feeling that, in refusing, I had done the wise thing.

My friend had said, "C'mon! Let's go!" I was as anti-fascist as he, but the idea of becoming a soldier, even in a good cause, had never been attractive to me. Basically I was, and am, a pacifist. Also the situation in Spain was confusing. The Republican Government was supported by a number of diverse and bickering groups: Socialists, Anarchists, Communists, as well as the Republicans (who had deposed the monarchy, but were not necessarily leftists), and a large part of the populace that was not associated with any of these political parties. Where would foreign volunteers, who spoke no Spanish, fit into the anti-fascist coalition?

A recruiter for the Abraham Lincoln Brigade had told my friend that there was travel money available. I think he was almost set to go, but wanted a little encouragement, and someone to go with him. He cooled off when I didn't respond with enthusiasm. I told him I doubted that the probable sacrifice of my life would help the cause. I didn't go and he didn't go either. I saved him from what at best would have been a harsh experience. Military adventurism never attracted me.

While I was walking around looking for another job, I bumped into a girl from my class who had a job for the summer in her family's business. She was on her lunch break. "What are you doing on this side of the river?" she asked.

"Looking for work – like everyone else," I answered. The last part of my remark didn't apply to her. She was going to college in the fall – her family was well off.

"Hopeless!" she said in reference to the job situation. "Come and have lunch with me?"

"I'm broke."

"It's on me – this time."

I had a hamburger. She had a salad. We talked of this and that. "I usually found you amusing when you spoke up in class," she said.

"Oh! Did you agree with me or disagree?"

"Neither. Your ideas are so far out. I can't take them seriously." She paused as if at a loss for words. "They don't seem to connect with me."

"Maybe you just need to hear more of them."

She laughed at that notion.

"My parents are on their vacation. I'm here 'cause I'm trying to earn some money to take with me when I go to college in September." She was going to go to a nearby Ivy League women's college. "I get tired of eating alone."

That seemed reasonable, and tended to explain her unexpected friendliness. I thought of how many times I had eaten alone in the restaurant beneath the Campion Hotel. "Yeah," I agreed. "It can be tiresome."

"Come and have dinner with me tonight?" The words came out of her in a rush, as if in a sudden inspiration. This was a surprise to me. We had been in some classes together, but we hadn't ever had anything to do with each other. To the extent that I spent any time with my schoolmates, it was with the group around the literary magazine, or the ones who spoke out in discussions in class, and she was not in either category.

"Sure," I said, "Thanks."

"I'll cook. You can wash the dishes."

"O.K. It's a deal."

Actually there were other tasks she gave me. I peeled the potatoes and set the table. It was a simple summer supper. When we had consumed it, her tasks were done, but I still had to wash the dishes. I ran hot water into one basin to wash the dishes, and cold water in another to rinse the soapy water off the dishes. She hovered behind me and without warning reached around me and splashed a handful of cold water up on my face. Instinctively, my hand came up to protect myself as much as possible from the splashing, but she was closer to me than I realized and my arm caught on her arm. For a moment our arms grappled with each other. Then somehow, without premeditated intent on my part, we were on the floor – and I was atop her. This would not have been an unusual position if I was wrestling with a guy from another team, but with a girl it was exciting. My heart was pounding so hard because I sensed that she was willing. The obvious thing to do in the circumstances, it seemed to me, was to kiss her. So I kissed her.

Soon her skirt was up, her panties down. "Don't come inside me," she said. I wondered – never having done this - if I could manage to control the emission. When the moment came I spewed sperm over her belly. She went to clean herself and I finished doing the dishes. We sat in the living room for a while talking aimlessly. Then she suggested, "Let's go upstairs." Her room had a narrow bed. "We can use my parents' room." It had a double bed. We undressed and got on the bed.

Before dawn, but not by much, she came down with me to the door – to lock it after I went out. I gave her a hug and a kiss. "Next time bring some condoms," she instructed me. Condoms were available, but not easy for a teenager to obtain. But there was no next time. That very day I found another job, and I didn't call her for a few days. When I did, her mother answered the phone. "Wrong number," I said. "Sorry." I was truly sorry, not for the phone call, but for the deprivation of what I expected was in store.

The girl shortly afterwards went away to college, but by that time my new temporary job had already ended and I had left town. Before that I did seek her out and we had lunch together again, and this time I gallantly paid. For a long time, almost all of which I was away from West Springfield, I thought that that lunch was, and would be, the last time I'd ever see her. But just as my first encounter with her had been fortuitous, so again eventually we ran into each other.

Decades later I returned to West Springfield to attend a funeral, my Aunt Gertrude's. I might not have gone but for my sister Ruth. Indeed I might not have even heard of her death if it weren't for Ruth. I was not in correspondence with any of the Sweeney's. Ruth was living then in New Jersey; she flew up to Boston to visit with me, and I drove her to West Springfield. I was surprised to see my former inamorata at the funeral mass for the deceased.

She had aged of course but was still recognizable. "Hello," I said.

"What brings you back to town?"

"She's my aunt."

"Small world."

That was about it, except that she was married, had three children, and was content with her life. I can't say what her thoughts were, but for me it was like meeting a ghost from the past.

FOUNDRY

The new job I found was at a foundry. Again, my job was an auxiliary task to the main operation. This foundry produced pigs of "white metals," which meant lead, tin, pewter, copper, and bronze. The yard had an accumulation of scrap metals. I was hired to separate the pieces of junk into the categories of their consistency: lead in one bin, copper in another, and so on. I had a bottle of acid and a file. The file cut through grime and corrosion to show a clear view of the metal. The acid by its reaction answered questions when my eyes were inadequate to make identification. It was a low-paying position compared to the men on the foundry floor, but I didn't envy them in the heat of summer pouring molten metal into molds, and breathing the air cloudy with fumes that had to have been unhealthy.

While I was working in the factory and then the foundry, Fitz was working at a company that produced greeting cards for birthdays and other occasions. The multi-colored cards required inks of various chemical compositions, and the printing plates had to be washed after a batch had been printed. The residue of the inks, now mixed together in the wash, was - in the perception of the owner of the company – waste, but Fitz with only his high school chemistry class recognized a way the mixture could be separated and some usable ink recovered. He explained the process to the boss, who was very pleased to be able to reduce his expenses by a certain margin. He gave Fitz a bonus, and promised him a job during the summers while he was going to college.

Since graduation I had not seen much of Fitz due to my awkward hours of employment at the factory. Now that I was working nine to five, it was possible again to get together in the evenings. It had, however, been months since I had seen Beg. A scheme concocted by Beg brought us all together for what turned out to be the last foray for us as a threesome. Beg had a job at the factory where his brother-in-law worked, and he had bought a second-hand car. He suggested that on a Saturday when none of us were working, he would drive us to Troy, New York, where we would visit the red-light district.

"You'll get the clap," I said. "Or worse – syph."

"Naw!" he rebutted. "We'll wear rubbers."

Springfield did not have a red-light district. Massachusetts was more restrictive than New York State. Troy, about a hundred miles west on Route 20, was notorious. Some of the guys Beg worked with talked about the whorehouses in Troy and gave him descriptions and preferences, and he was raring to go. "Remember," one of them told him, "Jerk off before your go. If you don't, you'll come too soon." Another added, "And that's a waste of money."

It was supposed to be a sort of initiation to manhood. Fitz was as ambivalent as I was about the health dangers of brothels, but after chewing over the idea, we – the three of us – went. We drove through the district, surveying the houses. Beg made a choice and we went in. The women were semi-clothed, sitting around on display. We made our choices and were taken upstairs and into separate rooms. "First time?" the question was posed to me. I admitted I'd never been in a whorehouse before. She said something to the effect that this was business, not a love affair. "No kissing, no playing with my tits, or feeling me up. Just fuck. Understand?"

That was off-putting. The whole atmosphere was bleak, the grubby building, the commercial setting, but what did I expect? I was there to buy sex. No extras had been promised. That was the one and only time I ever went to a brothel.

In a few weeks the pile of scrap at the foundry was consumed by my separating it into bins that were regularly emptied to go into the smelters. My job came thereby to an end. At this point my earlier hope of saving enough money over the summer to be able to accompany Fitz to Bowling Green fizzled out. The summer was nearly over and I couldn't find another job. This looked like it might be the parting of the ways for me and Fitz. Those who go to college and those who don't generally run in different tracks. My employment during the summer had been sporadic and my savings were insufficient for a year at college – even with Bowling Green's minimal costs.

Fitz's sister Betty, a nurse at Mercy Hospital, suggested I apply to be an orderly at Springfield Hospital. They did not pay much but provided a free room for orderlies. She had heard there was a shortage there. I did not apply, but tucked away the reference. At the moment, I wanted to leave Springfield. Unemployed and no job in the offing, I was determined not to hang around just waiting for something to turn up. Going to sea on a merchant marine ship was what I wanted to do, but only union members would be picked by the hiring halls, and even if I spent some of my small savings to pay dues to the union, I would not be picked when seamen were needed because too many old members of the union were "on the beach" waiting for a berth on a ship.

If not out to sea, why not inland? There were crops to be harvested. I had an idea that I might "go West, young man" in the nineteenth-century manner, and if not make my fortune, at least earn a respectable amount of money. But my idea did not find favor with Dad. From his point of view, the situation was too uncertain to take the chance and go so far, opening myself to who knew what possible dangers. Seeking a job was not my only reason; it seemed to me the time had come to get away – to leave the Park Street house where my disbelieving presence caused tensions that made everyone uncomfortable.

I wrote to the Department of Agriculture in Washington, D.C., and asked about jobs in harvesting wheat in the Dakotas. John Dos Passos, whom I had read, gave me the idea. I decided to hitchhike west and work in the wheat harvest. Dad didn't like the idea; that was why I wrote to the Department of Agriculture. The answer on Department letterhead paper came back with the information that there were indeed jobs, but they were temporary, and advised against going from Massachusetts just to seek such employment. The days of the big harvesting machines with gangs of men to work them moving north from Texas to Saskatchewan (as the grain ripened) were over. Farmers had been equipping themselves with smaller machines and therefore many farms were harvesting simultaneously. The farmers did not want to wait for the big combine teams to get to them and perhaps meanwhile lose some of their crop to rainstorms. If I got a job on one farm, when the crop there was harvested, such would also be the case with neighboring farms. So the likelihood of another job was minimal.

I read the first part to Dad, neglecting to read the admonition not to go. "So – there is work out there," I said. Dad looked troubled, but didn't try to refute what I said. "And I'm going," I concluded.

Ruth, who had selected the Park Street house, had been the first to leave. She married Ed and they lived in New Jersey. I left some months later, and was never again in that house. Robert the next year went to a seminary to become a priest in the Order of St. Joseph. Phillip, graduating the same year, couldn't find a job so he expanded his paper route until, taking over routes vacated by kids who outgrew that type of enterprise, he covered most of West Springfield and hired kids to deliver some routes.

Grandma Sheehan, alone finally when Willy married, came to live on Park Street. I never saw her there, but I wonder how she felt being in the same house with Dad. Not long after this Dorothy went into nurse's training. Barbara, when she grew up, was the first, and only, of Irene's children to attend college. She did so at Our Lady of the Elms in Chicopee, not far from home, but after getting her degree and teaching for a year, she went to France as a teacher for American G.I.'s at an Army Base.

The number at home decreased, and Irene eventually decided to find a lower rent and moved back to lower Main Street. Grandma Sheehan died at one or the other of these homes. Dad lived through the war years and most of my college years, and died from an embolism after being hit by a car that broke both of his legs. Irene lived a few years longer. After her death, Phillip moved to East Springfield. Dorothy's husband worked in Connecticut, so they lived a few miles south of the state line. Barbara eventually settled near her. No trace of the McCall family, except in dusty archives of school attendance, taxation, and other state, town, or church records, and the memories of some now elderly residents, former neighbors or friends of one or another member of the family, remains in West Springfield.

CHAPTER SEVEN

HOBO

My career as an employee in factories was brief: employed in the spring and laid off twice before the summer was over. If another job in the area had been available, I would have taken it, but other laid-off workmen, who had been employed for a decade or more, were looking for work. Many of them were married and, having families to support, they would usually get preference over a recent school graduate with no responsibility for others.

With an old suitcase packed with a change of clothes, a light blanket, and a few other items, I was ready to start hitchhiking west. Route 20 went right past our front door. Convinced now that I was really going, Dad offered me some pocket money. I showed him what I had saved, and told him I didn't need any more. Dad said, "Call collect if you have any problem."

I set out a little before Fitz would cover part of the same route on his way to Bowling Green. The area from Springfield to eastern New York was already quite familiar. Fitz and I had been over it several times, going to Watervliet where his sister Mary and her husband Mike Kerry lived, as did my relatives the Moore's. Beyond that the way was less familiar, but Fitz and I had been over it the summer before, when we scouted out

Bowling Green. I recognized places we had passed on that trip, and the memory reminded me that Fitz was going to college and I was going to find some temporary work. I shook off the negative feeling and concentrated on what I might find on the road ahead.

Now alone, I was impressed with how big a state New York is: from Albany, where I stayed overnight in nearby Watervliet, to Syracuse, to Buffalo. A few rides later, into Pennsylvania, through the city of Erie, and I was still a long way from the wheat fields. In Ohio, before I had got as far as Bowling Green and was still in somewhat familiar territory, a "rubber tramp" picked me up. The designation was his. He had no permanent place of residence; therefore he was a "tramp," but unlike those who hopped freight trains, he traveled on rubber tires. He had his own car and went from town to town, stopping wherever he found a bowling alley. He would bowl a few strings, leaving several pins standing. Some hangers-on would notice and suggest making it interesting by having a competitive round with a little betting on the outcome. Usually he would win. That was how he supported himself. He had to eat and buy gas for his car; if he had sufficient money he'd sleep at a cheap hotel, otherwise in his car, parked in some quiet place. He didn't tell me all this until I had, in response to his questions, told him I had left home and intended to work in the Dakotas harvesting wheat. I guess that made him feel that I was a kindred soul.

He stopped at a roadside diner. I said I would try to get a ride but that if I didn't, I hoped he would take me with him again as far was we were going in the same direction. "Come on in and have a bite," he said. The idea of spending some of my small amount of cash in a diner did not appeal to me, when I could eat for much less by buying bread and cold cuts and perhaps an apple in a grocery store. I told him so. "This one is on me," he offered. Thus began a journey in tandem with a rubber tramp that lasted until we got to North Dakota. Harry, my newfound friend, was lonely and pleased to have some company.

I watched him bowl and he had me bowl with him, knowing I had no experience and would look as amateurish as he pretended to be. Then when someone would challenge him to a contest, I would watch him lose the first couple of times, and then when he asked to let him try to make up his loses by upping the ante, he would gradually improve, never too sharply, but just enough to win. He got by on his skill in bowling, but it was a precarious living. I did not want him to buy another meal for me; I suggested we get the makings in a grocery store, split the cost, and have a picnic somewhere along the road. He was amused by the idea but agreed, and found that he enjoyed the *al fresco* meal. "I can save some money this way," he said, "whenever I need to." He did not intend to give up on roadside diners and truck stops.

Having no geographical goal for his travels, he agreed to go in the direction I wanted to go. In Minnesota we came upon a county fair. "We can make some money here," Harry declared.

How?

He arranged it with a man who had concessions to run. Harry stood behind a table with clusters of balls neatly piled in pyramids. Behind him was a stand where objects sat that could be knocked off if hit hard enough by a ball. My job was to be Harry's "shill." "You wander around in the crowd. Don't go too far away from this stand, but come up when you see that no one is throwing balls here. Then come over and ask me – don't shout, but in a loud voice, 'How much to play?' 'How many balls do I get?' 'What do I get if I win?' Anything you can think of to ask. If someone comes and buys a chance, you can go away. If not, throw some balls. We've got to make this stand look busy - and fun."

For a few days we ran this game, taking in a moderate amount of money. How much went to the concessionaire and how much Harry could keep, I can't now say. Harry arranged that. I couldn't complain; Harry had been feeding me on and off ever since I met him. He preferred to eat at a luncheonette or bar rather than make his own cold meal from things purchased at a grocery store. Especially in the evening we'd stop at a diner and he paid. Now he gave me a few bucks for my efforts at being a shill.

On the last day, there was a prize for the teen-age woman and teen-age man who came from furthest away. Springfield, Massachusetts, won for me. A girl from Missouri won. We were feted with a dinner together. Her parents watched us solemnly making sure that, though the scene looked something like a wedding, I did not take any liberties with their daughter.

On our way again, we were soon in North Dakota. We got a job on a farm. Harry opined that the farmer would pay less for inexperienced help than for old hands, so told me, "if he asks have you done this before, say 'yes.'" I followed his advice but was easily found out. Westfield, Holyoke, and Springfield are cities; even West Springfield was not rural. I'd grown up on city streets, and despite some stints of camping, I was totally unfamiliar with the commonalities of rural life.

"Hitch up this horse," I was directed by the skeptical farmer. I made an effort, but put the horse collar on backward. The farmer broke out in a hearty laugh, "That horse ain't a priest!" When he got over his amusement, he showed me how to do the job.

The wheat had already been cut; the tied-up sheaves stood in rows of stacks down the length of the field. Our task was to walk alongside the rick, and with a pitchfork pick up a stack of wheat and lift it onto the flatbed of the rick. We had to control the horse that pulled the rick. We halted the horse as we came to a sheaf and sent it on when the sheaf was on the rick. The reins were fixed to the front of the rick where we could reach them with the pitchfork; the horse was trained to respond to changes in pressure on the reins as well as to a human voice.

We had a place to sleep in a barn on a spread of hay, and were fed breakfast in the farmer's kitchen: steak and eggs, fried potatoes, bread, coffee, pie -- the biggest breakfast I'd ever eaten. Then in mid-morning the farmer's wife came out in the field in a pickup with a huge coffee urn and piles of sandwiches on a tray and pieces of cake on another tray. Around noontime, she was back with another supply, and again later in the afternoon. In the evening we ate in the kitchen, a sit-down meal more ample than the great breakfast we had begun the day with. It was a lot of food, but we worked it off in a long day "from can to can't," that is from the time you can see until you can't.

Harry lasted one day. "I can make a living in an easier way," he told me, and said goodbye. He was heading back to where there were more towns than farms and bowling alleys were more plentiful. I stayed on and when the crop was finished, I managed to get another job not too far away. This time I could verify that I was experienced.

The Department of Agriculture was correct. Jobs in any locality were soon over. Looking around for another job, I repeatedly heard a story from other men looking for work: A young boy from a farm was taken by his mother into town one Saturday to do the family shopping. "Look at all those bums hanging around," the boy said. "Shh! Those are not bums; they're harvest hands." Some weeks later, after the harvest was over, the boy was again in town, and said, "Those harvest hands are still here." His mother said, "They're not harvest hands, they're bums."

When needed in the local labor market, a man who would work was welcome; when work was not available, an unemployed stranger was considered a nuisance and was no longer welcome. Another story told me was about a hand who when hired was told he could sleep in the field. In the morning, the farmer opened his door and found turds on the porch just where he was about to step. He called the hired hand and said, "Did you do this?" "Yeah," said the man. "You didn't expect me to shit in my bedroom, did you?"

I had two short-term jobs, on two different farms, and then the harvesting season was complete. Dad's warning was verified: I had not earned enough money to make the trip worthwhile. But I had enjoyed the outdoor work, which I preferred to the factory and especially the foundry. Moreover, I found satisfaction in having learned to control the horse and rick. I would have been happy to go on to more farms if there had been any that still needed workers, but there were not.

Riding the Rails

It was time to move on. I heard that there would be apple-picking jobs in the Wenatchee Valley in Washington. I was not going to go back to West Springfield. So – on to Washington.

Up to this point I had been carrying the old battered suitcase I'd taken from home. It was fine as long as I was hitchhiking, but hitching a ride was more difficult now. There was less traffic, and what there was generally was not going far, and while a farmer would pick up a neighbor, he was less inclined to pick up a stranger. A guy about my age I'd met on my last job told me the only way to travel was by rail. He would show me how to do it. First I had to get rid of the suitcase because I had to have both hands free. Fortunately, I had my blanket folded in my suitcase. I rolled my extra clothes up in the blanket, tied the two ends of the blanket-roll together, and tied it in the middle also. Now I could put the loop over my head and rest it on one shoulder while the ends fell on the opposite hip. So accoutered I could grab the rungs of the ladder on the side of a freight train and still bring my few possessions with me.

We waited near the railroad tracks outside the freight yards for a train to emerge. The trick was to catch it before it got going too fast. Alternately, one could lurk by a bridge where the train would slow down. In either case, we had to watch out for the detectives hired by the railroads to discourage hoboes from getting free rides. Railroad dicks were reputed to have sometimes thrown hoboes off a moving train. I doubted that was really true, but who knew? I was also aware that one could be injured or killed by one's own misjudgment when getting on or off a train in motion.

Trains carrying grain from the harvests of the area were not of great concern to the railroad management because the cargo was unlikely to be pillaged, and even if some handfuls were taken, what could be carried off would not be of great value. But when small things of high value were aboard, such as cigarettes, any tampering with the cargo could be costly. Railroad management was said to be ambivalent about hoboes: transporting migrant workers to where the work needed them was good business even if they did not pay a fare for the ride. Without workers getting to where the work was, there would be no cargo of grain to be carried to city markets. But some hoboes were not workers and most of them, given the opportunity, management believed, were thieves.

Empty freight cars needed elsewhere for cargo were often part of the train. If there was one on the train you wanted to ride, the best thing was to get inside by an open door on the side of the car. If an open door was not available, you could catch the ladder on the side of the car and climb up and ride on the roof. We didn't see any open side doors, so we would have to take a ladder to the roof.

The first time doing something dangerous is rough on your nerves. I wondered, as the train accelerated and I was running next to it, if it wouldn't pull my arms out of their sockets when I grabbed the ladder. "Get on!" my friend shouted. I took hold of a rung, and got the other hand on also. My feet left the ground; I was being carried by the train. My arms were still intact. I reached up to the next rung and the one higher, and finally got my feet on a rung. Soon I was on top of the freight car. My friend had made his way to the top of the car behind me. He walked in my direction, jumped over the space between his car and the one I was on. "You did it," he said, approving my having accomplished the first feat required, but I was sitting, and wondering how he kept his balance on the moving train, which sometimes lurched and swayed. I didn't think I would jump from one car to another as he had just done.

We sat atop the car and talked. He smoked, offering me one. I declined. I had not yet ever smoked. Fitz had begun to smoke, but the idea did not attract me. It was afternoon when we got aboard. The sun was warm. As evening came on it got cooler and we were exposed to the air as the train hurtled forward. We began to get chilled.

"We've got to find a 'reefer'."

"Hunh?"

"A refrigerator car."

Refrigerator cars carried meat or other cargo that had to be kept cold. On each end of that type of car there was a compartment to hold ice. The ice was loaded in from a trapdoor in the roof. When there was no cargo that needed to be kept cool, the ice compartments were empty, and were a place to get in and out of the wind. The car we were on was not a "reefer." That meant we would have to walk over the top of several cars to find one. I was not anxious to do this. I undid my blanket roll and got my sweater, and was prepared to suffer the cooler air till we got to a place where we could get off. "No, no, no," he insisted, "You can do it." I was not really convinced.

"Look. I'll go and find one and come back and get you."

He went off toward the rear of the line of cars. I watched his body wobble along over a car, hop to the next and wobble on. After a while, he came back. "Nothing that way," he said and took off in the other direction, forward. He came back shortly and I hoped his comment would be the same, and I would not have to move, but he announced, "One just a few cars ahead."

I got on my feet, wondering if I could do what he had done in going from one freight car to another. I was feeling the vibrations of the moving train, and unsteadily walked to the end to the car, looked down at the coupling holding the car to the one ahead of it, and on either side of the coupling I could see the bright iron rails and the wooden ties that supported them. The rapid succession of ties appearing from under the car ahead and disappearing under the car I was on indicated how fast we were going.

"Don't look down. Look at the place where you are going to land." He had already gone on to that car and was allowing me space to join him. I took a breath and jumped. It was no big deal. To jump over that distance on the ground would have been nothing, but it seemed a great deal wider with that yawning space below, the wobbly landing spot, and the frightening speed.

The next gap I did without hesitation. By the time we got to the reefer, I felt initiated into the fraternity of hoboes. We opened the trapdoor, got in, and closed it over us. It was dark, but warm. When we felt the train slow down, we got out and looked around. We were approaching a town. We climbed down to the bottom of the ladders on the side of the freight cars; he had gone to the next car ahead. I watched him. When he jumped off, I held on till past him, then jumped.

We found a "jungle" in a clump of trees where other hoboes had a fire going. Something was being cooked, not in a pot but in a large tin can, the size used in restaurant kitchens. Any combination of ingredients, whatever was available, was dubbed "mulligatawny." We had no food with us, so we walked into town to buy the makings of a meal, and we rummaged in the waste containers behind a restaurant for a large tin can to wash out and use for our cook pot. Later we found an unoccupied space where we could stretch out and sleep. "Put on all your clothes. That way no one can steal them." With two shirts, two trousers, two pairs of socks, I hardly needed my blanket. One last piece of advice before we went to sleep: "If you take off your shoes, put them inside your blanket. You do not want to be shoeless tomorrow. Not good here to be barefoot!"

I had not intended to become a hobo. My intention was to work the harvest, make some money, and if I had enough, go to Bowling Green College, but I hadn't been really confident that was possible, and as it turned out, it wasn't. When the harvest was over, my earnings did not significantly increase what was left from my savings from working briefly, first in the factory and then in the foundry. It was not enough to last me through a semester's room and board, and anyway the semester had begun.

Fitz and I planned to room together if I managed to go to college, so he would have rented a room and I could have joined him there, even if it was too late to start classes. If I ran short, Fitz was willing to carry my share of the room rent for a while, but I needed to pull my weight over the long run. A part-time job would be necessary for me, and I had no idea how available such jobs would be. Perhaps I should have gone to Bowling Green after the harvest. I had the $50 for registration, but little excess. If I'd found some employment in the college town, even at minimal pay, I'd have been ready for second semester. One semester, even if I had to drop out afterward, would get me started.

Maybe. But if apple picking in Wenatchee Valley in Washington was more profitable than wheat harvesting had been, I might be able to start in the second semester. Following a will-of-the wisp, I went on looking for work, no longer a schoolboy hitchhiker, but now a riding-the-rails hobo.

The train we were riding stopped about two miles outside Missoula, Montana. The road from where the train stopped to the town was soon cluttered with men walking to town. The length of the line showed how many unpaid fares there had been on the train. I noticed a woman. She wore pants, jacket, and a man's hat, trying to look as much like a man as she could. Safer, no doubt, that way. Eventually I saw a few other women of various ages, and almost all wore men's clothing. I did not personally see anything untoward happen, but heard that their lot could be hard if some man, or men, got aggressive ideas.

Another category of trespasser on railroad property was Negroes. Leaving Missoula, we were about to get in a freight car that had an open door. There would be no need to get into a reefer. I was about to pull myself up on the floor of the car when my friend grabbed my arm and held me back. "Not this one," he said. "Don't ride with 'jigs.' Never know what can happen. Railroad dicks don't like them. Chance of getting hurt if you're with them."

We got another car to Spokane. There we separated. I am indebted to him for instructing me in how to hop freights, but I never learned his name. No one revealed their own names; nicknames were easily generated. Anyone like myself, tall and skinny, could be called "Slim." If you mentioned the town or state you came from, that could be added to differentiate you from other Slims. I was tagged Springfield Slim. Someone I got to know in one place would show up in another and hail me as Springfield Slim. Anyone of less than average height might be dubbed "Shorty." Red hair would get you the name "Red." A stocky man would be "Heavy." An elderly man with white hair would be "Dad." And so on.

The way I got the moniker "Springfield Slim" was that a man said to me, "You come from somewhere in the lower Connecticut Valley." I was surprised, and admitted that I grew up in Springfield, Massachusetts. "How did you guess?" It was not a guess, he told me; it is the way you talk. My pronunciation of certain words revealed my origin. This was amazing. I knew there were regional accents -- southern, Vermont, Boston, Brooklyn -- but I assumed I was speaking standard American English. Although my junior high course, General Language, was an elementary introduction to linguistics, I had never heard of "geographical dialectology." The man must have been a professional linguist, or at least been exposed to a certain amount of linguistic information. He told me the words that gave him the clue, but I'm not sure I can now repeat them. I think "water" was one. At any rate, I got my epithet of Springfield Slim from a linguist.

It shouldn't have been surprising to see a linguist who was a hobo. Doctors, lawyers, and men from many professions and occupations found themselves in those years on the road. Some were lawyers who had been disbarred, doctors who lost their licenses, or businessmen who went bankrupt. Some were fugitives from alimony or other obligations, and these were mixed in with all the jobless, homeless victims of the great economic depression of the 1930s.

Apples were not yet ripe, but there were hops to be picked. Hops grow on vines; the vines were strung up to hang from wires about seven feet above the ground. You cut down the vine, stripped off the hops into a hemp bag, and left the vine on the ground, moving on to the next vine. Hops are flowers. Imagine picking rose petals and when you have filled a great sack with them, take them to be weighed. If you get pennies for your load, you are not going to make much money. Where I was picking, a couple of Mexican families were working, even the young kids, picking hops. A young black man, a few years older than me, said, "You can't make any money in the afternoon. Let's go swimming." There was an irrigation canal nearby where he intended to swim. "Why not?" I said. It was a hot day. We swam in our underwear. It made sense to enjoy ourselves since we didn't need to grub for a few more cents. The Mexicans kept working. They had kids and more expenses than single men.

"You make your money in the early morning," my new friend, Henry, told me as we sat on the bank of the canal. Dew is heavy on the hops in the early morning; later, when the sun gets hot and the dew evaporates, the hops are dry. "You want to sell them as much water as you can," he said, "it's heavier than hops."

The owner of the hop field provided tents for his temporary employees. Henry had a tent to himself. I was in a tent with a taciturn man who sprawled all over the inside of the tent, so I moved in with Henry. He was from Frankfurt, Kentucky. He'd had one year of college before his money ran out. He'd saved for tuition and expenses from what he earned working in a mine. He wanted to go back to the mine, but No Hiring signs were posted at the entry, so he decided to "knock around" for a while, hoping to go back to college sometime.

When the hops had been picked, I went to Seattle. Where Henry went I don't know. This was the pattern of friendships on the road; they were short-lived. Homeless friends soon separated, going in search of the next job or whatever they might be seeking. I just wanted to see Seattle. I had heard it was an interesting port city. The waterfront drew me and I looked at the ships tied up at the docks. The great totem pole was a surprising monument. East Asians, dressed similarly to the rest of the population, and their storefronts seemed to intermingle with the downtown shops of white Americans, unlike other cities where a "Chinatown" is separate from the rest of the city. Here there were Japanese also. A section of the city was known as skid row, from the former practice of skidding logs (cut from timber in mountains in the region) in a sluiceway to where they could be loaded onto ships or trains. When that operation was displaced elsewhere, skid row became the poor section of town.

I found a job in a Coffee Ann, a food dispensary that featured coffee, doughnuts, sandwiches, chili, stews, and soups. The owner had bought cheaply some sacks of last year's potatoes; they were smelly because some of them had rotted. I sat in a back room taking a potato from a sack, peeling it, and tossing it into a bucket of water. Every now and then I had to chuck a rotten potato into a large garbage can. All day long I sat in the smelly room until I had worked my way through several bags, separating the good spuds from the bad, and peeled and diced the good ones. I was given a bowl of stew, made with some of the potatoes I had peeled, a couple of chunks of carrot, and a piece of tough meat. And a sandwich along with a cup of coffee.

I spent the money I earned that day on a ticket to a theater. The Garment Workers Union, the ILGWU, was putting on a musical, *Pins and Needles*. It was full of skits and songs promoting the union message. I did not belong to any union. Gilbert & Barker, a subsidiary of Standard Oil of New Jersey, would not deal with unions. There were no unions for the seasonal farm work I was seeking, except in California, in the vineyards where efforts were being made to organize workers into a union. Anyway, I was very sympathetic to unions. And I enjoyed the show. Whether it was there or elsewhere that I learned certain songs I cannot now be sure, but some lyrics still stick with me.

> *I dreamt I saw Joe Hill last night,*
> *Alive as you and me.*
> *But Joe, you're ten years dead, I said.*
> *I never died said he.*

Then he goes on to say he will always be (in spirit) with the people whenever a strike or demonstration is going on for workers' rights. I even picked up a Yiddish version of Joe Hill, which I can still remember, though I am unsure of the orthography to record it here. Some songs were silly, but carried a message: "This is the man, the very fat man, who waters the workers' beer." Some were frankly socialist: "Bandera rosa triumphera!"

In Wenatchee Valley, an orchard owner had a Help Wanted sign out. His apples were not yet ready for picking, but he was looking to get pickers before other orchards hired the best. Had I picked before? When I was a kid, I said, my house had apple and peach trees all around it. True, but I was not an experienced picker, and had not said so, but he evidently took it that I was. He had tents set up to accommodate pickers until the work began. He and his wife were Finnish and had set up a Finnish Bath, otherwise known as a sauna, and let his employees use it. It was a domed structure, just big enough to hold two persons. Stones were heated in a wood fire outside, brought in with tongs, and put on a metal sheet in the center of the little room. A cup of water, taken from a bucket next to the metal sheet and poured on the hot stones, sent up a burst of steam. After a couple of cups of water, the interior of the dome was filled with steam. I had never been in a steam bath before. When I broke out in sweat, I moved to get out. "Wait!" said the other hired picker who was sharing the heated stones with me. "You want to get whatever troubles you have out of your system." I stayed. Sweat rolled down my face and dripped to my chest, which was already running rivulets. When we finally came out, we took turns standing in a cold outdoor shower.

Ladders used in picking apples from a tree were different from any ladder I had ever seen. The series of steps between two uprights were the same as other ladders, but instead of two legs to be pushed out behind the steps to steady the ladder, there was only one leg, not two, hinged at the top of the ladder. I had to push that leg out, test the ladder for steadiness, never wholly satisfactory, and climb up until my feet were higher from the ground than my head had been when I was standing on the ground, and then reach out forward, to the right, to the left and get all the apples within reach. The picked apples went into a sack fastened in front of me suspended from my shoulders. When I could reach no more apples, I'd climb down, empty the sack into a slatted wooden box, move the ladder, and go up again. Pay was by the box. To prove that I was a good picker, I wanted to have as many full boxes by the end of the day as possible. That meant stretching my arm out as far as I could to get as many apples as I could on each time up the ladder. The problem was that the ladder would tilt when I reached for an apple far from the ladder. More than once the ladder fell sideways and I had to jump to the ground, and the heavy sack of apples hanging from my shoulders would pull me down so that I would land with my face almost to the earth. But I was never hurt.

I was writing letters regularly to Fitz, who preserved them. One from Tieton, Washington, dated 26 October 1938, summed up my experiences since leaving Massachusetts. My first stop, naturally, had been at Uncle Harry's and the following day I made 600 miles to Fremont, Ohio, about 30 miles from Bowling Green, were he would shortly arrive. It was in Fremont that I was picked up by Harry, the rubber tramp, who brought me over the course of a week to Fargo, N.D. A week was also consumed in the trip via freight trains to Yakima, Washington. I told Fitz that I might have made more money picking apples if picking hadn't had to wait exceptionally long for the first frost to bring out the color of the apples. During three weeks of waiting I ran up a bill for foodstuffs that I was then paying off. Strangely, I didn't mention picking hops. While in Tieton, I thought that I'd work in the bean harvest, which "pays $60 a month plus room and board, and lasts to the first week of December." Then I would return to West Springfield where I would get back in time to work in the Christmas rush at the Post Office. I expressed a hope that I would be able to enroll at Bowling Green College for the spring semester. None of my projections came true. I didn't pick beans, and Christmas came and went while I was still on the West Coast.

When the apples were picked, I left Washington and headed south for California to find work picking oranges, and also to escape the cold weather that would soon make Wenatchee uncomfortable. I rode a freight train across Oregon without ever touching the soil, just as I had crossed Idaho without setting foot in the state.

The word-of-mouth information before we even arrived in California was that the oranges were not yet ripe. That I saw for myself shortly after arrival when I slept under an orange tree on the edge of an orchard. A traveling companion and I answered a Help Wanted sign in a dry goods store, a branch of a national chain whose name I will not mention. It was a one-day job, breaking down some flimsy walls in the basement and carrying the detritus out to a dumpster. In another section of the basement there were shelves with piles of folded shirts, pants, and other items. "Time to re-outfit ourselves," my companion suggested as we finished the job. We had been left to ourselves, unsupervised, and before we went up to tell the manager the job was finished and collect our pittance of pay, we picked out some new things to wear. We took off our clothes, now dusty from the demolition, and put on a shirt, turning the collar in so that when we put on our old shirts, the new one didn't show. We did the same with pants, turning up the cuffs. Dressed again in our clothes, we went up to the ground floor and reported to the manager. He came down, inspected the job, paid us, and we left. As soon as we could, we stripped off our outer clothes, glad to be free of the feeling of being stuffed inside the double layers of clothing.

This guy, who I knew as Shorty, was familiar with the California scene. He led me to a shelter that had been set up in the vicinity of Fresno where we were permitted to rest for a while. We each had a bed in an airy dormitory, were able to take showers, and chat with guys coming from various directions, getting info on job possibilities, the assessment of the railroad dicks in that direction, and so on. It also was a chance to pick up some reading matter, magazines mostly, but a few books too. The shelter for homeless men was run by some charity. Men there, and those coming and going, sometimes were carrying a magazine or a book. Looking at them one would not expect them to be readers, but some were. Once read, a book was good only if you could swap it for another. I had a couple, and swapped them, but found one interesting, the other not promising enough to bother reading. I quickly swapped the second one. These transactions gave me the idea to become a collector. I solicited arrivals for books. Some just gave them up without asking for one in return. When someone requested a book in exchange, I'd give him his pick from the number I'd assembled. Under my mattress was a layer of books. When I had to leave, I turned over my library to the person in charge of the center.

I read more in the week I was allowed to stay there than I had been able to read since I left West Springfield. It was in a magazine article that I read about Eleanor Roosevelt, wife of the President, visiting "jungles" and talking to men on the road. The number was at an unprecedented high level, in the millions. Mrs. Roosevelt at various times went down in mines to see the conditions of miners, into ghettos to see the poor, black and white, and sponsored many causes, all of which I read about at one time or another, but I remember specifically the time and place where I read about her checking out and publicizing the plight of hoboes.

It was here, in Fresno, that I wrote again on 22 December 1938 to Fitz. I reported that oranges had been decimated by frost and I had used up my earnings looking for a job. I had managed for a while to get by with "spuds & raisons & things" scrounged from warehouse platforms. Currently, I was working in the kitchen of "a shelter camp for transients." I asked that he not divulge this information to my family because I had written them that I was employed in a cafeteria – I didn't want them to worry. But I revealed to Fitz that I received no pay, only "my eats and a bed." I don't even have money for stamps, I confessed, but "I get tobacco for working and swap it for money to buy stamps."

Again I laid out projections that didn't come to pass. I wrote I'm "on to the Gulf Coast, where the scuttlebutt is that there is money to be made in oystering. During the winter they plant baby oysters in the oyster beds. So if I get a job, I'll be out on a boat shoveling infant bivalves into the shallow water." This plan apparently died while I was crossing Texas. "Can't say," I wrote, "when I'll get up around BG. Depends on what luck I have on the coast. If I get a job, I'll be up there around April with my pockets jingling. Otherwise I'll be there but without any metallic accompaniment."

It was in Fresno that I got rid of the blanket I'd been carrying. I learned about "California blankets." The trick was to wrap newspapers around you under your clothes. It was good insulation, and discarded newspapers were available for the taking. A piece of canvas that I had obtained was adequate to hold my few possessions and this way they took up less room. I rolled the canvas and my things inside it. It made a compact bundle, less bulky that the blanket roll. Bundle was modified to "bindle" by hoboes. Tied at both ends with my piece of rope and the rope slung over a shoulder, the whole thing was on my back, nothing except the rope in front of me, leaving me much more flexible in hopping a freight. I was now a "bindle stiff."

Near Bakersfield I picked cotton. With a twelve-foot long bag hitched over one shoulder and dragging on the ground behind me, I moved along a row of cotton bushes, bending over to pluck the balls of cotton and shove them into the bag. When the bag was full, I took it to a man with scales who weighed it. "You can get more into your bag," he said when he looked at the scale. I should pack it in more tightly. A Mexican girl, by her appearance scarcely into her teens, was just ahead of me at the scales; she had a heavier bag than I had. This was more tiring than working with a rick in the wheat harvest – bending over all day strained muscles in a different way than upright work. The hell with cotton! The hell with waiting for the oranges to get ripe! I never did pick oranges.

I went south to El Centro in the Imperial Valley where it was all truck farming. On the train south in a boxcar, a group of men were smoking. The smoke didn't smell like tobacco. Someone said they were smoking "tea" and offered me a puff. "I don't smoke," I told him. "This ain't tobacco," he said. "Try it." I accepted the offered cigarette, took a puff, coughed, and handed it back, to the amusement of the group. This was, I realized, something that could induce hallucinations; it was not a substance I would consider wise to fool around with while riding illegally on a train with a bunch of men I did not know. Still coughing a bit, I moved to another corner of the car and pretended to sleep. It was my first encounter with marijuana.

I picked celery, heads of lettuce, etc. I did not like this work either, or California, as far as work goes. This state was a disappointment compared to Dakota and Washington. From the East Coast to the West Coast in search of work, I had skipped across several states, and found work only in four: Minnesota, North Dakota, Washington, and California. I had been a shill at a county fair, harvested wheat, hops, apples, cotton, and done truck gardening, all in the open air, plus scullery jobs indoors. Just enough to keep going; no profit. But I had seen the country: views of the Great Lakes, the Plains, the Rocky Mountains, the Pacific Ocean, and a few cities: Buffalo, Cleveland, Chicago, Seattle, Sacramento. I had missed San Francisco and Los Angeles, but I'd find them later.

One of the comments I heard from my traveling companions about Californians suited my perception of those I met, admittedly not a random sample. Put into a jingle:

The miners came in forty-nine
The whores in fifty-one
The offspring that they left behind
Is now the native son.

Californians who were born there were proud to call themselves "native sons" in distinction to those who flocked to the west coast from the "dust bowl" that had devastated some plains states. The owners of the farms where we worked were of course native sons.

I headed east again, through New Mexico, Arizona, and Texas. No work anywhere along the way at the time of year I passed through, and when there is no work, the local attitude by the authorities is hostile toward drifters. Texas had a bad reputation. A Texas judge, in one story, sentenced a hobo from the North saying, "Your granpappy came South with a gun, and now you come down looking for southern hospitality. Thirty days!" Thirty days on a chain gang would be a month of work without pay, and supervised by a deputy sheriff with a gun. Despite the scuttlebutt about how tough Texas could be, I traversed the state – as fast as I could – without any trouble. And so I came to Texarkana, on the state line between Texas and Arkansas, and headed north to Mena to investigate something I had read about.

COMMONWEALTH COLLEGE

When I was in high school and thinking of college as almost unattainable, *LIFE* magazine had a brief mention of an unusual college in Mena, Arkansas, called Commonwealth College. It was said to be a hot-bed of "communism, atheism, nudism and free-love." In making my way back east from the west coast, riding on a freight train approaching the town of Texarkana, I remembered the *LIFE* story. How could I not go a few miles north, especially since Mena was a rail junction, and take a look at it? Mena was a small town but it was a terminus of the Fort Smith and Western Railroad, which had been largely financed by an investment from Queen Wilhelmina of the Netherlands; Mena had been named in her honor.

It did not look like a college. There were no grand buildings with columns and porticoes. In fact, it was a farm with a number of houses where the persons attending the college roomed and a large hall that served as a dining room for students and staff. When it was not mealtime, the room was a meeting hall for discussions, and was used more regularly as a lecture hall. Some classes were held outdoors in good weather. The college president was readily available for a passing hobo, me, to interview. His name was Claude Williams; everyone called him by his first name. A biography of Williams, *South of God*, by Cedric Belfrage, was written not long after I left the college.

Williams grew up in the mountains of Tennessee, in what was then a whites-only community. Signs by the roadside told Negroes: "Nigger don't let the sun go down on you here." The local opinion was that blacks didn't have souls. As a young man Williams went to Nashville and saw individuals who were half black, half white in ancestry, or one quarter, or an eighth black. Did these people have half a soul, or some other fraction? Since he was attending a seminary to become a church minister, that was a troubling question. He decided the mountain opinion was unfounded; blacks and mulattos were fully human and had souls like anyone else. It was his first "radical" opinion. He was ordained and appointed to a rural church in the lowlands. Many members of his congregation were sharecroppers, who owned no land and worked someone else's land for a share of the produce. The landowner got the bigger share; the sharecropper got barely enough to feed his family. Claude heard grievances from his congregation. He helped organize a sharecroppers' union and negotiate better conditions from landowners in the district. The bishop removed him from the church. He made the union his fulltime occupation.

The union couldn't afford to pay him a living wage, but his activity brought him to the attention of Commonwealth College, which was looking for a president. A wealthy man, a Harvard graduate, had founded the college. His father thought Harvard had radicalized him. At any rate, he used some of his inheritance to create a place where unpopular ideas could be examined.

Was I interested, Claude asked, in enrolling in Commonwealth?

"I have no money," I told him.

"You willing to work?"

"I've been knocking around looking for work."

"Then you've found some right here. You can be helper to our farm manager, and when you have free time, you can sit in on any class you wish."

In this way I was invited to stay, and I did. I was hired, sort of, but for no salary. I thought that I was working off my tuition, but Stephen Smith, writing a history of Commonwealth College, tells me I'm listed as recipient of the John Field scholarship, given by Ralph Field, whose son was killed in Spain in the war against Franco. I would work mornings and be free in the afternoon to participate in the activities of the college.

The students ranged in age from late teens (few of these) to seventies (only one or two), and it was hard to distinguish between student and staff (I hesitate to call any of them faculty because no academic degrees were required, though some may have had them; experience was more important). A person could be the teacher, or discussion leader, in one class, and a student in another. It is true that there was a class in Marxism, much the same as the class at the Benjamin Franklin Institute in Springfield that I had once briefly attended, but many of the persons at Commonwealth while I was there were not communists, but some other kind of radical. There was an elderly man who proclaimed himself an anarchist. I was not the only one who preferred to be known as a non-denominational socialist. And there were not a few who were uncommitted to any particular ideology, but found the ambience congenial. One man, about sixty, was

Ralph Field, my scholarship donor. He had fought in Spain, as had his son who had been killed there. Another man had lived in a commune in Wisconsin; these pre-1960s communes were not founded by hippies but by followers of nineteenth-century reformers: Owen, Saint-Simon, Brisbane, etc. One young guy may or may not have had any political leanings; he had recently been released from a prison in Oklahoma where he had served a term for passing counterfeit money. How he made the transition from prison to Commonwealth I never learned. Lee Hays, a tall stout man in overalls, led singing of any cluster of singers who cared to participate in song. He was also a storyteller and had something of a reputation as a folk singer and raconteur.

Charlie Brown was the man who ran the farm and set the tasks I had to do. He was grey-haired but vigorous, perhaps fifty or so. Mostly I worked alongside him and I was impressed by his skills. He seemed to know how to do anything. He was a good boss to work for and I admired him greatly. Every morning he woke me before daylight and we went to the barn. I milked several cows, don't remember how many, but my wrists were tired when I finished. Finished is perhaps the wrong word. Charlie finished the milking, following me from cow to cow because I didn't get every last drop of milk from the teats. Then we carried the large metal milk cans to a refrigerated room.

After milking we could have breakfast. We were usually alone; hardly anyone else was up yet. Then we would go on with whatever job needed to be done. We cut down trees with a crosscut saw, he on one end, me on the other. When the tree was cut through and toppled, Charlie would say, "Let's cool off by lopping off the branches," and he would pick up an ax and start swinging at a branch. I was so pooped from the sawing, I could hardly hold an ax, but I attacked a branch. Whereas Charlie severed a branch with one blow, I hacked at one a few times before it was detached from the trunk. The trunk was sawn up in lengths that would fit into a stove, but these cylinders had to be split by ax into segments of smaller width, and the branches had to be similarly reduced to kindling size.

We were clearing a forested section to make another field for planting, and in addition to cutting down the trees, we had to get the roots out. That meant severing the roots that were visible, fastening a chain around the stump and using mules to pull the stump loose. As it came up part way, more roots could be seen and they had to be cut. Rocks also had to be removed from the area cleared of trees. Digging around a rock outcrop to expose enough rock to get purchase for a chain, the mules would again do the heavy work, but the few great stones and many littler ones had to be rolled onto a stone boat by human hands. The stone boat was simply a wooden platform without wheels that the mules would haul away to the edge of the field, where a stone wall would be built.

One morning after breakfast Charlie got a rifle. We're going to butcher a hog, he told me. We went to the fence around the pigpen. On other days, the pigs, expecting to be fed, would come to the side of the fence where Charlie was. This morning they got as far away as they could and turned their backs to him. They know, Charlie said, what this rifle means. It was not the first time one of them was sacrificed for the college larder. Charlie wanted to get a shot into the brain. He moved around the fence, the pigs scattered, each time he moved, some went one way, some the other. It took awhile before he had a line on a fully-grown pig, but he eventually got a shot, right into the center of a pig's forehead. The pig went down and was still.

We went in and dragged the animal out of the pen. Charlie hosed it down to remove the mud caking the skin. We already had a metal barrel full of hot water; it was set on a wood structure that held the barrel at a 45-degree angle, making it easier to dip the animal into the water. Charlie slit a hole between the bone and the ligament of the hind legs, threaded a rope through and, with a pulley suspended from an overhead branch of a tree, we hoisted the body of the pig, head down, into the air and maneuvered it into the barrel of hot water. When the bristles were softened, the carcass was lifted out of the water and hung in the air while we scraped the hide clean of bristles with a knife.

A stick was put between the legs near the hooves to keep them apart. Then Charlie neatly disemboweled the animal by cutting a line down the center of the ventricle side, being careful to make a loop around the anus so the intestines could be detached intact. Guts, liver, kidneys, lungs, and heart were placed in basins to be dealt with later. The body cavity was hosed out. Now the body could be lowered onto a table where it could be cut up. The head was detached, brain removed, and both set aside. The butchering proper now began with legs, hams, ribs, shoulders segmented.

A smokehouse was a long-established part of the farm. We prepared hams and bacon to be smoked. We scraped off whatever flesh there was on the skull to make headcheese. Other scraps went into the cleaned intestines to make sausages. "We hate to waste anything," Charlie said. "We tried to get Mr. Ford to take the squeal of the pig to put into his horns, but he didn't like the sound." Actually, he did not use the bristles of the pig we slaughtered though he mentioned they were used in some brushes. Working with Charlie was an education for a city boy; he was a good teacher.

I soon made friends. I liked to listen to the man who fought in Spain, Ralph Field. He was more concerned to explain the composition of the Loyalist forces and the politics therein than he was with the military events but he did speak about both. The elderly man who had been in the commune should have been interesting to talk to but his English was rudimentary; he preferred to speak German, but that was a language with which I had not yet had much experience.

A guy with a shock of brown hair, a rich baritone voice, and a muscular body was the cynosure of most feminine eyes. He was not much older than me; most of the men were older than either of us, so perhaps we found ourselves a natural pair. He had grown up in Hell's Kitchen, just across the East River from Manhattan, a big city kid with street smarts and a quick repartee with a colorful vocabulary. Somehow he had managed to get a year or two at Columbia University and had become fascinated with modern literature. He had ambitions to be a writer. He had been inspired by e.e. cummings to drop all capital letters and most punctuation. He admired James Joyce and had adopted from him the "stream of consciousness" style. Someone had nicknamed him "lower case jim." That had to be before he came to Commonwealth; everyone here was too seriously committed to politics to be concerned with literary monikers.

He knew a great amount of poetry, which he would recite in his resonant voice. My fund of poetry, not always to his taste, may have been one of the things that drew us together. He also was able to sing well enough to be in a barbershop quartet. He was a good storyteller and had a hearty laugh that invited accompaniment. I moved to share a room with him and we talked incessantly whenever we were together. He told me about books of which I'd never heard and recounted the contents. I especially remember e.e. cumming's novel *the tin derby*. The title referred to the helmet worn by World War I soldiers. He had a copy of *Ulysses*, though it was still illegal to import into the U.S. because of its supposed pornographic passages. It made amazing reading.

A large man from New York City, Marc was tall and weighed about 300 pounds, with a size 17 collar (I remember the collar size because when I resumed my journey after my stay at Commonwealth, Marc gave me a shirt – mine were totally worn to tatters). The collar flopped around my skinny neck. Marc was jovial, but I can't recall that he ever said anything that I bothered to remember. He attached himself to jim as a fellow New Yorker, and that attached him to me as well.

There was a novel in the works. A portable typewriter was frequently in use but jim didn't let anyone see what he was writing. The story was based on his own experience. What experience? He seemed too young to have much. But he was the one who had recently been in prison in Oklahoma, a state abutting Arkansas, and thus not far away from Mena.

Intending to earn some money in the summer vacation from Columbia, jim had answered an ad in the newspaper for a driver. "Businessman who travels frequently requires a driver for his Chrysler car." It sounded like a chauffeur was wanted, and he did not have the special chauffeur's license, and he feared he would not be acceptable. However, the man who placed the ad chose from among the applicants the young man from Hell's Kitchen.

"Well, James. Would you like to see the country?"

"Sure," said the youth who had never been out of southern New York.

"Here's a gift to start off as friends." The man handed jim a twenty-dollar bill.

"Thanks."

"Suppose I told you that the bill is counterfeit. What would you do?"

"Spend it. Get rid of it as soon as possible. At some bodega where they don't look carefully at the money except to see how much it is."

"You wouldn't call the cops?"

"Naw!"

The man had a suitcase full of twenties, all counterfeit. The scheme was to go from city to city, leisurely but not slowly enough for the local banks to find numbers of counterfeit twenties appearing in deposits and cause an alert. Also, there was no particular direction of travel; that would have aided in the capture of the passer of the bogus bills.

The man and jim took turns driving, but jim was the sole passer of the twenties. He would buy some inexpensive item, get fifteen or more dollars in change – money they could spend without cautions. The man would pick jim up at a designated street corner at a specified time. If jim was not there, that would mean he had been picked up by the police, and the man would drive to another state and put in an ad for another driver. They got as far as Oklahoma before jim was caught. He served time.

Marc, jim and I serenaded, if that is the appropriate word for some of the songs we bellowed, the building where some of the women lived. I do not know who created the lyric of a song featuring Commonwealth:

> *When you go to Commonwealth College*
> *Be sure to bring a queen*
> *'Cause the women at Commonwealth College*
> *Are few and far between*

It held some truth. The women were outnumbered by the men.

There was a young couple from New Jersey. The husband, Paul, was usually off in some quiet place reading while most of the students were enjoying the leisure hours; the wife, Ruth, a short, plump Jewish woman, hung around with jim and me. She had an interesting story: her parents came from Russia after 1905 when there was a general repression and anti-Semitic outbreaks. They were anarchists and found their way from Ellis Island to New Jersey. They worked until they had enough money to buy some land that included a few farm buildings. One had been a chicken house. Her father fixed up the chicken house as their home. The purchase was made collectively with other anarchists who had accompanied them and joined in the purchase of a large piece of property. They farmed, happy to have land because in the old country Jews were not permitted to own land. Having grown up on what was in essence an anarchist commune, in which the younger generation had drifted from the founding ideology, Ruth was immune to political ideas; her husband, from a different background, was intent on exploring whatever ideas might be relevant to solving the socio-economic problems of 1930s America and the world.

Charlie had another rifle that he loaned to me, saying, "We're going to get ourselves some rabbit stew." We went out in the woods. There were plenty of rabbits around. Rabbits are not smart. They seemed to think that if they do not move, you won't see them; that may work with hawks hovering above, but it makes a human hunter's success easier. Charlie got a rabbit and so did I. He showed me how to skin it and get to the meat. We cooked the rabbit in his house and ate our stew there away from the others in the mess hall. It was delicious, but I have another reason to remember the rabbit.

A day or so later I began to run a fever. The college nurse gave me some medication intended to bring down the fever. It did not have much effect. A doctor from the town was called. He thought I had typhoid. He prescribed a new drug, just released on the market, called sulfanilamide (the first of the sulfas). It did no more than the nurse's earlier medicine. I developed swellings under my armpits and on my neck. The doctor, called back, lanced the swelling to release the pus. My lymph glands were picking up something alien in my blood, but what the infection was he couldn't say. My temperature remained dangerously high, and he proclaimed that I would soon die. Nurse asked me where she should write to notify my family. Thinking of "home" as Irene's house, I gave her my sister Ruth's address in New Jersey. I also asked the nurse to write to Fitz at Bowling Green College. Fitz hitchhiked from Ohio to see me on my deathbed in Arkansas. I was delirious; I didn't even know he was there.

But I didn't die. Nurse had taken a blood sample and sent it to some facility in Chicago. Word came back that I had tularemia, a blood infection spread by squirrels and rabbits. It had been identified in Tulari county, California, hence its name, and was not previously known to be in Arkansas. Fortunately for me a serum for tularemia had just been approved by the health authorities. This treatment was given to me and I speedily recovered. Nurse's initiative saved my life. Her face is still clear in my memory, but strangely I can't remember her name. I had been unaware of her before I fell sick; she didn't ordinarily wear a nurse's white uniform outside the dispensary, which I had had no occasion to visit. Professor Smith informed me, from his study of the records of Commonwealth College, that her name was Mary Rader, and that before coming to Commonwealth she had served in Spain as a nurse.

As soon as I was well, I left Commonwealth the way I arrived, with only a bindle. I hitchhiked away from the Mena area headed for Springfield, Massachusetts. I am grateful to Claude and Commonwealth for paying for my sick care, the fee for the local doctor, the serum that cured me, and above all to nurse Rader. Having no money, except perhaps a few dollars I'd had when I arrived, I had no choice except to travel as I had done previously.

A car stopped to pick me up. There were two guys in the front seat, so I got in the back. There were empty beer bottles rattling around my feet. We were speeding on a macadam road when the guy in the passenger seat said, "Take this next turn. It's a short-cut." The driver took the advice and turned on to a dirt road. The car began to swerve in loose sand. Before the driver could slow down or get the car under control, we plunged into a thicket of young saplings that bent, gave way, and let the car through.

The vehicle came to rest on its side. I was jostled but unhurt. The driver had his foot out of the door, which must have swung open as the car hurtled through space, and now the weight of the car held it pinned so he could not pull it free. "My foot! My foot!" he kept screaming. His friend in the passenger seat was knocked out and far from being any help, his weight was slumped on the driver. I was able to climb out of the door now on the upper side of the tipped car, and tried to heave it up in order to enable the driver to extract his foot, but it was too heavy for me to do by myself. I ran out to the paved road to stop a passerby to help.

The supple saplings sprang upright and no one would ever have noticed that the car had entered the thicket. A pickup truck stopped. I explained what had happened and pointed to the thicket. The scene looked serene and the farmer, who was apparently untrustful of city people, was skeptical of what I told him. Suspecting some scam, he drove off faster than he had been going when I flagged him down. There was not much traffic on this road. A number of cars passed me by. I was getting worried that no one would stop.

A big fancy car did stop and the driver, in a business suit, believed my story. He turned on to the dirt road, stopped, and followed me into the thicket. Together we righted the car. The passenger had come to. He had probably passed out as much from drink as from injury though he had somehow crushed an arm and it hung limply. The "Good Samaritan" drove all of us to the nearest hospital. The driver and his friend were kept for a while to have their injuries treated; I was allowed to leave almost immediately with only the addition of a band-aid to my elbow where some skin had been scraped off.

I walked to the edge of town and started hitching again. Two or three days later I was home. Everyone was surprised to see me because no further news had come after they had been notified that I was on my deathbed.

I did not stay there long. The lawsuit from the Rood & Woodbury grocery truck accident had been settled while I was away. R&W got some compensation for the damage to the truck. The lawyer took his share. The doctor who had bandaged me was paid, and there was $50 left over for me. Ironically, $50 was exactly what I needed to pay the registration fee at Bowling Green. So I had returned from death's door to receive the cost of going to college. Not for the first time nor for the last, I told myself I was lucky to get through the dangers that came my way.

After a short rest, with the end of summer approaching, I hitchhiked with Fitz to Bowling Green, Ohio.

CHAPTER EIGHT

COLLEGE FRESHMAN

The college in Bowling Green was one of four set up in each corner of the state of Ohio to supplement the Ohio State University; this one was in the northwest corner, a few miles south of Toledo. In terms of the number of students at the time, it was not much bigger than West Springfield High School, but in terms of facilities – libraries, dorms, cafeteria, gyms, buildings, and space, it was more grandiose, but definitely not one of the substantial institutions of higher education in the United States.

While not overly impressed, I was happy to be there. It was, at last, a real college. But the admissions office was not particularly happy to have me. The person who interviewed me said, "Your marks look like the temperature chart of someone who had a series of fevers." I had a number of A's and B's but also some C's, even a D. I had done what interested me and paid little attention to what didn't. However, the A's indicated I could do college level studies if I made the effort. I knew I could do it, and the admissions official was persuaded that I was now in a serious frame of mind and allowed me to register. Thus began a happy year of study and college life.

Fitz and I rented a room in the home of a garage mechanic who owned a two-story house. He and his wife lived on the first floor and rented out the upstairs to students. The second floor had a separate entrance on one side of the house. It was such a small house that there were only two bedrooms, one bathroom, and a hallway on the second floor. The other room also had two occupants so there were four guys to share the bathroom, which could be a crunch trying to get to early morning classes. However, it was not a problem for me since I adjusted my schedule so that I had no eight o'clock class, and therefore could stay in bed a bit longer in the mornings. I preferred to stay up late and prepare for the next day's classes or write term papers before going to sleep, and this arrangement suited me fine.

In the hallway was a narrow table with a gas ring for cooking. The guys in the other room, New Yorkers, ate out and did not use the gas ring. Fitz and I ate some of our meals in our room. I did all the cooking. With three older sisters and a younger sister, Fitz and his brothers had never been required to do anything in the kitchen. I had once earned a Boy Scout merit badge for fire building and one for camp cooking. And there was my experience cooking in tin cans in the hobo "jungles." Plus I had always done the cooking when Fitz and I went hiking on the Long Trail. So naturally it fell to me to become the cook.

Fitz agreed to wash the pot, frying pan, dishes, and cutlery whenever necessary. The source of water for cooking and cleaning was in the bathroom. Nothing was ever washed until I said I needed it to prepare the next meal. We had uncomplicated meals when we ate in and usually not more complex out. Generally that was a burger and fries at a diner called The Giant Hamburger.

Attending classes and studying are sedentary tasks, so it was good to be able most days to go for a walk around town and out into the surrounding farm area. This was always a half hour or more of exercise and relaxation and Fitz and I would do our usual talk-fest while walking.

Sometimes we would go past the house where Betty, a girl Fitz had become acquainted with the year before, lived. If she was in, a coke bottle would be on the windowsill. If Fitz saw a bottle he'd call to her, and her head would pop up from her desk in front of the window. She'd wave and come down and join us. Betty had a keen mind and she added to the intricacies of our conversations.

Charlotte was Betty's roommate and soon she would come down when Betty did. Now a foursome, we tended to walk two by two. Fitz and Betty, old friends, walked together, and Charlotte and I, getting acquainted, followed after them. For some time, we talked only of quotidian things, but one day, Charlotte said – out of the blue – "Dan! If you say you love me, I'll let you do it." What the "it" was – was never in doubt. "It" did not relate to anything said previously, but flowed from the fact that we were male and female and young. For a moment I could say nothing. I hadn't expected this, but still I was not surprised – because we were young and male and female.

The proposition certainly was tempting, but what *exactly* was being offered? The "if you say you love me" clause was the hazard. After we did "it," how long would it be before she'd say, "Why don't we get married?" How could I then say "No" when I'd already attested that I loved her?

I said I liked her but love takes time to grow, and *maybe* if we did "it," love would blossom. That, she averred, was not good enough.

"O.K." I said, and figured that was that. I was not going to be implicated in her plans for matrimony. I had heard that some parents sent their daughters to college so they could find a husband, but I hadn't thought the quest would be so direct. Subsequently, Charlotte did not accompany Betty when Fitz called. We were back to three again, which I noted marked an improvement in the conversation.

Late one afternoon, Betty unexpectedly came over to our room. I was just about to start cooking supper, so I made a little more and she ate with us. The problem was we didn't have an extra plate, so she had to eat off our plates and use our forks or her fingers to do so. Betty volunteered to wash the dishes, not a big job, but for once it was done immediately after the meal.

We talked for hours and eventually the talk turned to sex. "One could be 'tender' with another person," Betty noted, "without being married, but if married that would be 'legal tender.'" This pun set us all laughing. "I'm not concerned with legality," she added. Soon we were all three in bed - Betty in the middle, flanked by Fitz on one side and me on the other.

In the morning, Betty looked out the window and in the daylight saw her girl's bike leaning against a tree in front of the house. "Oh!" she said, "I shouldn't have brought my bike." A girl's bike parked overnight in front of a house that rented rooms only to male students was likely to be noted. "It's a dead giveaway!" she added.

And apparently it was. Not generally perhaps, but to our landlady at least. The following morning, Melba, our landlady, came into my room a little after eight. My first class was not until ten. All except Melba and I were out of the house. Melba was bringing me some coffee. "Had some left over," she announced. "Thought you might like a 'cuppa.'" As she held out the coffee, her negligee fell open, revealing that her pubic hair was as blond as that on her head.

"Thanks." I took the cup and drank some of it while Melba seated herself on the edge of my bed. I placed the cup on the floor beside the bed. She raised the blanket and sheet and got under them with me.

The next morning she brought toast and jelly with the coffee, and the day after some scrambled eggs.

Melba's younger sister, who lived in Toledo, a few miles north of Bowling Green, came down for a visit. Somehow it was arranged that the two sisters and Fitz and me would go roller-skating at a rink in Toledo. I had never been in a roller rink before, but had done a lot of ice-skating on Van Horn Pond. We skated as couples and changed partners when the music changed. We saw the girls to their parental home, where the sister still lived, and where Melba was going to stay the night. Fitz and I started hitchhiking back to Bowling Green.

Unfortunately, the traffic that late was light and what there was of it passed us by. In the dark hitchhiking was never as easy as in the daytime. From about midnight until dawn we waited for a ride or walked a ways and were still not back to Bowling Green. In the daylight our luck was better, but we didn't get back until just before eight o'clock. Fitz had a chemistry class at eight, which he wanted to attend because he was a chemistry major. He suggested I go with him and then we'd both go to our room and get some sleep. I agreed.

We were a little giddy after being up all night, and we'd been talking of all kinds of things, some of them humorous. Sitting in the back of the class, we made *sotto voce* comments to each other about the lecture, which of course was serious, but in our silly mood seemed hilarious. The professor told us to leave the room because we were distracting the class.

"Jeez!" Fitz said when we were out of the room. "That's my faculty advisor." It would have been better to have missed the class than to have been kicked out of it. However, no real harm was done. Fitz passed the course, and eventually received a B.S. in chemistry.

Freshmen were supposed to wear a brimless cap called a "beanie." I did not like the idea because it was a signal that upperclassmen, if they wished, could harass the wearer – a game they called hazing. I never bought a beanie. I was not going to waste any of my scarce cash on a useless thing for a practice of which I did not approve. Whenever not in a class or working I was almost always with Fitz, an upperclassman, so I was usually taken to be at least a sophomore. One evening the two of us were walking on the campus where two walkways crossed and at that juncture a fountain in the center of a pool spurted water into the air. Two upperclassmen were tormenting a freshman. The freshman, who was in one of my classes, saw me and to distract his tormentors shouted, "There's McCall! He's a freshman and he's not wearing a beanie." The two hazers converged on me, allowing the cornered freshman to get away.

Before they could say anything, I told them, "If you try to make anything of this, you'll find yourself in that pool." I was not at all sure that I could carry out my threat. Seeing Fitz with me, they may have assumed that he would help me. It would then be two against two, a fair fight, but the tormenters did not want a fight in defense of their supposed right to haze any freshman. They backed off.

The dean's daughter was in one of my classes. She was a dark-haired beauty and I feasted my eyes on her while listening to the lecture. Somehow I got her phone number and called her late one afternoon when classes were over. She was at home and answered the phone. I told her who I was and invited her to go to a movie with me.

"When?"

"Tonight."

"I would never go out with anyone who asked me on the same day!"

"Why not?"

"It isn't proper."

"Oh! Then how about next week?"

"No."

"Why not? Isn't that enough warning?"

"Yes, but I do not wish to go anywhere with you."

"Wow!"

An older woman who had worked for some years after high school and then come to college as a freshman sat next to me in the library one day. There were a series of long tables stretching nearly across the long reading room. Suspended lamps over the center of the tables provided light to readers on either side of the table. Students read assigned readings that could not be taken out of the library, or researched material for term papers. In the days before Xerox we had to copy passages we wanted to quote. The tables were always occupied almost to capacity, so it was not surprising that the empty seat beside me should soon be taken after I sat down. She said "hello" and I looked up from my book. I recognized her as someone in one of my classes, and acknowledged her greeting.

"I hear that you are from Massachusetts," she said.

"Yeah. Springfield. Why?"

"I'm from Massachusetts, too. Just outside Boston."

I nodded, acknowledging our neighborliness, but said nothing, anxious to get back to my reading so I could finish and get out of the library to do something else. But she went on talking, and despite my wish to ignore her, I found myself in a conversation. Somehow, what was on my mind came out – I told her about the dean's daughter's haughtiness in the way she turned down my invitation to see a movie.

"She's telling you that you are not in her class."

"I wasn't asking to marry her. Just go to a movie."

"But if a man that she might consider marrying saw her with you, in your inexpensive clothes, he might cross her off his list of girls whom he might woo."

"Really?"

The conversation went on and got around to what she seemed to have had in mind. She told me about the advice Benjamin Franklin gave to a young man on how to select a mistress. Consider an older woman, Franklin suggested, because she can teach you what you need to know to please a woman – and yourself – and she will be more grateful for your attention than a woman your own age is likely to be.

It hit me that there was something pertinent to the two of us in this story. She was an older woman and I was a younger man. The implicit message was to forget the dean's daughter, who was unobtainable anyway, and share some pleasure with a willing older woman who was now sitting beside me. All this more or less whispered conversation came to a stammering end. I was stymied for a reply. She realized my confusion was equivalent to a refusal, and said something to put me at ease again. It was a good offer and if I'd been wise enough to see Franklin's wisdom, I'd have accepted her projected gift of herself, but I was too immature to realize what I was turning down. I was looking for a young woman, not an older woman. Not fazed by my rejection of her offer, she remained friendly and we frequently thereafter had lunch together in the cafeteria.

Classes

Being a freshman, I did not have a lot of choices in available courses. Freshman English and a couple of other required courses left me only a little room for electives. Freshman English could be a bore, but as I'll explain in a moment, it turned out to be the most exciting course of the semester. There were, however, some points of interest in other courses.

An historian, apparently feeling alien -- out in the mid-west -- one day told the class, "In New England there is culture; west of the Hudson River there is only agriculture." I guessed he was a New Englander who would have liked to be teaching at a New England college and felt exiled out on the flatlands of Ohio.

His account of the Civil War surprised me when he said, "the war was not to end slavery" but to "preserve the Union." Later I learned this was a common opinion. My immediate reaction was: what was the reason the Union was threatened with dissolution? It was nothing other than slavery! So the professor's distinction was – if not one without a difference – at least not wholly true.

My second reaction was: Adam Smith, in the previous century, had demonstrated that slavery was not an economically efficient way to get a labor force. The slave owner had to feed, clothe, and provide shelter to a slave and his/her small children. These needs might be minimally met, but they were expenses that were year-round, whereas hired workers were paid wages for what they did and laid off when the tasks were completed. Therefore, Adam Smith concluded slavery was on its way out of existence. So – should the Civil War have been fought?

Considering that the Civil War was the bloodiest in U.S. history, *if* the only purpose for the war was the "preservation of the Union," one should ask – what would be lost if there were two countries where previously there had been only one? Today one might say that -- divided in two – the influence of either, or perhaps even together, their weight in world affairs would be limited. Those who take pride in being part of a superpower would regret this diminishment, but those who yearn for more comity in international relations probably would not lament the division.

Also, seeing that after the Civil War a temporary real freedom for the slaves ended, and a system that suppressed the former slaves and their descendants was instituted and perpetuated into the period of our class discussion, it seemed to me that a great mistake had been made by President Abraham Lincoln and his administration in going to war. Despite the effort to separate the policy of preserving the Union from the policy advocated at the time by abolitionists, the Emancipation Proclamation was issued by Lincoln's administration before the defeat of the Confederacy. Freeing the slaves was brought to the forefront of the Lincoln cabinet's deliberations not by the moral concern for the injustice of keeping human chattels, but by the military argument that the North needed to encourage the slaves to flee the South and thereby reduce the labor necessary to support the Confederate armies.

Although Britain had eliminated slavery in its dominions a generation earlier by buying out the slave-owners' chattel property, no one in the Lincoln administration made a serious case, before the war began, for emancipation by cash payment! Perhaps the U.S. Treasury did not have sufficient cash on hand for so many purchases, but proceeding one state at a time, this transaction of gradually freeing all slaves everywhere in the country might have been negotiated and accomplished without bloodshed. No doubt some owners would have been reluctant to sell their "property," but the government, if persistent, could have prevailed over individual opposition to legal emancipation.

Slavery did die out in the Western Hemisphere in the nineteenth century, and the industrial system of wageworkers replaced it, as Adam Smith had predicted, but it lingered in some corners of the Old World, particularly in agricultural economies. One might argue that, without the Civil War, slavery in the U.S., being in the agricultural southern states, could have lasted at least as long, for example, as it did in Brazil; that would have been another twenty years or so. One year is too long for the person enslaved. In terms of actual misery of the freed slaves, and their children and grandchildren, given discrimination and segregation, one may wonder if all this was an adequate remission for years of the suffering of slavery.

The defeat of the Confederates created such animosity between whites and their ex-slaves and between the two regions, North and South, that the Civil War bequeathed more hatred to succeeding generations than would have resulted from ending slavery in the manner Britain ended it. The South resented the Union forces changing their social system, and the memory lingers. If, however, slavery had been given up by slave owners for their own economic reasons, there would now be less regional tension between North and South, and more importantly Blacks would have been, in time, more readily integrated into American society.

So what if we would now have two countries instead of one? A smaller United States and a Confederate States, each independent of the other, and by the end of the nineteenth century with slaves emancipated in both countries, they could have been as friendly with each other as Canada has been with the U.S., and there would not have been an unnecessary bloodletting of a Civil War. Lincoln was a great man, but great men can make mistakes, and I am still convinced Lincoln made a whopper of a mistake in preserving the Union.

My opinion, I admit, is part of my feelings about the stupidity and brutality of war. At the time my attitude was merely an intellectual reaction to a college lecture, but not long afterward I would see some of the horrors of the reality of war. My juvenile criticism of the Bowling Green history professor's presentation of a defense for the Civil War has remained a part of my adamant assessment of war in general.

A friend from Arizona, with whom I occasionally dine, is vociferously opposed to my point of view. He came north to study at MIT and never left the North except to travel widely during his vacation times. His travels include visits to the sites of Civil War battles at times of re-enactments. Many individuals in these performances own their own uniforms – Rebel or Union – and other military equipment. Why is war so popular?

A course in political science, taught by a man born and educated in Germany, was mainly memorable for his heavy accent and his attempt one day to explain the word "pugnacious." His effort to derive it from "pug-nosed" (the result of being punched in the nose, he thought) was laughable as an etymology.

Despite whatever shortcomings there were, I enjoyed being a student again.

Freshman English courses require a lot of writing of theme papers. For an assignment to tell about some event before coming to college, I wrote about being in a boxcar in a freight train where a group of men were smoking marijuana. The paper came back without a mark. I asked the professor why it had not been graded. He said, "You did not do the assignment. You were supposed to describe one of your experiences. Instead you wrote about an imagined situation. Creative writing is fine, but that was not the assignment."

I had a bit of difficulty convincing him that I had actually ridden on freight trains, but when I supplied him with more details, his incredulity faded. He took a flyer from his desk drawer announcing a competition for a "youth novel." The prize offered by a man named Kauffman in Pennsylvania for the best first novel submitted by someone under 40 was $5,000. That sounded like a lot of money. Under 40, however, didn't seem to exclude a lot of competitors that I considered to be beyond "youth."

"Never mind what the assignments are," the professor said. "From now on, you write about what you know of riding the rails. I will accept it in lieu of the assignments. Make it into a novel. My comments will help you edit it before submitting it to Kauffman." This was heady stuff. In high school I had aspired to become a writer without being sure that was a possibility. Now as a college freshman, a professor was urging me to write a novel!

Curiously, this professor, who was – for me -- the most significant one I had at Bowling Green, is without a clear name in my memory. It is not just that that encounter was 65 years ago, but I've mixed his name with the male English teacher I had in high school. It is either Hayes or Hughes, but I'm not sure which is which. I was happy to follow the suggestion. John Steinbeck's *The Grapes of Wrath* had just been published. The prospect for a realistic novel about hoboes seemed propitious.

I named my protagonist Alan. Alan replicated most of what I had done, including the incident when I had been walking along a highway and came to a warehouse where a man on a platform, from which trucks would be loaded, was getting boxes of pears ready for shipment. He was removing a pear from one box and putting it in a barrel with other pears. I stopped to talk with him; the road ahead looked long and devoid of buildings on either side. I asked, "How far to town?" He stopped what he was doing and thought for a minute. "I don't know," he said. "Takes about five minutes driving. I've never walked it." My face must have registered some disappointment. "Sit in the shade for a while," he invited. "The sun's a scorcher today." He was back to eliminating the odd pear from the boxes.

"What are you doing?" I asked.

"Getting rid of the fruit that will not be salable by the time it reaches the market." I looked in the barrel; the pears looked fine to me. "We'll make preserves of those," he told me. "But if you want some, help yourself."

My stomach was empty, and hunger urged me on as I ate several slightly overripe pears. When I started walking again, the warehouseman gave me some more to take with me. I walked down the long road, flagging passing cars for a lift, but didn't get one. Maybe I looked too ragged.

Soon I felt the fruit churning in my stomach. It was going through my digestive system in a hurry. It wasn't long before I had an irresistible need to relieve my bowels. I looked around for a tree or a bush to hide from the passing traffic. Not a one in sight. Before getting to the warehouse there had been innumerable trees. An orchard lined the road. Now there was an open field.

I was desperate. Beside the road was a ditch. I jumped down into the ditch, hoping it would provide me some privacy, and dropped my pants and did what I had to do. Cars whizzed by. I do not know how many saw me in the act, but by that time I didn't care.

One difference: Alan did not leave home because he was considered a "heretic" there, but Dad's bankruptcy, if updated, provided a plausible reason. Alan worked at various jobs, and eventually was able to enroll in an inexpensive land grant college. Thus the story had a transformation from "down and out" to the beginning of a personal success. What the story lacked was a love interest. I played around with trying to create one, but was not really satisfied with my efforts. I introduced a character who resembled Charlotte in the way he met her, but in appearance she was more like the dean's daughter. She even had a touch of the wantonness of Melba.

NO FEES OR CREDITS

At Commonwealth, I had been able to attend some lectures and discussions, but had a schedule of farm work that took priority. Now classes took priority, but I had to earn some money for food and room rent. My first job, which I kept all year, was dishwasher at the Women's Club, where lunch, but no other meal, was served every day. The good thing about this limited dining service was that there were often a few leftovers that could not be easily integrated into another day's luncheon menu, and the employees were given handouts of these remainders. It didn't happen every day, but what I did receive as my share helped with my food bill.

The woman who managed the Women's Club would come up to the sink in which I was washing dishes, stick a finger in, and say, "Not hot enough!" and turn on the hot water faucet before going away. I immediately turned it off. My hands were red and blubbery from the hot water, and could stand it no hotter. The Women's Club job enabled me to pay my share of the rent and to contribute to buying food for the meals we ate in our room.

The second semester was coming up, and I did not have the $50 to register. Late in the first semester, I had found a second job – setting pins in a bowling alley. The kid who had the job was hit by a flying pin that badly bruised his shin. The job was only for Saturdays, but it made it possible to put a little aside toward the registration fee. However, the second job had become available too recently for me to have saved much, and when registration came due, I was short of what I needed and was unable to register.

One way of dealing with the situation was to try to get a fulltime job, save money and return the next fall and register. But time was a factor. War was raging in Europe, and I could not believe the U.S. would stay out. People made fun of FDR's statement, "I hate war." And students added, to make it a couplet – "And so does Eleanor." To me it seemed I had to get as much as I could of schooling before I got drafted and sent off probably to die in the war. What I would learn would be useless if I were going to be killed, but before that I'd have had the pleasure of learning.

I thought of a plan. I selected some courses that I would like to take and went to the professors giving the courses asking permission to audit. Most professors were inclined to grant such permission, assuming that the petitioner had a full slate of courses he or she was taking for credit. No one suspected that all the courses I was attending were only being audited. In effect, I was stealing a semester of college education, but since I got no credit for the courses, I was not getting anything that had any dollar value. And the English professor who had been reviewing my efforts at novel writing continued to do so, even though I no longer was registered in his course.

At the end of the first semester some students dropped out, or transferred to another college. One transferee created a vacancy in an unusual residence that had nine places. My friend Abe Hoffman from Springfield was one of the nine and he had introduced me to a student named Haberstein, who lived there. He was called "Hobby" by his friends. Hobby was a senior and sociology major. I found conversations with Hobby stimulating, and we had become friends. Hobby suggested that I take the now-empty place in this residence. It would save me money both in rent and in food. The nine ate together and managed to create substantial meals for low cost. Buying for nine instead of two, as Fitz and I had been doing, allowed buying the large cans or packages that were generally sold to restaurants. Moreover, the cooperative nature of the group attracted me.

After discussion with Fitz, I decided to accept Hobby's invitation. Fitz's room rent would be the same. The owners would get less, but Fitz would not have to make up for what I had been paying. We would still see each other for our daily walks and at other times. Even if another place had been available, Fitz would not have been interested in joining; he did not like the "crowding" he imagined in this fraternity of nine.

The dwelling had been constructed in the upper level of a barn behind a house on the edge of town. The lower level still had some farm machinery stored there, although no farming was being done anymore by the owner of the property, a widow of a farmer. Thus a few years before, she had agreed to allow a group of students to build some walls of plywood to create a number of rooms and install a kitchen stove, sink, table, shower, beds, and desks.

One room was for the student who proposed the idea and directed the work of dividing the space into rooms for different functions. Now a senior and older than any of the others, he was dubbed "Poppa" and had a small room to himself. The remaining eight all slept in one room hardly larger than Poppa's room. Two-by-fours were the supports to put one double bed above another. Two of these large bunk beds provided sleeping space for eight guys. To ensure that everyone had adequate air to breathe, the upper part of the window had been taken out. In the winter no one went into this cold room except to sleep;

the door was sealed to keep cold air from seeping into the rest of the rooms.

Another room was the dressing room. A pipe was run across the width of the room, and everyone's jackets, pants, and shirts were hung on the pipe. The rule Poppa instigated was that one's clothing, so long as one lived here, was communal. "First come, first served." This was certainly to my advantage. I had hardly anything except what was on my back. I could vary my appearance now by being quick in the morning to make my selection. Of course we were different sizes, so a couple of guys about my size were the victims of my getting there before they did. One of them protested to Poppa but was told that if he wanted to stay, he had to follow the community rules.

One large room had nine desks, made mainly from plywood, and in that room for some specified hours after dinner there was to be no loud talking or radio to disturb studying. Some might gather around the dining table in the kitchen for coffee and quiet chatter if they had no urgent studying to do.

Tasks were rotated each week. We had four teams of two. The tasks were cooking, washing up, sweeping and dusting, and dealing with trash and garbage. The job considered the heaviest was cooking because it had to be done every day at a certain time, and it required some planning and even some skill. Hobby and I were a team. We were acknowledged to be the best of the teams at cooking. Everyone went Saturdays to do the shopping for food in order to have enough hands to carry everything back. The shopping was a two-stop trip: to an A&P and then a farm outlet where we could get milk by the gallon. We usually got the milk from which the cream had been skimmed off – for 10 cents a gallon. And eggs, butter and cheeses.

There were fraternities on campus. We were not a fraternity, but someone had made a sign that read "I Phelta Thi." The phony Greek-sounding letters were an in-joke seldom mentioned outside the house; we were concerned not to arouse curiosity about our exceptional residence. We were unsure our habitat, cobbled together in the upper level of an old barn, would pass muster with the college's standard for housing. The slogan was probably originated by Poppa, who had a habit of telling lurid jokes. But the implied boast of "I felt a thigh" was more than extravagant since we were living essentially sexless lives as far as I could see. Chris, the youngest among us, made claims of "scoring," but I was skeptical, even though he was handsome and energetic.

The course I most enjoyed in the second semester was a philosophy seminar with Professor Slater. In one discussion I held forth for "equality." Women are equal to men in intelligence, I maintained, and it is a waste of half (or more) of the population's intelligence to bar women from positions of management, public office, or scientific research. A couple of male students disputed this, and only one or two female voices came to support me. There were no blacks in the seminar (there were exceedingly few in the college at that time), so when I espoused equality between blacks and whites in mental ability, and otherwise, there were several demurrers who felt free to reveal their attitude. When I argued for social equality, e.g., eliminating, or at least reducing, class distinctions, almost everyone was opposed. The whole session that day was most of the members of the seminar on one side and me on the other, with a little help from Fitz and a couple of others. Slater was a moderator who interrupted only to keep the discussion going.

Slater introduced us to semantics. Both Fitz and I thereafter had many discussions about the concepts in this discipline. When the weather warmed up in the spring, Fitz and I one day happened to walk by Slater's house when he was sitting on the porch. He recognized us and invited us to come have a glass of lemonade.

During this spring, news of the war in Europe came over the radio. A political science professor invited students to come to his house at the time Raymond Gram Swing was reporting the news. Early comers might get to sit in a chair; most would sit on the floor. When the newscast was over, the radio would be shut off and we'd all have a discussion of our opinions about events. Outside this gathering little talk about the war was heard. We were a long way from the Atlantic shore, and the ocean was wide. Most Ohio students on this campus seemed to be able to ignore the international news and feel quite safe in their supposed isolation. I was convinced that "Bundles for Britain" (military aid to Great Britain) would soon be followed by American troops – with me among them.

I was not the only one aware of the war. A professor in the Theater Department called for volunteers to try out for a part in a play to be put on in the university theater. The play was *Bury the Dead* by Irwin Shaw, an anti-war drama.

I tried out for a part though I was not registered as a student. No one seemed to know that. To my surprise, the director called me aside and asked me if I would like to be the student-director. I hadn't known that there was such a position, but the opportunity sounded too good to turn down. He gave me some hints as to how I should manage the job, and thereafter he never interrupted during rehearsal, but afterward would go over with me how things had gone during this rehearsal and often how they might go better in the next rehearsal.

Being an apprentice director was a wonderful experience and renewed my fascination with theater. The substance of the play, however, intensified my worry about being sucked into the war. The concept of *Bury the Dead* was that the dead from the Great War of 1914-1918 were rising up from their graves and protesting the slide to war again. The things they said reflected the failure of the settlement of the armistice conditions that were supposed to maintain peace. Meanwhile, warmongers screamed to *bury the dead* to stop their voices. On the eve of World War II it was a powerful message, but of course it made no difference in the outcome of events.

One course I audited was on German poetry. Of course, I didn't know any German, as I admitted to the professor when asking permission to attend the course. Poems typically are short compositions, and I could make my way through one with a dictionary. "What I want to discover is the music and rhythms," I said. I still recall bits of Goethe's *Kennst du das Land, we die Zitronen blühn?*

LEAVING BOWLING GREEN

When exam time had everyone grubbing far into the night to get ready for four or five exams, I left Bowling Green and hitchhiked south. A woman who had been at Commonwealth while I was there lived in Tennessee, almost directly south of Bowling Green. I had written to her and she invited me to visit. She had grown up in China; her parents were missionaries. She thought it amusing that the Chinese called them *gwai lo* (foreign devils). Having been considered by most of those around her as a "foreign devil" as she was growing up made her, she said, indifferent to criticism. She did what she thought she should do and did not concern herself with disapproval from others.

Her husband was a lawyer. He had not been to Commonwealth. He greeted me jovially and took his wife and me out to dinner in an elegant restaurant. Driving home after dinner, he unbuttoned his vest and his shirt while driving to be ready to go to bed as soon as we were back in the house. He always liked to get to bed early.

The next day, a Sunday, my friend suggested we go for a picnic on Lookout Mountain, not far away. Sounded good to me. She invited a friend, a young black woman. The car we had used to go to the restaurant was a big car, appropriate for a lawyer to impress his clients. The wife's car was a roadster, and that was the one we took for the picnic. The husband drove, his wife beside him in the front seat, leaving the rumble seat for the black woman and me. We had a wonderful view in several directions from the mountaintop, and enjoyed a sumptuous lunch of cold meats and salad, washed down with a white wine with fruit for dessert.

We were not far from Black Mountain College across the state line in North Carolina. It was described to me as a different sort of college, largely run by refugees from Germany who had fled Hitler's fascism. Their philosophy was referred to as *werklehre*, which connoted learning by doing (or working). "You should stop there before you go north," my Commonwealth classmate suggested and the others concurred. I decided I would.

On the way back, getting into town just before dusk, I had my arm over the black woman's shoulder. We had become acquainted during the day and that seemed allowable, but when the car stopped at a traffic light with people crossing the road looking at the two of us out in the open in the rumble seat – a white man and a black woman, I wondered what their reaction might be. This was a southern town, and I had not grown up as a *gwai lo* and could not be as undisturbed by public opinion as my friend took for granted. There was no problem as it turned out.

Before visiting Black Mountain College, I stopped to see Thomas Wolfe's home, the boarding house his mother ran that he described in *Look Homeward Angel*. He described his fellow townsmen so stringently that a later book was entitled *You Can't Go Home Again*. I finished reading that book just before I started hitchhiking west.

Black Mountain College reminded me, in some respects, of Commonwealth College. It was part farm, part college, without pillared and porticoed buildings. I walked around with no intention of being more than a sightseer, but was invited to speak to the director, who asked me about my academic background. I told him about Commonwealth and Bowling Green. He said I was welcome to stay and sit in on some classes. The only one I now recall was a literature discussion where I heard reactions to Thomas Mann's *The Magic Mountain*, which I hadn't yet read. And with the other students and teachers I spent some time working on the farm that produced much of the food consumed in the dining hall.

The next day, the director told me that he had good reports of my participation in classes, and asked me what I thought of the college. I was full of enthusiasm. "Would you like to apply for admission for next fall?"

"I do not have the money for tuition."

"We are not as expensive as most other colleges, and we have some scholarship monies. How much could you put up?"

"Whatever I can earn during the summer – if I can find a job."

"Take this application form and request a scholarship. As soon as you are employed, fill it out and send it to us. We will be happy to see you here in September." I intended to comply with his instructions, but as it turned out my luck at finding a job that paid an adequate salary was no better than it had been since I was laid off at Gilbert and Barker.

Heading north, I stopped in New York City, where I called "lower case jim," my friend from Commonwealth College. He told me to meet him in a certain bar. He got off work at 5 p.m. Shortly after five, I entered the bar and looked around. I didn't see him until he stood up, waved his arms, and called out in his resonant voice, "Over here! I want you to meet my new cunt." As I approached his table, I saw that a "pleasantly plump" woman was sitting next to him. "This is Margie," he said by way of introduction. She was all smiles. She was apparently accustomed to his ways, and New Yorkers, at least in this bar, were also, for no one seemed to pay any attention to what elsewhere would have been seen as rude and obscene.

The job jim was working at was elevator operator in a ritzy apartment building. He had a room above the top floor of apartments, next to the machinery for the elevator. The noise in the room when the elevator was moving was thunderous, but during the hours when most people were asleep the elevator did not move very often. This I know because jim insisted I stay over. When I saw how small the room was and how narrow the only bed, I said I would keep on hitchhiking. It was not a long haul from NYC to West Springfield. "Naw! It's nighttime. You don't want to do that. Stay. We'll manage. And tomorrow Margie can show you around the big city."

That claim of being able to "manage" was hyperbole. Margie was living with him. The two of them were sleeping in that narrow bed. For one night three of us somehow managed to squeeze onto that tiny space. The next day Margie called a woman who was a friend and an artist, introduced me, and said I had no place to sleep. The friend got the hint and invited me to sleep in her studio. Not mentioned at the time, the invitation was also to sleep with her. She gave me a charcoal drawing when I left.

Finally, after a roundabout route from Bowling Green, I was again walking the streets of Springfield looking for work. Suddenly I remembered the suggestion of Fitz's sister Betty, who months before had suggested that I become an orderly at Springfield Hospital.

CHAPTER NINE

HOSPITAL ORDERLY

The job of hospital orderly did not get much respect in the hospital or outside. I heard it said that the job was usually held by alcoholics. That may have been generally true though none of the orderlies at Springfield Hospital were habitual drunks while I was there. The position of orderly doesn't seem to exist in today's hospitals; there are volunteers of various kinds who do some of the tasks, and male nurses are more common and eliminate the occasional need for a male orderly's strength.

For me in Springfield again, it was a good job. Having been away for a couple of years had cooled the tension between Irene and me. But not wanting to live "at home" and revive the problem of having an atheist under her roof, a room provided by the hospital for me as an orderly was ideal. A building behind the hospital had storage on the first floor, and rooms above for orderlies and other single male staff. I had a small room with a comfortable bed, chair, closet, and bookstand. I ate my meals at the hospital cafeteria. Good food, cheap. The essentials were taken care of. Pay was minimal but the Depression was not over and jobs were scarce.

When I started to work at the hospital I had great respect for doctors, thinking them dedicated do-gooders, and probably they were mostly, but listening to doctors scrubbing before an operation gave me a less admirable view of them. They talked of their expensive automobiles, their big houses, fur coats for their wives, and other material things. They saved lives but they sounded like money-grubbers.

Nonetheless, the profession of medicine fascinated me. I bought a copy of *Gray's Anatomy* and *Materia Medica* and spend a lot of my free time in my room browsing through these texts, looking up things relevant to patients I saw during my time on duty. What my duty consisted of was mainly pushing a gurney with a patient to or from the operating room, or X-Ray, running an errand for the charge nurse of a ward, such as getting a medication from the pharmacy, assisting a nurse with a patient, emptying bed-pans and urinals, or just about anything the head nurse on the floor asked me to do. Sterilizing instruments in an autoclave was not a regular duty for orderlies; it usually was done by a nurse, but the head nurse on the floor where I was assigned had shown me how and given me the task.

I was a member of the hospital community, not that I socialized with doctors. John Lamoreau, the night telephone operator who lived in the house where orderlies slept, said the hospital was organized like the Catholic Church: The Head Surgeon was the Pope; other surgeons were the cardinals; diagnosticians were the bishops; other doctors such as dermatologists were priests; nurses were nuns; orderlies were altar boys. Actually, that put orderlies too high in the hierarchy. Most doctors paid no attention to orderlies, and didn't speak to them except to give orders. Floor polishers who kept the floors waxed were not considered part of the hierarchy, and it seemed to me that orderlies were essentially on that level. As far as the M.D.s were concerned, we were just above inanimate.

There was certainly a definite distance between orderlies and nurses, but we were male and they were female and some of them were amenable to having a date with a presentable orderly to go to a movie. A teaching hospital had nurses being trained. The first year they studied and spent some hours in the hospital doing cleaning tasks. They wore a uniform indicating their probationary status. They lived in the nurses' home on the hospital grounds and were strictly supervised and limited in their options of what to do in their free time. The Hospital took a quasi-parental responsibility for them. Other nurses, if they wished, could live in the nurses' home, and they were freer in their movements.

One day as I was taking the sterilized instruments from the autoclave with a pair of sterilized tongs, someone "goosed" me, and in my surprise, I almost dropped what I had in the tongs. I turned, indignant, and saw one of the nurses with a grin on her face. When she saw my expression, her smile faded, and she said, "I'm sorry," and stammered something about, "we all play grab-ass, you know." I didn't know, and I wasn't happy. The story of my anger went the rounds, and a pretty nurse who didn't approve of this disorderly playfulness told me that my disapproval had put a quietus on the practice. She had gone to Sacred Heart School and when I said I had also, that seemed to create a kind of bond (I didn't tell her my true feelings about Sacred Heart), and it was good to have a nurse around who was simpatico.

Ed Shea, an orderly who was about my age, had a car, which made him more likely to get a date than an orderly without a car. He and I became friends and both went out in his car with a couple of nurses and necked somewhere on the way back from the movies. Going to the movies was always a disturbance to other moviegoers. No matter what we did, it was impossible to get the smell of chloroform out of our clothes.

Exiting the hospital by the most convenient route to get to the building where I roomed took me past the shops where electricians, painters, and repairmen of various sorts had their tools and supplies. They had nothing to do with the medical side of the institution; they simply made repairs and worked as far as possible out of sight of the medical personnel: two worlds co-existing but with little contact. I only became acquainted with one of them because Kelly was different. The first time I walked past the open door of the paint shop, he said, "Hello." I returned the greeting, but kept walking. "What's the hurry? Stop and chat a bit!" I turned and leaned in the doorway. "Come in. Have a seat. Want a cup of coffee?" There was a pot always available. I declined. He was cleaning his brushes. What we talked about that first day I'm not sure. Probably not much of any consequence, but every time thereafter when I went by I tarried a moment if he was there.

Before long I became aware of his ulterior motive in stopping anyone who would pause and engage in a little dialog. He was a sociable person but he was also a propagandist. Kelly was a member of the Workers Socialist Party. Other orderlies brushed him aside, but I was open to discuss his ideas. What was the difference, I wondered, between his doctrine and that of the Communist Party? "We are the Second International.

Communists are the Third International. Both Marxist, but they are Leninist and we are not." It had to do with schisms rather like the Mensheviks and Bolsheviks, but older. WSP'ers were open and hoped to succeed in changing the system by constitutional means. They did not conspire to subversion in order to gain their goal. Sounded like the Fabians.

Kelly invited me to his home for dinner. His wife was dead and he had three kids, the oldest a girl about twelve who helped him cook supper. The boys set the table. He gave me a beer and took one himself, swigging while he worked at the stove. I sat at the kitchen table while the places were set around me. Like normal proletarians we ate in the kitchen. He talked all through the meal. As far as I remember the kids never said a word. Kelly loaned me a book, *Ancient Society* by Lewis H. Morgan. It was a book that influenced Karl Marx, he told me. I looked at the table of contents and saw Iroquois, Greece, Hawaii and wondered what all this had to do with contemporary social revolution. I read it because it appealed to my interest in history, but why it was so important to Kelly's political beliefs remained vague.

When a patient died, he or she would be removed from the ward as quickly as possible. An orderly was called to move the body. The announcement over the loudspeaker was "Pratt Street on Ward Nine (or whatever designation)." Pratt Street was the back entrance to the Hospital by which cadavers were taken out to be brought to a funeral home. There were no houses on Pratt, which was only yards long. Use of the term "Pratt Street" was to avoid saying "dead," "deceased," "corpse," or any such word that might upset patients or their relatives.

The autopsy room was next to the Pratt Street exit. Not all who died in the hospital were autopsied, but some were and when that occurred an orderly was called to assist. The orderly simply had to hold a hose and direct it where the doctor indicated to wash away the blood and other fluids, and later clean up the table on which the autopsy had been performed and the floor around it. We got a dollar for this extra service, but most wanted to avoid being called. To most it was a ghoulish experience, but to me it was an opportunity to learn some anatomy, physiology, and witness diseased conditions of organs. It was a bit of free medical education. Orderlies were supposed to be called one after another in regular order, but all were happy to let me take their turns when I said they could get the dollar. When the public address system announced that orderly so and so was to report to Pratt Street, I went instead.

Usually there was one doctor, occasionally two. The extra doctor was oftener than not a young doctor and was learning something from this particular operation. Or perhaps he was the doctor of the deceased patient being autopsied. Whenever there were two doctors, the one doing the autopsy would have a running commentary of explaining, pointing out conditions that were significant in regard to the illness or injury that led to the death. This helped me to see things I wouldn't have noticed otherwise. The doctors doing the autopsy never talked to me about what they were doing, so unless there was a second doctor present, there was silence. One doctor did more autopsies than the others. He noticed I was always the orderly assisting. One day, he may have been in a hurry to get somewhere, and he said as he was putting the organs back in the body cavity, "Do you think you can sew him up?"

I had seen the sewing up many times; it did not seem difficult. I gave him an affirmative reply. He handed me the needle already threaded with suture, and watched me do a few stitches, then left. I felt pleased to be given the responsibility, especially since doctors generally took the position that a little knowledge is a dangerous thing, and would never explain anything to an orderly.

While I was working as an orderly, I received a form from the U.S. Government to fill out indicating my occupation and whether there was any reason I might be eligible for a deferment from the draft. My thoughts had been on declaring myself a conscientious objector. If I had been a Quaker, that would have been easily done, but how to prove, as an individual without any affiliation with a recognized body that held to a pacifist position, that I was not merely a coward?

Sitting at an unoccupied seat in the nurses' station, I was completing the form for the draft board. The question to be answered: Is there any reason your job should qualify you for deferment? I answered affirmatively: "I empty bedpans and if they were not emptied, the accumulating shit would be a smelly, unsanitary mess and disease would proliferate."

The Head Nurse on the station came by and inquired what I was doing. I showed her the form. "You can't say that!" she said in horror. "You are responding to the government."

"Yes, but it is *our* government. This is a democracy."

It must be (or there is inefficiency of a grand order), because I never heard anything about my irreverence.

The Draft Board informed me of my number. It was quite low, indicating it might not be long before I was called up. That was part of the reason I took the job at the hospital instead of going to Black Mountain. I started working as an orderly in the spring. It was now late summer of the next year and the draft board had not yet sent me "greetings." The idea occurred to me to take a vacation before the draft notice arrived. But where? And how to afford it?

Then someone told me of a fishing shack on the Connecticut River opposite Northampton. The rent was quite low and I had some savings since my room at the hospital was part of the compensation for my employment and my meals had been inexpensive. The only other thing I had spent money on was movies and a few books.

I rented the shack and enjoyed swimming from the dock. And I had lots of leisure for reading. The once polluted river had largely recovered during the years of inactivity of the paper and other mills that had polluted it. It was not far from Springfield if one had a car, and Ed Shea did. On his day off, he and a few friends from the hospital would come up with a case of beer, some hot dogs to BBQ, and potato chips or other munchies. We'd swim, lie in the sun, swig beer, gorge on the food they'd brought, and they'd tell me all the news about the hospital personnel.

The shack, my new home, was hidden in a clump of trees along the riverbank. Behind it was a truck farm. I occasionally helped myself to a carrot or an onion, but my main supply of food came from Northampton just across a bridge. Northampton was an interesting town, home to Smith College, and there were several secondhand bookstores and cafes and hangouts for young people.

Summer passed and fall was drawing on toward winter. I would have to do something to counter the increasingly chilly weather if I didn't get drafted soon *and* if I was going to stay here exposed to the winds that blew down the river. Should I buy an oil heater? Wouldn't I be notified to report as soon as I bought it, and the money be wasted? Better wait till the last moment. Bundle up and wait. When the damn letter came, it was almost a relief. The first thing I did was to go to the Coast Guard Recruiting Office and sign up. The Coast Guard came under the Treasury Department (because it had been designed in part to prevent smuggling and thus to ensure the collection of customs duties), so it was not primarily military. It had pragmatic duties like maintaining lighthouses, buoys and other aids to navigation, rescuing persons in distress at sea, and so on. Yet it was quasi-military in organization and joining this branch of the service would get me out of the draft. Even better, my time would be spent on the water, not on dusty parade fields. Given my circumstances, the USCG seemed a good option. Besides allowing me to avoid the Army, enlistment gave me ten more days of freedom.

CHAPTER TEN

U.S. COAST GUARD

Coast Guard boot camp at Curtis Bay, Maryland, was not notably different from what I expected to have if I had gone to an Army boot camp. Endless marching. Of course, I had no experience of the army except for that summer at Fort Devens when Fitz and I went to the Citizens Military Training Camp. But I had heard from friends who had been drafted and wrote from Fort Benning, in Georgia, where recruits from our region of Massachusetts seemed to be sent.

Although men were being drafted into military service, we were not yet at war and civilian opinion of men in uniform near military bases was generally not positive. On liberty from boot camp, we went into the town and were served in taverns, but old timers told newcomers like me that until recently there had been signs in some barroom windows, "No Dogs or Sailors Allowed." The signs were gone, in view of patriotic recognition of the national mobilization, but we did not sense a welcoming.

The only memorable event of boot camp was guard duty one blustery winter night on the midnight to four a.m. watch. With a rifle on my shoulder, I had to march to and fro on a wharf on Curtis Bay as if a German U-boat might come up the Chesapeake as far as this insignificant Coast Guard station and attack it instead of more important targets, for example, on the Potomac. I was not worried about being attacked by frogmen, nor was the CG, apparently, for they gave me no bullets for the rifle.

I was annoyed with the useless ritual of guarding this small stretch of waterfront from nothing. My hands were cold, especially the one holding the stock of the gun, my fingers hurt, and my face was frosted by the winter wind off the water. Even my body inside my navy blue wool uniform was chilled. My nose was dripping, and I had to pee. I could get a handkerchief out of my pocket with my free hand and wipe the snot, but I couldn't leave my post to go to the latrine unless I was relieved, and no one was around to relieve me. I walked to the end of the pier as I had been doing, but before turning around to walk back, I opened my fly and pissed into the sea. That was a relief, not only lessening pressure in my bladder but also getting rid of water in my body that the frigid air was trying to turn to ice.

To distract myself from the sensation of freezing as well as to pass the time, I started to recite poetry to myself, whispering in case an officer came to check on me. Trying to remember the lines of the stanzas, some very familiar, others hazy but with effort retrievable, made the time go by. I loved the music of Edgar Allan Poe's lyrical, lilting verses, and started with

Once upon a midnight dreary
As I pondered weak and weary

I finished reciting "The Raven" and then, going on to other birds, went over Shelley's "Ode to a Nightingale" and the albatross in Coleridge's "Ancient Mariner." My sister Ruth had once left a library book on a table where I saw it and picked it up. It was *A Few Figs from Thistles*. I was so taken with the poems in that volume that I sought others by Edna St. Vincent Millay. So now I tried to recall one of her long poems:

All I could see from where I stood
Was three long mountains and a wood;
I turned and looked another way,
And saw three islands in a bay.

I did not get all the way through it, but didn't mind – it soon got too mystical for me, but I loved the naturalistic beginning. And on and on. Poems Aunt May had recited to me. Some e.e. cummings:

my sweet old etcetera
aunt lucy during the recent
war could and what
is more did tell you just
what everybody was fighting
for,

Even Robert Frost ("Whose woods these are I think I know"). And of course the first poem I ever learned by heart, Shakespeare's XXIX Sonnet. At the time I was not yet familiar with poets I later came to enjoy like A. MacLeish, R. Graves, and – as cummings would say – etcetera. Thus, I got through the watch with less discomfort than I would have if I'd let myself dwell on the cold.

From boot camp, I was sent as an "apprentice seaman" to Staten Island to report for service on a buoy tender. Seamen were divided into two watches, each under a bosun (boatswain mate). One had the nickname "Bull" and he was big and husky as a bull. The other was accorded the nickname "Tiger" – probably to counterbalance the accolade of "Bull." Tiger was physically a counterpart of Bull, fully as brawny. I was assigned to Bull's crew, perhaps because I was from Massachusetts and Bull was from Maine and several of his crew were also from Maine. Tiger's crew had no New Englanders.

The two crews alternated the work of getting a buoy out of the water, hauled high over the deck by the ship's crane, and released on the deck. Then it was secured so it was out of the way of the workmen and would not roll about. Another buoy fresh from the station -- where it had been scraped of its barnacles and old paint, repainted with anti-rust and anti-fouling paints, and finished with the proper color for its type and function – was put in the sea in place of the one removed. It was exciting work. One had to be alert and know what to do; it was dangerous if one did not. And it was team work, each man working with other men, like players in a basketball team clued to where the ball was at any moment; the buoy in movement was the place where we focused our attention. Everyone had to be ready for the unexpected. A shift of the deck due to rolling seas could cause an unscheduled movement of the great, heavy, barnacle-befouled metal giant of a buoy dangling in the air over us, dripping slimy seawater, and we had to keep it under control by the lines we had attached to it, and not let it swing wildly about and bash one of us.

Before long my rating was advanced from apprentice seaman to seaman first class. This was what I wanted – to be on a ship, even if only a little tub doing buoy tender duty. Better by far, to me, than being in an army camp. And what we were doing was something worthwhile. Hanging around an army base, "being prepared" in case war "broke out" was for me hardly above the category of waste of time. I had never been happy with the idea "they also serve who only stand and wait," even though I granted there was a value to that kind of service – at least in some circumstances. I was glad I had joined the Coast Guard despite having committed myself to a longer period of service than if I had simply let myself be drafted.

A tall and rangy Texan who answered to "Mac" was the only one in the deck crew in either watch whose conversation ever mentioned a book he had read. He suggested we go into New York City and go to an opera. "I've never been to an opera," he declared. "Neither have I," I admitted. So we went to the Metropolitan Opera with USO tickets and saw Lily Pons in *Der Rosenkavalier*. Mac was very pleased with the experience; I was ambivalent. Was drama and singing a good mixture? I was already dubious, but had to see other examples before my opinion solidified. From my point of view, a dramatist's perspective, it seemed that stopping the action of the story for a singer to belt out an aria was an uncalled-for interruption. But in some cases at least, the drama was of little significance, merely an out-dated story preserved in the music.

At a nearby bar, Mac ordered a Singapore Sling. Someone next to him at the bar said, "That's a woman's drink." Mac turned and gave the guy a disapproving look, and the man, no doubt noting Mac's size, turned quickly away and minded his own business. The Sling had a number of different kinds of rum but derived its "feminine" orangey-pink color from a splash of Grenadine; what any of it had to do with Singapore was never explained to me. My question was dismissed by the bartender as not worth the bother of a reply.

On the subway, Mac and I were seated when a black woman holding a young child in her arms got on, and I got up and gave her my seat. Mac, in high dudgeon, jumped up rather than sit by a black person.

"Why'd you do this," he hissed at me.

"She had a baby," I said as I sat in the seat he had vacated. The child looked at me, and I noticed the mother's hand around the boy exert a little pressure, causing the infant to turn his attention from me to her. She gave a little shake of her head, which was to indicate that he shouldn't stare at me. Was the lesson "it's not polite to stare," or was it "don't be caught looking at white people?" I suspect it was the latter, and it seemed it was never too early to teach a child the rules of the American color caste.

It was easy to get to New York City whenever we were at Staten Island, just a ferry ride, but our territory was all around Staten Island, New York Harbor, Long Island Sound, down the Jersey Coast, and up the Hudson River. We might be tied up anywhere in that extensive region after a day's work.

In a Connecticut seaport one night I stood at a bar drinking a beer. The place was relatively quiet, though a jukebox played and one or two couples danced. I turned my back to the bar, leaning against it, watching the dancers. At a table just in front of me sat a family. It looked like a father, mother, daughter, and a young man who might have been a brother or a boyfriend of the young woman. In any event the youngsters were not dancing. They all sat with glasses of beer and a large pitcher of beer waiting to replenish anyone's glass that needed it. No one was talking. It seemed like a sad group. The girl was looking at me. My elbows were hooked on the bar behind me, my hands drooping downwards. I turned my palms up and drew my fingers up and inward, a gesture of invitation. The girl got up. Everyone else at the table gave looks of surprise. I walked around the table and led the girl to the dance floor. When the music stopped, I took her back to her table. Everyone got up as we approached, and the older man said they had to go. They led the girl out, leaving nearly half a pitcher of beer on the table.

Another night somewhere on Long Island Sound, when our pocket money had run out, I walked around town with a shipmate. Neither of us had the purchase price of a glass of beer. Many of the crew who had liberty did not bother to go ashore, for it was the wrong time of the month; when payday comes once a month and it is only $21, the usual situation at the end of the month is to be broke.

We stopped to look in the large plate glass window of a tavern. A man stopped behind us and said to our backs, "Good evening, sailors!" I turned and responded to his greeting. My companion also turned, and the man saw - for the first time - that he was a Negro. There probably were not many persons of color in the town, and however many there might have been, this man clearly had little contact with them. A Negro in uniform whom he had hailed without realizing his identity was a surprise to him. He was at a loss, momentarily, for what to say. Then he said, "Joe Louis is a great boxer, isn't he?" He invited us to join him inside where he would treat us to beer. We accepted.

We replaced buoys in the Hudson River all the way up to Albany, and that was a change, threading our way in the narrow water of a river. But it was at Perth Amboy, on the Jersey coast, that I had the most exciting experience during the time I was on the buoy tender. We tied up for the weekend and I got a 72-hour liberty. This was not far from my friends, Paul and Ruth, from Commonwealth College. I phoned them and got directions and went out to the farming community where they lived.

We sat around and talked for a while. Paul asked if I wanted to go out with him on his little sailboat. "Sure," I immediately agreed. "You go ahead," Ruth said, "the boat is not big enough for three. It's really only a dinghy." Paul drove us to where he kept his boat. We set out in bathing trunks, and sailed out into the bay. The sky was strewn with clouds but had not appeared threatening. When we were well out from shore, the clouds closed and the sky darkened, a wind came up, and rain began to fall. We were in one of those sudden squalls small boat sailors are warned about. Paul turned and headed back, but the wind was against us, and our only power was the little bed-sheet-sized canvas the boat carried.

"I'm going to tie up to that buoy," Paul announced and told me to catch it with the boat hook as he steered us as close as he could. I reached for the buoy with the boat hook but just missed. Paul grabbed the bowline and jumped into the sea, swam to the buoy and secured us to it. He climbed back into the boat, hardly more wet than I was in the drenching rain. It was so dark we wondered if anyone would see us. However, it was not long before a Coast Guard cutter came and towed us to shore. An officer had to make a report and wanted our names and addresses. I gave my name and my family's West Springfield address for I did not care to tell this officer that I was in the Coast Guard.

NY SOCIAL LIFE

I don't know how she found me. She was Chris's sister, and I had never met her. Chris was the most junior of the Cleveland trio that formed the center of the nine-member boarding house of students at Bowling Green. But how did Chris know where

I was? I certainly had not written to him; he'd have been out of college by this time, and I had no idea where he might be. I guess I must have written to Hobby, the one of the nine I had been partnered with for the chores we had to do, and he likely had mentioned it to Chris – they came from the same town and were old acquaintances.

Chris must have written to his sister Ellen working in New York City, and she had written to me on Staten Island. I was happy to phone the number she gave me, and we arranged to meet. To my surprise, her mother was with her when I showed up at the designated place. "Mom is here for a visit," Ellen said as we sat at a small round table. We were served whatever it was Ellen wanted to drink. Her mother had the same, and I said, "Me, too."

The table was so infinitesimal that it hardly provided cover for our three pairs of legs vying for space beneath it. Therefore I was astonished when Ellen's hand landed on my thigh and worked its way toward my crotch; it is a wonder that I didn't make some facial expression that would have alerted the mother. That scene when I first met Ellen is unforgettable. It made me wonder if I had not been wrong when I doubted her brother Chris's tales of some of his risky sex exploits.

That was the only time I saw "Mom." Apparently she returned to Ohio before my next date with Ellen. This time there was no need for even miniscule cover for her aggression. My faulty education had insisted that sexual advances were made by the male and that the woman parried his efforts. It was with amazement, but willingness, that I submitted to this reversal, as I considered it, of gender roles.

For the next couple of weeks, whenever the ship was at Staten Island and I had liberty, I called Ellen and she always was available for the evening and always eager to go to bed with me. On a Sunday morning when I had a weekend liberty, we awakened and repeated what we had done the night before. When I rolled over after we finished, I looked out the window next to the bed and saw a pubescent girl leaning out a window a floor higher on the next building, observing us. Her curiosity reminded me of my own – at approximately her age – when I lived in the Campion Hotel, but it made me uncomfortable.

Then Ellen had news for me. She was pregnant. This was plausible, but I had understood that she was using a diaphragm. She wanted to have an abortion, and she wanted me to help pay for it. How, on $21 a month? Actually, I had a small savings account in a Springfield bank, accumulated while I was an orderly at the hospital there. I cleaned out my account and gave the money to her, and I visited her in the place she told me the deed would be done. I brought her flowers and sat by her bed. She was only there for a day or so. Subsequently I resumed my visits to her apartment.

As I was turning on the landing to go up the stairs to the top floor, where Ellen's apartment was, I saw a man just beginning to come down. He looked embarrassed as we passed each other. There was no other apartment on the top floor of this narrow building: he had to be coming from Ellen's apartment. She denied that anyone had just left her apartment. Her attitude changed when I affirmed that I had seen him on the uppermost flight of stairs. She might have said he was a salesman or something, but she apparently was not prepared to give a plausible explanation – or was she ready to make a confession?

Finally she told me that he was the one who had "knocked her up," as she put it, but they had been unable to afford an abortion. Her mother had been summoned to help, but she had been only moderately helpful. This was surprising! Mom had sat there while her daughter enticed me into a plot to swindle me out of my fortune.

I was the succor, or sucker, who supplied the requisite sum.

Angry at being deceived, I was nonetheless so interested in the whole sordid story that I felt empathetic to their plight and my anger cooled, but it was the last time I saw Ellen.

It took me some time to locate "lower case jim." He had moved from the tiny room he had when he ran the elevator in an elegant apartment building. Fortunately, I remembered his girlfriend Margie's sister worked in a bank. She was able to tell me where jim was; Margie was still with him. They had an apartment now, and jim worked in a department store. They were not married, but they appeared to be essentially settled.

And of course, they had a coterie of friends, including a blind man, Walter, who went about New York without one of those long red and white canes. "How can he do that?" I wondered, being myself still cautious of the city's automobile traffic. "Crossing streets by himself? And how does he know which subway car to take?" You will see, they told me. Walter was legally blind, and had been from birth. Perhaps he saw darker outlines of persons and objects in the general obscurity, I suggested. "No," they told me. "He's totally blind."

One evening we went to Walter's apartment. When he unlocked and opened the door, he immediately turned on the light. "When I first lived here," he confided, "I never thought to put on the light. I didn't need it, and I was not used to thinking about another person's needs. In the school for the blind where I grew up, they taught me a lot but did not really prepare me to be on my own in the city." Then he pointed out prints of paintings he'd bought at museums, and asked me my reactions to them. He knew the painter, the contents of the picture, the critics' comments, and liked to discuss art he had never actually seen. It was eerie, but it also was impressive as an example of what a person can do to overcome a handicap. I never did get to understand how he maneuvered around Manhattan without a blind person's cane. I didn't ask him, though he probably would have taken the question in his stride. There is a difference, as I learned, between being legally blind and totally blind. Which he was I'm still not sure.

One of jim's friends had obtained a Mexican divorce, one that was done by mail, and the guy had not left the city. Now he wanted to remarry but New York State did not recognize Mexican divorces obtained by mail, so he could not marry in the state without becoming a bigamist. However, if he went to New Jersey, which recognized Mexican divorces, he could marry his fiancée, return to New York City and live there without having broken any law. The couple and witnesses went to New Jersey, were married by a Justice of the Peace in the afternoon, and returned to celebrate in an evening party at jim and Margie's.

Margie's sister had a friend who was an actor, who only occasionally had work on the stage. He supported himself, I was told, by pushing a machine polishing floors at night in office buildings. All aspiring actors have intervals of unemployment in their chosen profession, and work at other things meanwhile, hoping for a break. For Earl it was at least that difficult, but probably more so inasmuch as he was black and there were fewer parts calling for a tall, muscular black man.

A woman who danced with Earl at the wedding party kept apologizing for being clumsy when *he* stepped on *her* feet. "Don't apologize!" said jim, "everybody knows Earl can't dance. Just because he's black doesn't mean he's got rhythm!" It was the kind of statement, stereotype contradicting, jim liked to make. I wondered how Earl felt about the remark.

The problem of not being an accomplished dancer was one I was familiar with. It was a problem that became acute when the USO opened up dance halls for servicemen. I had never really learned to dance, but that didn't stop me. Ask a woman, put arms around her, get awkwardly through one dance, sit out the next with her sipping soft drinks (all that the USO permitted), and discuss taking my erstwhile dancing partner home when the dance was over, exploring verbally the possibility of a more serious dancing, horizontally, in her bed. Usually it was a no go. USO rules forbade making dates to go elsewhere, but it was done by some of the women who volunteered to be USO hostesses. They could not depart on the arm of a serviceman, but they could meet the sailor, soldier, or marine at the nearest corner and proceed from there.

One evening, as the dance was nearing closing time, my enquiry about "seeing her home," got the reply, "Do you have cab fare?"

"Yes," I asserted, hoping I would be able to cover the cost of a taxi ride.

We rode to somewhere in the Bronx, almost clearing out all the cash I had, and I did indeed see the door of her apartment.

We had some kisses, and a bit of a tussle in the stairwell, but she would not let me in. "C'mon," I urged, "why not?"

"My husband might come home."

I didn't know if she was married or not, but I was not concerned. She was a woman who had volunteered to entertain servicemen at USO events, and she had illegally left there with me, which created some kind of expectation. There were married women whose husbands were away, perhaps in the service, who decided that if the military took their husbands away, some man in the military could substitute for the absent husband and satisfy their needs. From my point of view there was the ever-present realization that at any moment I might be shipped out to sea, torpedoed, killed outright, or drowned. Before that happened, it was only sensible to try to sample the joys that might soon be unattainable to a casualty of war.

"If you are patriotic enough to entertain a serviceman," I said in desperate frustration, "perhaps your husband will be patriotic enough to let you service a serviceman?"

She put her hands on my shoulders and pushed me away. "Go!"

It was a long walk to a subway station. Somewhere on the long ride to South Ferry I fell asleep. The car reached South Ferry, turned around, and headed back up-town. I woke up as we were coming into Columbus Circle. I got off and got the next train south and this time made an effort to stay awake.

Getting off the ferry from Staten Island at South Ferry one evening, I encountered a teen-aged girl who put herself in my path. "H'lo, sailor! Looking for a good time?"

"Always," I said and took her arm. I'd been scouring bars and USO dances looking for a willing woman, and here was one coming to meet me! She wore a Navy pea coat and a white sailor's hat sat at a jaunty angle on her head. Below the pea coat that protected her from the cold, damp air of the harbor, a bright red and dark blue plaid skirt flared around her knees, indicating that, despite the ship's store outfit, she was not a WAVE. She led me to a hotel where, "they won't give us any trouble." I paid for the room. Once inside and the pea coat doffed, I saw that her underwear was a Navy skivvy. "I'm a seagull," she declared. "I follow the fleet." She had been "shacked up" with a sailor in San Diego. His ship was transferred to the Atlantic and she had hitchhiked cross-country to meet him, but then his ship had been sent into European waters. He would find a girl in some port over there, and she was momentarily on the loose – an opportunity for me, she implied. She handed me a rubber. "You gotta wear this. I don't wanna be left with shit in my pocket."

As we lay on the bed afterwards, she outlined her scheme. "If you pay for it each time, you'd soon be broke. If we shack up, you can get all you want. All you have to do is pay the rent on a room in Brooklyn. There's some cheap ones there around the Navy yard. And buy a little chow once in a while. I'll cook for you. Just sneak out a couple of knives and forks from your ship. I've got a frying pan and a sauce pan, all I need, and I can make a swell meal on a hot plate."

"Sounds good," I said, "but I'm just a first class seaman. Twenty-one dollars a month is all I earn." Twenty-one dollars a day – once a month, that's how we usually put it, but I didn't want to joke at this moment. "I couldn't pay a month's rent, much less buy some food. You need a petty officer."

"Yeah, I know," she admitted. "I couldn't tell your rating with your pea coat on. I thought you were a little older than the

269

average draftee. I took you for a regular enlisted man." She had been seeking a sailor at the Brooklyn Navy yard, but there was a lot of competition with women more mature, more curvaceous and busty than her slim schoolgirl figure, and so she had tried to snatch a "Hooligan." She had typical Navy biases; the Coast Guard was a Hooligan Navy.

In the morning, I gave her what cash I had, keeping just enough for fare to get back to Staten Island. I never saw her again. Perhaps she found someone to shack up with.

QUARTERMASTER STRIKER

Captain Robertson announced there was an opening for a quartermaster striker and if he could not fill it with a volunteer from the crew he would put in a request to headquarters for one. What does a quartermaster do? In the army, quartermasters keep track of supply, in effect - a storekeeper. I did not want that kind of a job. I was happy on deck. But I was told that a quartermaster stands the wheel watch, he steers the ship when he is on duty, and he corrects the charts (maps of the sea lanes) when changes are made in the navigational aids (lighthouses, buoys with or without lights or whistles). Ah Ha! That sounded more interesting. Perhaps I could learn navigation? I volunteered. And I got the job and became "striker" (apprentice) to the quartermaster.

On this small ship there were only two officers, the Captain and the Exec, and there were four quartermasters, two on each watch so they could relieve each other round the clock, four on, four off, because one of us had to be on the bridge at all times, even when the ship was not underway. On my watch there was one quartermaster, third class, and me, a striker. When the quartermaster on my watch came down the ladder to get me to relieve him, I would awaken at the sound of his footsteps and be sitting up when he reached my bunk, but when I came to wake him, I had to shake and shake him before he reluctantly awakened.

I realized we were different kinds of sleepers, but I thought he was only lazy. Later I found out about research on sleep, that there were two contrasting types of sleepers. One goes immediately into a deep sleep and comes up gradually to wakefulness. That was me, already half awake when I heard his feet on the ladder coming down into the sleeping quarters. The other type descended more slowly into sleep, came up to wakefulness even more slowly, and was sleepy for a while after being awakened. That was him.

Until I came up to the bridge, I had not been particularly aware of the first lieutenant, also known, since he transmits the captain's orders, as the executive officer. The Exec seldom found it necessary to speak to a seaman; he told the bosuns what he wanted the seamen to do. The officers and the quartermasters were the only six on the ship that were ordinarily on the bridge. It was now impossible not to interact with the Exec.

Being at the wheel when underway and keeping the ship on course is something one has to learn. It is not really difficult but takes a bit of practice. What I had to learn was how far to turn the wheel to get a particular compass reading. The ship continued to turn for a moment after one had stopped the wheel. I turned too far and then had to compensate, but went a bit too far and had to adjust again. My learning did not occur under ideal conditions. On a calm day with a smooth sea, there is little difficulty but with a rough sea on a blustery day, it is something else for a beginner.

"Your course should be as straight as a string," the Exec proclaimed.

"For a string to be straight, it has to be taut." I replied. I do not think the Exec liked puns, and anyway, a seaman does not talk to an officer like that. He did not put me on report, but I had started off on the wrong foot with him, and we never got along comfortably with each other, though fortunately there was never a real run-in.

If the Exec was difficult and "by the book," the Captain was friendly and cordial. He liked to sing *sotto voce* to himself. He was standing next to me at the wheel. On the narrow bridge there was not much space. He was looking ahead, sometimes using a pair of binoculars, and I could hear:

I'm looking over
a four-leafed clover
that I overlooked
before.

When he wasn't singing or busy, he did not mind talking to me, a mere first class seaman, striking for Quartermaster, a nobody in nautical terms, and he was the only officer I met during my service who spoke to me as a person, not as an underling.

"I was born on the Orkney Islands," he told me. "When I was a boy, I ran away from home. If you're on an island and run away from home, you have to go to sea. I've been at sea ever since." And he now had silvery hair. Confiding this story encouraged me to tell him about riding the rails when I left home. He was interested and questioned me about details. Eventually, I learned that in the merchant marine he had earned a "ticket" (i.e., license) to command a ship "of any tonnage" in "any sea." But at some point he had married and wanted to be closer to home, and so had joined the U.S. Coast Guard. Although he had the highest ranking in commercial shipping, the Coast Guard gave him only a chief warrant officer rating, because he had not gone through the Coast Guard officer training school. His rank was only one step above the Exec, a warrant officer, who had risen within the CG from seaman to chief bosun mate before being awarded a warrant, but not a commission, to be an officer.

Usually only one officer was on the bridge, and it was quite different when it was the Exec's watch. He never spoke to me except to give commands to alter the ship's course, or some other ship's business. Occasionally both officers were on the bridge at the same time. One morning we were chugging slowly along the Jersey shore in a thick fog. The Captain had come on the bridge to add another pair of eyes. We were just creeping along. The two of them were passing the binoculars back and forth between them, each trying to identify something in the fog ahead. "It's a pennant," suggested the Exec. "I don't know," said the Captain. After a moment, thinking to be helpful, I said, "It's a branch of a tree with a cluster of leaves."

"Leaves?" said the Exec in a tone that suggested that what I had said was impossible, but probably it was only that my speaking without being spoken to had annoyed him. The ship was inching forward and as we neared the object, the two officers kept peering at it. Finally, the Captain announced, "It's leaves on a branch of a tree!" I said nothing aloud, but did to myself say something about the Exec's uncalled-for sarcasm. "How did you ever see that with your naked eyes when we couldn't make it out with the glasses?" the Captain asked. "I'm farsighted, sir," I told him.

"The eyes of a frontiersman," the Captain exclaimed. I felt good about the description then but in later years, when spending hours with my nose in a book, and seldom looking at the horizon, I found little advantage in being farsighted.

Being in the New York City area it was easy to get to Bayonne, New Jersey, where my sister Ruth had been living since she was married. I went there for a visit a few times. I got word one day that Ruth had given birth to a baby boy. I went to the hospital to see her and the baby. She asked me to be godfather to her son. The way she put it was that it was contingent on my being a church member. "Do you feel that you want to go on being a Catholic?"

What a hell of a position. She is sitting up in bed, very happy over the birth of her baby, and in that emotional state I had to disappoint her. "I'd like to but I'm afraid the Church would not approve. I no longer consider myself a Catholic."

Her husband's nephew got the job, which was no doubt better that way. The position was confirmed by the Church for someone to be responsible to oversee the little one's religion and morals and not necessarily his economic condition.

On a Sunday, 7 December 1941, the news came that Pearl Harbor had been bombed by the Japanese, and we were now at war. It soon turned out that we were not only at war with Japan, but with Germany and Italy as well. Hitler had declared the Japanese to be "honorary Aryans" when the East Asian nation had been accepted into the Axis nations.

"Oh, we'll kick their asses," said one of my shipmates, and that seemed to be the general opinion. "In a few weeks," someone allowed, as the time required. We would probably win, I thought, for the triplicate of Axis powers were already bogged down, each in its own morass: Germany in Russia, Italy in Ethiopia, Japan in China, but it would nevertheless be a long war.

With the outbreak of war, the Coast Guard was moved immediately from the Treasury Department and now became part of the Navy.

Kumer was a first-class seaman; he was also a twenty-year man, that is, he intended to stay in the Coast Guard for twenty years and retire, still a young man, with a pension. He had a couple of hash marks on his sleeve, indicating he was about halfway to his goal. Any member of the crew who wanted to know something about how to perform a particular feat of ship's lore, or the intricacies of CG regulations, went to talk to Kumer. He was our encyclopedia of maritime knowledge. Officers had urged him to take a petty officer rating but though he could have qualified for virtually any one of the ratings, he always declined. He wanted no responsibility for anyone but himself. He worked on deck with other seamen.

When he had liberty, he was not at the gangway, ready to go ashore as soon as liberty began. He would take it easy until about ten o'clock, and then in his tailor-made uniform, and his little kit with his equipment to protect him from venereal disease, he would go ashore. "Why do you wait so long?" I asked him.

"Now is the time other sailors have liquored up the women in the bar, and in doing so have often become too drunk themselves to get a woman into bed. I arrive and take my pick, and save the expense of buying lots of drinks for the women."

One Monday morning we were at the base on Staten Island and some of the crew had had "seventy-twos," that is a weekend pass of 72 hours, which meant that all the crew should be aboard by eight a.m. The Captain had received orders to go out; for some reason the schedule had been changed, so despite the expectation that this Monday would be a day spent working at the base, that was no longer so. There was a lot to do, preparing the buoys to be put back in the water, and it was not unusual to spend a day at the station, but this Monday would – suddenly – not be one such.

I was on the bridge. The bosun on duty had submitted to me the report of who had gone ashore and who had returned. Captain Robertson came in and asked, "Is everybody aboard?"

"All except Kumer, sir," I replied.

We both knew that if the ship remained at the station that day, as everyone had thought it would, a little lateness would not be considered a big deal, but if the ship departed and someone missed the ship, he would not merely be tardy, but would be AWOL, absent without leave, and in wartime that could be considered desertion, a very serious charge indeed. What, I wondered, would the Captain do?

"Get out the chart," he told me, designating the waters of our destination. I did as he asked, set the chart on the table for him, and went back to stand by the wheel. Captain studied the map. I knew that he knew these waters like the back of his hand, but he now examined the chart as if he had never seen it before. "Tell me when you see Kumer," he ordered. I looked at the corner of a building that anyone coming from the gate would come around in order to come to where the ship was tied up. He apparently was sure Kumer would not be very late, and I thought that a good bet. But how long could we wait? The Captain had orders to go – how much delay would be tolerated? I stared and stared and wondered.

Finally I was able to say, "He's just coming around the corner, sir." Captain didn't say a word, but was out the door on the flying bridge, facing astern, not able to see Kumer, now running, and called out, "Let go the stern line." The seaman who had been waiting by the bollard around which the stern line was looped did as commanded. "Let go the spring line," Captain called out a few moments later. Then Captain turned and looked forward. Kumer had just cleared himself over the railing at the bow, as the ship now was touching the wharf only at the bow, and in his blues looking out of place among the crew in dungarees, was scurrying to get to his locker and change into work clothes. "Let go the bow line," the captain ordered.

Some of the other crew, like me, must have known what the Captain had done. Those who had been standing by the bollards waiting for the command to remove lines, and who had waited there longer than usual, had seen Kumer running to get aboard the ship. Captain never said anything to admit he had saved Kumer's neck, and no one could ever prove that he did. Of course Kumer was a valuable member of the crew, and that may have been a consideration, but I was convinced that Captain Robertson did it because he was a humane man.

Free tickets were available for men in uniform for cinema, theater, opera, ballgames, and other entertainments. But there was also the option of going to nightclubs and ordering a beer at the bar, and standing there with your beer while the show was on. At Café Society Uptown, Zero Mostel, as Senator Claghorn, demanded to know, "What the hell was Pearl Harbor doing out there in the Pacific?" Jimmy Durante ended his spiel, as he did on the radio, with "Good Night, Mrs. Calabash, wherever you are." Martha Scott, ebony shoulders gleaming in the spotlight above her strapless white gown, appeared by the piano, bowed, and sat to play exquisitely. Quite different was Café Society Downtown where Fats Waller sang his insouciant songs to his own piano accompaniment.

I was suddenly able to take in more of the delights of New York due to my job typing up the liberty list. What happened is that the ship's yeoman, who was the one to do all the ship's secretarial jobs, got seasick every time we were at sea, even when the sea wasn't rough. He had gone to the hospital two or three times, but the doctors, after giving him a seasick antidote to no avail, could do nothing further for him, and he was transferred to permanent shore duty.

The yeoman's name was Poet, and perhaps it was his name that began our acquaintance. "It does not mean a poet," Poet explained, "it's Dutch and means potter, a person who makes pots, as I suppose one of my ancestors did." The yeoman shack was on the upper deck, behind the officer's quarters, which were aft the bridge, so we both used the ladders that gave access to the upper deck (which seamen usually didn't ascend), and we had become accustomed to hanging out together when not working, either in the yeoman's tiny office, or if we were tied up somewhere, on the bridge, if I was on watch.

When Poet was transferred from the ship, the captain said to me, "You are the only one aboard who can type, and you know something about your friend Poet's duties, so you must take over until we can get another yeoman assigned to us."

What could I say? It was not a request but an order, and in a military organization one does not have a choice in such a situation. The quartermaster job was interesting to me, but the yeoman's job seemed to me just drudgery, and meant being cooped up during working hours in a narrow office. The compensation I gave myself was liberty every night I wanted it. As quartermaster I was in the starboard watch and had liberty every other night, alternating with duty on the bridge other nights. Poet had put himself in one of the watches and did not take advantage of his position. But there was no watch for a yeoman on a buoy tender after the day's work was done, so I went ashore with whichever watch had liberty. The officers went ashore; both had homes to go to, so they would not notice. Neither of the bosuns seemed to notice, or if they did, did not mind.

When Poet was transferred to shore duty, and we knew he wasn't coming back, I soon became discontented with substituting for our seasick yeoman. I hatched an idea. I would try to become an interpreter. My French was conversational and that would be my primary qualification to offer, but to become an interpreter in government service, one had to be proficient in two languages other than English that were pertinent to current wartime needs. Could I quickly acquire another language? It was not impossible. German was in demand, but there were many Americans of German descent and they would qualify at a higher level than I could hope to attain quickly. The Soviets were suddenly our allies: Russian was pertinent to American collaboration with Russia, and there were, I thought, fewer Russian speakers among Americans, so the competition would be less tough. Where could I study Russian?

"Russian classes are given at the evening school run by the Communist Party," jim told me. Hmmm! I didn't doubt that the FBI watched the coming and goings at a Communist Party school, and they would certainly note my uniform. That would be crazy, wouldn't it?

"Hey, they're our allies now."

"Yeah, but ..." Anti-Communist feeling domestically was no less heated whatever international alliances might be.

"Walter takes classes there. He can show you the ropes."

I met Walter at a restaurant near the school. He had a stack of mail. I read his mail to him while he ate. I had already eaten on the ship and only had a cup of coffee. His mail consisted largely of comments on the reviews of the musical events he wrote for one of the New York City newspapers. Many did not require answers. He asked me to write a few words on the envelopes of those that did. Someone at the paper would read my scribbles to him and the address and he would type an answer, extrapolating from the key words he'd told me to put on the envelopes. Well-trained typists do not have to look at the keyboard to type, so it was not surprising that a blind man as competent as Walter could type, but he still needed somebody's eyes to give him the address and the clues he had dictated to me to write on the envelopes. Walter went to listen to a lecture on "proletarian literature," and I went to the Russian class.

A woman who was in the restaurant one evening saw me reading to the blind man and thought that was a kind thing for a young sailor to be doing instead of going off carousing somewhere (as she expected sailors to do). She spoke to me as Walter and I parted. She asked me to meet her after my class was over. Naturally, I did. She was tall, dark haired, and had a pretty face and good figure – how could I have refused?

We went for a drink somewhere. She asked me about myself. I gave her a brief run-down of my life. "You *ran away* from home?" I remember her exclaiming. "I didn't run," I amended. "I hitchhiked."

She was born in Argentina. Her mother had been sent with a group of other Jews out of Germany by a Jewish philanthropist to escape European anti-Semitism. Ironically, she, Rachel, the daughter, grew up in the midst of Argentinean anti-Semitism, and now in New York when she heard Spanish spoken, she cringed.

Rachel took me home with her. The apartment was dark and quiet when we came in. I thought she lived alone. In the morning, however, her mother made breakfast for us. I felt embarrassed to see the mother – who knew of course that I had slept with her daughter, but neither of the women gave any sign that they were embarrassed. I was invited back. The mother said, "Rachel is just over a long sickness. I'm happy to see her happy again." The situation seemed peculiar to me, but if it was OK with the mother, it was fine with me. I became a regular visitor.

The teacher in my Russian class was, I assumed, a Russian. Eventually I found out she was Ukrainian and in effect was teaching what was her second language, albeit a closely related one. What I learned may have had a Ukrainian accent, but in the long run it didn't matter because my study of the language was interrupted and never really completed. As I informed the teacher, I would sometimes miss class because my ship, a buoy tender, might be anywhere in the waters worked by the buoy tenders of the Staten Island Coast Guard station, and that might be too far away to make my way to class. And I did not know when I might be transferred away from New York. It was the latter factor that finally did in my pursuit of competence in Russian.

At almost the same time that I met Rachel, a woman in my Russian class began to chat with me before and after class. In no time at all we continued our conversation in her apartment. Her name was Esther. "Esther is an alcoholic radical," she quoted some chemical definition. She drank a lot but no more than everyone else I knew, and most of my friends (outside the service) were radical, so I felt at home with her.

Esther was in her forties. I was barely into my twenties. Her friends, she told me, accused her of robbing the cradle. I didn't mind. I remembered what Ben Franklin said about having an older woman as a mistress -- she can teach a young man what he should know about pleasing a woman (and himself), and will be more grateful for his attention than a younger woman would be.

She did have a lot of friends. One was a painter who had done a mural in a nightclub. He took a small party of us there and the owner picked up the bill. "He'll do that if I don't come here too often," he told us. Another was a cinematographer. He showed us a film he'd just made. A nude woman was riding a bicycle and a naked man on foot was chasing her. He caught up. She did not really want to get away from him. They embraced. A woman who was a friend of Esther's was married to an unknown writer who produced scripts for radio dramas. His name was Arthur Miller. I saw him at a party but he did not make any more of an impression on me than the others at the party.

Someone broke into Esther's apartment and stole her typewriter. Companies that made typewriters were now turning out munitions and typewriters were impossible to find for sale. That explained why a typewriter was valuable enough for someone to steal one – nothing else had been taken. Esther needed a typewriter if she was to be able to do some work at home, as she had been accustomed to do. I told her about my Corona portable. She was used to an upright, but a portable would be better than nothing. I hitched up to West Springfield and brought down my portable typewriter and loaned it to her.

I kept Rachel and Esther apart by pretending I was on a port and starboard liberty schedule. On port liberty, I would see Rachel and on starboard liberty I would see Esther.

This worked fine until New Year's Eve. Each wanted me to celebrate with her. I had told Rachel about hot buttered rum, a drink described in a novel by Kenneth Roberts. Rachel was giving a party and wanted to provide some hot buttered rum. The rum was easy to get, but butter was rationed. I could get some from the cook on my ship, I told her. So it was arranged. I went to Rachel's party with a pound of butter. We put the great lump of butter in a large bowl of rum, stuck a hot poker into the butter, melting it, but the lump kept skittering away from the hot poker, floating off across the surface of the rum, and it took awhile before the rum was buttered. The unusual drink was, nevertheless, a success, and the party was merry.

Unbeknownst to me, a friend of Esther's was at the party. Of course, she couldn't wait to tell Esther, who was hurt by my deception. Her door was henceforth closed to me. I should have felt some remorse, but New York was so lively that I hardly had time to muse over the situation.

Just before this debacle with Esther happened, I met Sarah, a showgirl who sang in a musical comedy currently running on Broadway. She was also a student at the Julliard School of Music. She took me home and let me sleep on a couch in the living room. Her mother was a light sleeper, and left her bedroom door open so she could listen for any suspicious sounds. I had two lovers at the moment, so I did not try too hard to seduce Sarah. In fact, I found her mother more interesting! Momma had come from Hungary by herself as a twelve-year-old with the name and address of a relative in New York stitched to her coat. She was full of stories about the old country and of New York in earlier days. Her husband was dead, but a photo showed him to have been exuberantly mustachioed. She had three children, two boys and a girl. The boys were older and both professional musicians. I saw little of them; they lived elsewhere.

PHARMACIST MATE

Captain Robertson was aware that I did not want to go on being a substitute for our absent yeoman. He knew because I kept reminding him to request a replacement for Poet so I could return to being a quartermaster striker. He did so several times, to no avail. It seems that this rating was in short supply at the moment. I would have to go on as acting yeoman. The Captain came to me one day with information that any enlisted man with one year of college could apply to officers' training school. "You have one year of college, don't you?"

"Yes, sir," I said, grateful for his offering me a way out of a job I did not want even though he knew it was going to be difficult to replace me in that capacity. But I explained to him, "No disrespect, sir, but I do not want to be an officer. I have all I can do to be responsible for myself. I do not want to be responsible for other men in a wartime situation."

He understood my position. After all, he had the similar situation with Kumar, the most competent seaman on the ship, who wouldn't even take a promotion to petty officer. My objection, however, left a truth undisclosed. I had studied at Bowling Green College for a year, but I had only one semester's credit. I might have got by if I applied, but perhaps not. My feeling about not being an officer, nevertheless, was deeply felt. In any case, the Captain's offer gave me an opportunity to ask for something else. I requested permission to apply to go to the Coast Guard Pharmacist Mate School at New London, Connecticut. "Make out the application," he said, "and I'll approve it."

Not long after that I was transferred from the buoy tender to the school at New London, and spent three months learning to do the duties of a pharmacist mate, or hospital corpsman. School was school, classes, lectures, textbooks, exams. I was used to coping with all this. A bit of on-the-job training in a hospital ward was also familiar to me from my experience as an orderly at Springfield Hospital. My marks put me at the top of the class, but I left the school with the same seaman first class rating that I had arrived with. The reason is a disgraceful one, not for me but for some of my superiors.

We were housed two to a room. My roommate was Mufson; I do not remember his first name because I always called him just "Muf." We often discussed our studies. Therefore I knew he was as familiar with the material as I was. When I passed the final exams and Muf did not, we both knew the reason. The Warrant Officer, who mustered us and marched us to class, was an anti-Semite, and had picked on Muf from the first day. Mufson's family came from Sweden. He looked like a Swede. No one would have known he was Jewish unless he had access to his records, where his religion was listed as Judaism. There was also a first class pharmacist mate who was assistant to the warrant officer. Casey was his name and he was proud to be Irish, and denigrated me for being Muf's friend. "You're shanty Irish!" Casey taunted me. "Your family keep pigs in the house?" And he wondered aloud how any Irishman could associate with a Kike.

I went to the Commanding Officer of the school and presented the charge that Mufson had been discriminated against because he was Jewish. I could vouch for him that he knew as much as I and yet had been given a failure on his exam. "If his exam papers are reexamined," I stated, "it would verify what I am saying."

The CO assured me it would be looked into, and I was dismissed. Nothing happened as far as I knew before we were all shipped out to our new berths. Mufson and I were sent away without a pharmacist mate, third class, rating as others who passed the exam had received. No one claimed I had not passed the exam but I was apparently being punished for creating a disturbance by contesting the decisions of my superiors. Where Mufson was transferred to I do not know, nor what became of him subsequently.

To my surprise, when the training period was over, I was transferred back to New York, not to a ship, but to the sickbay of a machinist mate training school located in the Half Moon

Hotel at Coney Island. The subway ride was long but I could be in Manhattan on every liberty. This was "good duty" and I wondered if I had not been favorably treated, perhaps because I had stood up for Mufson and exposed the injustice. This idea seemed especially possible when my third class rating came almost as soon as I arrived at my new post. I wondered -- did Mufson also get the rating in short order? Was anyone disciplined because of participating in blatant discrimination?

I renewed my visits to lower case jim and his girl friend Margie to find that jim had demonstrated a do-it-yourself model of a welding gadget in a department store that sold the implement. He had acquired enough familiarity with welding that he had applied for a job as a welder at the Brooklyn Navy Yard and had been hired. Now he was packing to go to Pearl Harbor because he was being sent there as a civilian employee of the Navy. Ironically, he could not have enlisted in the Navy because he had a record as a felon, having served a year in a federal prison for passing counterfeit money.

The New London interval, between my two New York assignments, was in the springtime. The Half Moon Hotel assignment was in the summer. What better time to be at Coney Island? The men being trained to become machinist mates were marched off after breakfast to the subway, where they went en masse to a stop near a public school where there was a machine shop. They were away from the hotel all day. After Sick Call before the men left in the morning and Sick Call in the early evening when they returned, there was nothing that needed doing unless a sailor was confined to a bed in the sickbay, and that seldom happened that summer. When it did, he was usually up and out after a day or two; if not, he was transferred to a hospital. So I spent most days on the beach in front of the hotel.

Again I was supposed to be on duty one night and one night on liberty, port and starboard, but Drew, the first class pharmacist mate who was my only superior, was engaged to be married and was saving his money, so he stayed in almost every night, allowing me, with his permission, to be free virtually every night. It was a long subway ride into Manhattan, but I got used to it, and in addition to my usual entertainments, I renewed my attendance at the weekly Russian course, this time with no absences because the ship was out of local waters. The Half Moon Hotel was stationary.

One result of my reappearance after a three-month absence was that the teacher decided my showing up again, with a reasonable excuse for being away, indicated seriousness, and she invited me to come to her home and be tutored. She also told me where I could rent a typewriter with Cyrillic letters. I had previously bought a Russian grammar and a dictionary; now I compiled a Basic Russian vocabulary on the basis of the vocabulary of I.A. Richards' *Basic English*. My Basic Russian, a handbook of typed pages in a folder neatly clipped together, did not help me because my only copy was displaced, permanently lost, sometime during my subsequent sea duty.

New York, with its many cinemas, was another resource. There were three theaters that sometimes showed Russian movies. I went to see as many as I could. Some of them were hard to follow, but one was about children, and they spoke in simple terms, and I understood more than I usually did. This was a lesson that helped me later: when I went to West Africa, I found children gathered around me, an *obroni* (white man), as a curiosity in the town I selected to study, and talking to them helped me greatly in making progress in speaking Twi, the local language.

Mussorgsky's "Boris Gudunov" was at the Metropolitan Opera. I went expecting to hear Russian, but the lyrics had been translated into Italian. Movies and opera were not the only options. There were two Russian newspapers. *Ruskie Golus* was the one I read. Early in my efforts, I painstakingly spelled out a headline to find out it was "footballny match."

The only memorable event in my new duty as hospital corpsman at the Half Moon was a sailor who complained of a pain in his abdomen. I examined him and found that the pain was at McBurney's point, a spot midway between his right hip and his pubic symphysis. It should be his appendix. But theory is one thing. Reality may be another. Was it really his appendix? And was it really ruptured? I called the hospital on Staten Island, where we were to send anyone needing hospitalization, and told a doctor there what I had found. He said, "Send him over." I arranged for a CG boat to take him and when he was gone worried that his problem was just an odd pain. When the doctor came in that afternoon, I told him about the sailor. He called to find out the man's condition, and told me he had been operated on for appendicitis, and was doing well.

Coney Island had not been ideal as a location for the machinist mate school. It was too far from the place where the men got their daily training. Another hotel was taken over in the fall, and it was on the East Side in midtown Manhattan! Timing was great: the weather was getting too cool for swimming, and the theater season was beginning.

A week or two after I took up residence in Manhattan, Rachel suggested we get married. This shouldn't have been a surprise, but it was. "The country's at war," I pointed out. "I may be killed. How does it make any sense to get married now?" My protest did not deter her. We kicked it around for a while and remained at an impasse. She said she couldn't go on as we were if we did not get married. "In that case," I said, half to myself, "Sorry." Then added, "Thanks for the memories." It was goodbye. It was unfortunate to end that way. If she had waited a few more weeks before making the demand of marriage, it would have been too late -- for I would have been out to sea on my way to the Pacific. I still had her picture and when I was transferred to the ship, I put her photo up on the inside of the door to my locker. Several shipmates asked, "That your girl?" Ignoring time, I said yes, and did not use the past tense as I should have done. An indication of how pretty she was, someone stole the picture.

I had been dividing my time between three women, and two of them were now out of my life. The one remaining, Sarah, was not sleeping with me. But at least she wasn't asking to get married.

Five o'clock in the morning the phone in the sickbay rang. I answered it. It was Miriam, a friend of Rachel's. "Rachel tells me you two broke up."

"Yeah. She wants to get married. I don't."

"Why don't you come over right away and let me console you."

I knew she had a great capacity to console sailors. I thought of three, in particular, that she'd consoled a couple of weeks previously.

Rachel and I had been walking with Miriam on the way to Miriam's apartment. She had invited us over for a drink. Coming up the street toward us were three French sailors. A Free French battleship had managed to break out of the German blockade around Dakar harbor and had crossed the Atlantic to put into the Brooklyn shipyard for repairs. The red pompoms on French sailors' caps were to be seen all over the city.

"Allo!" One of them said to us.

"Hello," the girls replied. I said "Bon soir."

"Ah, tu parle francais!" said the one who had greeted us. "Are these both your girl friends?" he inquired in French.

"No," I told him. "One is. The other is her friend."

"Then, perhaps," he smiled broadly, "she can be my girl for this evening?"

"I don't know. Ask her."

Miriam was already sizing him up, sensing what was being said. She entwined her arm in his. Thus we started walking again, two couples now, with two other pompomed sailors following behind. When we got to Miriam's place, the two straggling sailors caught up and were about to enter with us. I started to explain to them that they were supernumerary, but Miriam ushered them in. "I've got enough drinks for everybody."

With a glass in everyone's hand, we wanted to hear about Dakar. I translated the girls' questions as well as giving my own and they replied, each adding details. I had all I could do to keep up with translating. They were from Toulon, but that naval base was now controlled by Vichy, collaborators with the Germans. Their ship had got out when the Paris government fell and had gone to A.O.F. (Afrique Occidentale Française). Dakar was full of refugees from Europe. Men and women, but who cared about the men. Women were plentifully available. "We jig-jig all night." No need to translate "jig-jig."

Eventually, Rachel and I were ready to leave. I began to explain to the two stragglers that they should leave too. It was clear Miriam expected that the one who had been the spokesman would remain. Miriam, however, told me to forget my advice to the other sailors. All three remained.

"You know," Miriam greeted me when I arrived fifteen minutes after we got off the phone, "that I would never cut in on Rachel. But now that she and you are split, I want you. I had my eye on you and I guess you knew it." She was in her filmy white nightie, which quickly disappeared. She helped me undress. She knew the thirteen buttons of the frontal flap of the sailor's trousers. She undid them all while I pulled my kerchief off and got rid of the top part of my uniform. She pushed me onto her bed and got on top of me, taking me into her without delay. "I've been waiting since you hung up, thinking about you." She was ready, apparently her forethought was ample substitute for foreplay, and juices in amazing quantity flowed out of her onto my belly.

Ten days after the early morning telephone call my transfer order came through. I was to report to a ship just built and about to be commissioned, an APA (Attack Transport), that after a shakedown cruise would return to New York for one last time before heading for the Panama Canal and the Pacific Ocean. I would join the ship's crew with an advance in rank from third to second class pharmacist mate.

Every night during that interval I spent with Miriam, getting back to the sickbay in time for the morning sick call, and taking a long nap before the trainees returned and the afternoon sick call. I slept more in the day than in the night during that time. While Drew, my boss, talked on the phone to his college girl-fiancée in Philadelphia, I was doing what he would have liked to be doing.

From the time I met Rachel, and immediately afterwards Esther, with the exception of the three months hiatus in New London, this had been a period of intense sexual activity, but what followed was over two years of abstinence. At Colon, before we entered the Panama Canal, in Honolulu, and on Leyte, in the Philippines, there were whorehouses, but the lines of soldiers, sailors, and marines waiting their turn to enter was off-putting, and I supposed the chance of venereal disease too high. As it turned out, Miriam would be almost the last woman before multi-months in the vast Pacific.

CHAPTER ELEVEN

IN THE PACIFIC WITH THE NAVY

I was transferred to a ship just out of the shipbuilding works at Bath, Maine; it had just been commissioned as an APA. Someone had given it the strange name of *Cavalier*. It was designed to carry troops and land them on islands in the "Pacific Theater of War" by means of landing boats dubbed LCPVs (Landing Craft Personnel Vehicles). Three APAs and one AKA formed a Transdiv (transportation division). The K stood for "cargo." The cargo was tanks and other heavy armor and equipment. An AKA carried larger landing craft necessary for tanks; an LCPV could accommodate a jeep but nothing larger.

We went on a shakedown cruise to ascertain that everything was in proper working order and that the newly assembled crew was familiar with their duties in handling the vessel's operations. We returned to New York. Suddenly the city, from the deck of the ship, looked different to me. I was no longer a denizen of its streets but a being detached from land yearning to get ashore. A last liberty – saying goodbye to friends. Then out to sea again.

We proceeded down the Atlantic coast, rounding Cape Hatteras in rough weather and many of the crew suffered seasickness. My stomach had been hardened by my time on the buoy tender and I managed not to lose my breakfast. Mona

Passage between Puerto Rico and Cuba let us into the Caribbean and on toward the Panama Canal. Liberty was granted before entering the canal. It was not my first time in a Spanish-speaking locality; when I had crossed the border into Mexico by paying two cents to walk over the bridge across the Rio Grande River at El Paso, I had not stayed long enough to learn any vocabulary. English was commonly used there, but I had to experiment with what few words I could grasp. I saw the word "cerveza" on a beer bottle on the bar. Somehow I knew the words for a few numerals, and ordered for myself and a friend, "Dos cervezas, por favor."

"You speak Spanish?" my shipmate asked.

"No. But I might as well try."

The passage through the canal was interesting and beautiful. I enjoyed the process of getting into a lock, having the water level raised so that the ship rose, giving more of a view of the surroundings, and then after a while doing the same thing again to get higher, and then into a large lake in a verdant countryside, and later to pass into locks where the water drained out, letting the ship sink down between the walls, losing visibility of things beyond, and coming out into the canal, now closer to sea level.

We sailed up the Pacific coast to San Diego, California. For some time we stayed in the San Diego area, practicing landings on Santa Catalina Island, and returning for liberty in San Diego. I picked up a woman in a bar. She was a few sheets to the wind, and carried a plucked chicken by the legs, the butcher's paper wrapped around the bird in tatters. She took me to her home. I noticed some children's toys on the kitchen floor. In the morning, I heard a child's voice coming in the open window, "A sailor's in bed with momma." The woman, now awake and sober, shouted, "Jimmy! Come here." A door slammed as Jimmy came into the house, and in a moment a preadolescent boy appeared at the door. I tried to make myself inconspicuous under the covers. "What did I tell you? You don't say anything to anybody about what you see in the house."

I wanted to get out of there as soon as I could. She offered me breakfast. I declined. As I departed I realized I was in a Navy base. I must have been almost as blotto as my pick-up not to have noticed when we came in. My night's companion must have been the wife of a guy out to sea. I was late getting back to the ship and given a few hours of extra duty.

Pearl Harbor was our next stop. Honolulu was chockablock with sailors, soldiers, and marines. In front of various buildings on certain streets were lines of servicemen. "If the line goes in on the ground floor, it's a bar. If the line goes up stairs, it's a whorehouse," I was informed by someone who had been there before my ship arrived. I didn't intend to spend any time in either line.

My friend, lower case jim, was here in Honolulu. He had increased his skills and now had a better-paying job enabling him to have a comfortable place to live in the wartime city where decent accommodations were scarce. He had made friends among the local people. With him I went to a *luau*. Pigs, chickens, fish, taro, bananas, and other things were steamed in a pit in the ground lined with stones that had been heated by a wood fire. While the meal was being cooked by the heated stones, *okelehao* was offered to drink. The Hawaiian word is a corruption of the English "alcohol." Hawaiian speech doesn't allow two consonants to be juxtaposed and words must end in a vowel. Given these rules, *okelehao* is obviously "alcohol." *Poi* was a gloppy substance that tasted like glue, but to be polite we ate a small amount watered down with *okelehao*. The other foods were great; lots of fruits as well as the cooked stuff, mangos, pineapple, oranges, and coconut.

A Chinese friend of jim's invited us to his home and the friend's mother served us a Chinese meal with several dishes I'd never seen in a Chinese restaurant. One that made an impression was golden brown cubes that turned out to be fried tofu.

Another friend of jim's from New York was in the army, stationed at the moment on Oahu, so we had a threesome for some of our gatherings. Sometimes we just sat on the porch of jim's house and drank the local Five Islands Rum, affectionately called "five ulcer rum," and talked of memories of New York, or of the war, and prospects of how soon it might end. The soldier and the sailor in this triumvirate wished for a quick ending of the war, but I'm not sure how the well-paid shipyard worker felt. He had never made so much money in his life.

Our stay at Pearl Harbor was too good to last, and we were soon out to sea in a formation with aircraft carriers, battleships, cruisers, destroyers, DEs (destroyer escorts), and a number of transdivs, the latter loaded with troops and armament. These were so spread out we couldn't see them all. Some were scheduled to arrive at the target before the troop carriers. Kwajalein Island was the destination. Aircraft bombed it; battleships shelled it, and so did cruisers for three days and nights. One would have thought that with so many explosives dumped on the island, no one could be left alive there, but we knew that would not be so. Tarawa, the island attacked just before Kwajalein, had been hit as hard, but the Japanese were dug in so well that they were waiting for the Americans to try to come ashore. The American casualties had been heavy.

The APAs were to send the troops ashore, after which the vacated spaces in the APAs would be readied to serve as a hospital for the wounded who would be ferried back from the island. Hospital ships, painted white and brightly lighted at night with a red cross emblazoned on the sides, were not permitted by the Geneva Convention to enter the battle zone until the third day. Then the wounded, if still alive, would be transferred to the hospital ship that would immediately depart from the area. Pharmacist mates became important once the fighting on land began. Some pharmacist mates, with supplies of bandages, disinfectant, and morphine, were to go ashore with the troops and administer first aid to the wounded. The rest of the pharmacist mates remained on the ship to care for the wounded evacuated from the island. I was one of the pharmacist mates selected to be in the shore party.

The evening before the landing we were advised to get to sleep early because the landing would be at dawn. The advice was not easy to follow. The experience of Tarawa suggested that our chances of dying the next day were better than even. Would you spend your last night sleeping? A signalman, also on the beach party, and I sat on deck trying to enjoy as best we could what we expected would be the last few hours of our lives. An officer came by and told us to go to our bunks.

Awakened before dawn, we were dressed and up on deck in the dark. I had packs of medication. We waited for the command to go over the side and clamber down nets of stout rope into the LCPVs. Once a landing boat was loaded, the bosun drove it away from the side of the ship to wait for the other boats to receive their cargo of armed men. The darkness had been lessening and color was emerging on the eastern horizon. I was surprised to see green on a lower edge of a cloud. Green was not a color one expected to see in the preliminary phase of a sunrise. It puzzled me. Later I learned that the shallow water of a lagoon reflected this tint upward to be captured by clouds. Even later I learned that this was one of the signs Polynesian navigators looked for on their explorations: a greenish shade of cloud told them there was a lagoon under it, and if they steered toward it, they would find, if not an island, at least an atoll. Usually before they saw the greenish cloud, they would have seen land birds that ventured far out from the island to feed on fish.

Time to meditate on colors of the sunrise was brief. The landing craft, in formation with others, went at full speed for the shore. The flat-bottomed craft slid up on the beach far enough so that the ramp at the front of the craft could be lowered on to dry land – if all went well – but sometimes because of the formation of the shoreline or other reasons the ramp came down and dropped men knee-deep, or deeper, in water. This time I did not get wet and ran up the beach. As soon as I was within the trees and bush I fell to the ground in order to make less of a target and slithered forward. As a medical corpsman I had a red cross painted on my helmet. The enemy was not supposed to shoot at medical corpsmen but they were shooting bursts of bullets in our direction without paying much attention to who, or what, was in the line of fire. Besides, would the shooter even see the little red cross on my helmet?

Stopping the bleeding of a wounded man was the first concern. I cleaned a wound as well as I could under the conditions, bound the wound with bandages, and gave the man a shot of morphine if he was in pain, which we assumed was always the case. Being busy with tasks I knew how to do, and seeing the urgent need of mangled men for my help, I almost forgot the shooting. The hours went by uncounted.

Having survived the first battle, I laughed at my fears with the friend that had sat solemnly with me on the deck the night before. The marines secured the half of the island assigned to them in 48 hours; the army secured their half in 72 hours. The marines were exultant in their superiority in this operation over the army, but their casualty rate was much higher. The army's efforts, which spared risks, made more sense to me.

A hospital ship gleaming brilliantly was steaming away. The admiral sent a "well done" to the crews of all ships. Immediately after this approval was announced, a muster in the sickbay was called. A warrant officer just arrived from stateside was taking over from the chief pharmacist mate. He looked at the line of pharmacist mates, standing at attention, not in uniform, but in fatigues, and the floor of the sickbay strewn with wrappings of the gauze rolls of bandaging that had been used during the hectic time of the battle. "This place looks like a shithouse," he said. That was a fine thing to say as his first statement to us, and unfair with the battle just over, especially right on the heels of a compliment from the admiral. I felt annoyed and said, "We've just secured from battle."

"Who said that?" He knew who it was. He looked at me as I was saying it.

"You do not speak unless told to do so." I was given 30 hours extra duty.

My extra duty was to chip the old paint in the "head" in the sickbay. Working confined in the narrow room, I was stripped to the waist, sweating in the heat of the tropics. Over the entry to the head was a sign saying "BATH." I put a piece of tape with the word SWEAT printed on it in front of BATH. The warrant officer gave me some extra hours of extra duty for this decoration "defacing government property." I hated him as an arrogant son of a bitch, and I guess he hated me as an insubordinate underling. It was hard to disguise my feelings, but I tried to keep my mouth shut. However, I did run up over 100 hours of extra duty, but not all for talking back.

At Eniwetok I was again assigned to the beach party. The Navy had decided that the Japanese were not observing the Geneva Convention and were actually firing on hospital corpsmen. We were henceforth to be armed with a handgun. One was offered to me. I said I did not want it. "Take it. That's an order!"

I hesitated. "How can I use it when I'm doing my job as a hospital corpsman?"

"Take it." The officer was steaming with anger.

I took it, and went down on deck where marines were waiting to be sent ashore. "Anyone want a sidearm?" I asked.

"How much?"

"It's free. I'm giving it away."

Someone close to me grabbed it. I turned and left the area.

Back on board after the battle, I was told to turn in the pistol that had been issued to me. "I don't have it," I told the officer.

"You lost it?"

"No, sir. I gave it to a marine. I told you I did not want to carry it."

"You gave away government property?"

I was given a lecture and some additional hours of extra duty. Supervising my extra duty was still carried out by the warrant officer who had given me my first deck court.

ABOARD THE *CALLAWAY*

The *Callaway*, another APA, was short of its full complement of crew. I was transferred. I was glad to get away from the *Cavalier* with its cavalier warrant officer. Probably he was glad to be rid of me; that may be why I was transferred. Somehow the extra duty that I owed did not follow me. A new beginning.

It did not occur to me at the time, but eventually I wondered if some officer higher in the ship's command structure might have noted the mounting number of hours of extra duty being doled out, discovered the obvious personal vendetta as one causative factor, and in order to improve morale on the ship, and perhaps to give me a chance to avoid that particular warrant officer, ordered the transfer. At the time, my attitude was that I was fighting a two-front war, one against the Japanese, and one against the American officer class. Not every enlisted man felt that way but there was a fairly widespread feeling of hostility against officers with gold braid on their caps, which we called "chicken shit." That term also served to cover the various irritations we felt at unnecessary make-work, for example, moving some stores from one hold to another and the next day, or whenever, moving them back again, just to keep men busy. A few felt so strongly anti-officer, especially toward the "90-day wonders," ex-office-boys with three months officer training, now ensigns, or lieutenants, junior grade. Officers were aware of the antagonism. It was noted that we never saw an officer on the fantail after dark; he might, it was said, be thrown overboard. There was undoubtedly bravado and exaggeration in that threatening claim and I never heard of such an occurrence, but the statement represented a definite attitude among a certain number of sailors.

The *Callaway* was steaming along one evening shortly after I had come aboard. Out at sea, no lights could be shown, not even a lighted cigarette. I was standing on deck, leaning on the rail. The deck above extended out over my head, shutting out even the glimmer of the stars and increasing the darkness. Someone came and stood beside me. We began talking. He was William Wheeler from New Jersey. We were two men from the Northeast, our accents were not notably different, and we began to realize as we talked that we agreed on points of view on the topics we covered: the war, military service, politics. We talked a long time. When we went inside into the light, I was surprised to see that my new friend was African American. There had been a black pharmacist mate in the sickbay on the *Cavalier*, but we had not been close. I had not had an African American friend since Henry whom I knew only during the brief time I picked hops in Washington. Wheeler and I were shipmates and our friendship would endure longer – as long as we were on the same ship. Unfortunately after that, the war over, and the G.I. Bill making it possible for me to go to college, I became so engrossed in studies that I – never a good correspondent – lost contact with Wheeler and all my former shipmates.

Wheeler was a gunner's mate, a rating he could have because of an executive order by President Franklin D. Roosevelt that required the Navy to permit Americans of African descent to have the same opportunities as white Americans. E. Philip Randolph, head of the Brotherhood of Railway Car Porters, had threatened a march on Washington if Negroes were still confined to being officers' stewards as they had been until then. Nevertheless, there were still officers' stewards and these stewards were still Negroes or Filipinos quartered in a segregated compartment.

Wheeler and I were billeted in the same compartment. We swapped bunks with others so that we were next to each other on the same level. It was not hard to get someone to swap since we both had had bunks not far above the floor; there were seven tiers of bunks, one above the other, in that compartment. Most men did not like the high levels; we didn't mind, at least one did not have so many others climbing up to bunks above and stepping on your bunk to get there. By sleeping so that our heads were at the conjoining ends we were able to talk quietly without bothering anyone.

He had a subscription to the *Pittsburgh Courier*, a Negro newspaper, and I had a subscription to *PM*, a liberal tabloid from New York City. The papers came with other mail, at intervals weeks apart due to the problem of supplying moving ships. We would each receive armfuls of wrapped newspapers. We'd open them up, lay them out in chronological order on our bunks under the mattress. When I finished one of my papers, I'd give it to Wheeler. When he finished one of his, he gave it to me. We had a shifting line of two kinds of newspapers as the ones received in exchange replaced those read and handed on. And we discussed some issues in what we read.

There was news, but nothing of a type that was new to me, in what I gave to Wheeler, but what he gave me was a revelation of a world of which I had been only partly aware. I was not unaware of the attitude of many whites toward blacks; that much was obvious even in the limited contact I had had with "colored," or "Negro," or "blacks," or "African Americans," as the preferred terms shifted from time to time. But living in the North, where local newspapers did not cover much news from another region, I was until then ignorant of the prevalence and the extent of discriminatory exclusion, even in the North, of blacks from employment in jobs for which they were qualified, or of the frequency of police brutality against members of the black community.

News of Africa was not prominent in the *Courier*, as far as my memory goes, but Wheeler had a concern for the peoples of that continent. This became apparent when we read that Sir Stafford Cripps was being sent to the British colony of India to discuss with nationalist leaders what the post-war conditions might be. One vocal leader, Subhas C. Bose, was openly proclaiming that Japan was an Asian nation, and Indians should help this neighbor, Japan, against the Europeans and this would result in the end of colonialism and thereby independence for India. Ghandi and Nehru were for negotiating with the British, but there was not unanimity among the followers.

Africa had a nascent independence movement, not as advanced as India's, and it would not become newsworthy until after the war when African troops returned from battle scenes in Burma and elsewhere. I was just becoming aware of Africa but Wheeler was better informed. Together we wrote a "letter to the editor" saying Cripps, or someone, should be sent on a similar mission to the African colonies. Wheeler sent a copy to the *Pittsburgh Courier* and I sent one to *PM*. Whether either was ever publisher I can't say, but I never saw one in print.

That was the first action on my part that had anything to do with Africa. Later, after some twists and turns in my college career, when I became an Africanist, that is – a scholar concerned with Africa, I decided that I owed some of my decision to Bill Wheeler. I recognized race relations as a major problem for the United States and I thought that recognition of Africa as a cultural reality in the world would help to resolve some of the tension between whites and blacks in the U.S. I still think that perhaps it has, but no doubt is less significant than the civil rights movement, which has not yet completed its goals.

In addition to newspapers there were letters in the mail. Many of the letters I received were either from Fitz or his brother George, who had undertaken to supply me with books. In the newspapers I read reviews of new books; I would write to George and include a check so he could buy and send those of special interest to me. I think I read as many books in a year in the Pacific as I did later in a year in college. At one point my locker was so full of books that I had to get rid of my pea jacket to make room. I did not need the pea jacket in the tropics, but we received orders to sail to Attu Island in the Aleutian archipelago because Japanese troops had occupied it. Fortunately for pea coat-less me, we received a recall order because the Japanese had departed, realizing they could not hold this American island. Ship's store did not have a pea coat to sell me. Letters also came regularly from Irene, with news of the family, and from Ruth in New Jersey.

"Let's get some good chop!" Wheeler said to me one day. I looked at him wondering what he meant. "The best food on this ship," he informed me, "is in the stewards' quarters." The stewards cooked for, and served, the officers. "Naturally they keep some of the best for themselves." He took me down to the stewards' quarters, introduced me to the occupants who were there at the moment. After a bit of chatter, someone went up to the officers' galley and brought down some food for Wheeler and me. A steward who hadn't been present when I was introduced came in. "What's this honky doing here," he glowered in simulated great dudgeon. "That's Chandler," Wheeler told me. Chandler was to become, after Wheeler, my closest friend among the black members of the crew.

One day I was sitting on someone's bunk in the stewards' quarters talking to Chandler and an irate officer came in. There was no coffee in the wardroom, and no steward was up there as there should have been. Who's on duty? One of the stewards hopped up and volunteered to go up and right the situation. The officer, partly mollified but still annoyed, turned his attention to me. "What are you doing here?" He did not know who I was, but obviously I was not an officers' steward.

"Talking with my friends," I answered.

"Well, get out," he snapped, "or clean up this mess." There were cigarette butts and other detritus on the floor.

"Aye, aye, sir," I replied with mock deference, and found a broom. The officer watched me sweep for a moment, then turned on his heel and stomped out.

"Way to go!" Chandler slapped me on the back and took the broom away from me. He did not, however, finish the sweeping, just tossed the broom in a corner. The cleaning up would be taken care of in due time by whoever had the task to do so. We sat down and went back to our conversation.

SAIPAN AND LEYTE

We were on our way to Saipan, an island not far from Japan.

The pharmacist mate contingent in the shore party included me and a kid barely old enough to enlist and just out of pharmacist mate school. Everyone called him "Red" for the obvious reason, and I no longer know him by any other designation. He had come aboard with unruly red hair and an officer had told him to get a haircut. "Yeah, it's kind of wild, isn't it?" he said with a grin as if he were talking to a buddy rather than an officer. But the officer, seeing no disrespect in his manner, merely youthful exuberance and newness to the military, did not take umbrage. After the haircut his omnipresent smile and good humor prevailed. I came upon him and another sailor exchanging words that were incomplete sentences that made no sense to me. "What are you doing?" I asked. "He tells me the piece on one side of a record, and I tell him what's on the other side." Two jazz aficionados were trying to stump each other.

One of the landing craft that had carried tanks was anchored offshore and its long and wide inside deck was now used as a hospital area. We had evacuated wounded from the island to this emergency set-up. The wounded were on folding cots, rather than beds, but better than the ground, and with a deck over our heads we could have electric lights at night, which we couldn't have had on shore while the fighting continued.

The sounds of an airplane engine and then anti-aircraft firing resonated through the night. Someone said, "If they hit this hollow contraption with a bomb, the whole thing will plunge to the bottom of the sea." That stimulated a lot of excited talking by both wounded and hospital corpsmen. Red said in a loud voice with a hint of fear, "I'm getting out of here!" and started for the ladder to go topside. I grabbed him by the arm as he was about to go by me. "We're not going to sink," I told him, despite my uncertainty about what I was promising. "If we leave there'll be panic among the wounded, and they'll try to follow us."

Red calmed down. "Yeah," he agreed. "Can't do that."

Our gunners may or may not have shot down the enemy plane, but it was no longer sending us the menacing rat-tat-tat sound, and we went on with our ministering to the wounded. Dr. Kaufman, who had observed my exchange with Red, said something to me. His words elude me now, but they were to the effect that he appreciated my effort to prevent chaos. The wounded would not be able to flee but might try to get out of their cots and in doing so would loosen their bandages and start bleeding again. Later he recommended me for the Medal of Honor, citing my being active for over 70 continuous hours and leadership in the hospital corps. That was too great a designation as even I realized and I was awarded the Commendation Medal. The captain pinned the ribbon on my chest when the award was approved. I never bothered to pick up the medal and don't know what it looks like. A pacifist can't wear a military metal; that would be glorifying war.

We had been three days and two nights working, at first on the beach, under fire much of the time, and then on the floating tender. Seventy-something hours working without sleep. About a dozen of us all working without sleep; no one else got a ribbon for their efforts – I didn't see that my efforts were significantly different from theirs.

A picture of the ribbon pinning was sent out to some newspapers. Irene saw the picture and wrote me a letter. She wrote that the priest at her church said, "There are no atheists in the foxholes." She informed me that when I came back from the war there would be no further discussion in the family about my stance on Catholicism. That was certainly a welcome letter and I admired her for making a decision that must have run against the grain for her. But I already knew that I would not "go home" again.

Three prisoners were taken aboard. They were to be interrogated for any useful military information that might be obtained. Generally, prisoners of war were reluctant to talk, but it was always worth the effort to try. Two of the men were wounded. They had been bandaged on shore before being brought aboard, but their wounds would need attention. In the sickbay we were asked for a volunteer to tend to them. I stepped forward. I heard some guffaw behind me. They were enemies, the feeling seemed to be, let them die.

The interpreter and I had become acquainted. I told him of my blighted effort to become an interpreter by studying Russian. He had had an intensive course in Japanese at a college in Colorado set up precisely to supply the armed forces with some Americans who could speak Japanese. He showed me his dictionary, explaining how to look up a word: each character had one or more components called radicals, and the words were arranged, for lack of an alphabet, by the number of radicals, and within each radical by the number of strokes in a radical. Just for the fun of it, he taught me a few words.

When I went into the brig where the prisoners were kept, I said, *Ohayo gozaimasu,* which I understood to be a friendly greeting. One turned his face to the wall; neither of the others said anything. While I was removing the bandage, cleaning the wound, and re-bandaging it on one of the prisoners, I told him, in words I had obtained from the interpreter, that he would recover. He smiled but said nothing. I assumed he was afraid to say anything friendly in the presence of the others. The other wounded man was sullen. I told the interpreter of the distinctive reactions of each of the three, and suggested he get the one who smiled out of the brig, away from the others and he might get some response.

He did not initiate interrogations; his job was to put an officer's words into the prisoner's language and then the prisoner's into English. But he would convey my suggestion to his superior. What became of this, if anything, I never heard. The unit to which the interpreter was attached was the commodore's staff, and the commodore was transferred to another ship. After the war was over, I read that in Japan a soldier was considered dead if he was taken prisoner; his family would be so informed, and a funeral would be held. Captured soldiers, realizing they could not go home again, often decided to make the best of the situation and volunteered information that prisoners of other armies would resist giving even under torture. I wondered if the smiler had been of that type.

There were pauses between assaults in the island-hopping strategy the U.S. was following. Preparation had to be made, and supplies of munitions and soldiers and/or Marines had to be moved into place for the next battle. Sometimes while these activities were under way, the ships idled in some convenient spot. Occasionally on such a waiting period, about half of the enlisted men were permitted to go ashore on some island for recreation. The only time I remember, we were deposited on an uninhabited islet with baseball bats, balls, gloves, etc. We could play ball and drink two cans of beer before going back to the ship. A few who didn't drink beer could sell or give theirs to someone else so a few men had more than the two, but no one had enough to get drunk.

There were many who would have liked to have more alcohol. One scheme was to distill it: several sailors brought back coconuts with the idea of fermenting the juice. The plan was to get some sugar from the galley and funnel it into the coconut through a hole bored in the outer casing of the nut. The problem was that to get the sugar one needed the cooperation of the cooks, and that could be obtained only if part of the alcoholic product was shared with the galley staff. Consequently there was never much of the stuff when the fermentation was completed and no one ever got more than a taste. We had doctored coconuts stashed under bunks in the sickbay, and were afraid some officer would come by and smell the rich aroma, but few officers other than the doctors ever came into the sickbay, so our illegal actions were not discovered by anyone in authority.

The one non-militarily trained officer who might have detected our bootlegging was the Catholic priest who was a chaplain on our ship. We had two chaplains; the other was Protestant. The contrast between them was more than theological. This particular Protestant chaplain was aloof from the troops and the crew. I heard him referred to as "Lieutenant," deliberately not using the title "chaplain." The Catholic chaplain was always among the men who were not commissioned officers; he had the knack of being a companion, talking and listening to any who had problems or grievances, and he was always welcome in any part of the ship. He was a regular visitor to sickbay, checking on the progress of the sick or wounded, and joshing with the pharmacist mates. If his nose ever whiffed the fermenting coconut juice, he never mentioned it.

He was a young Irishman, quite happy in his profession. I thought as I watched him how much more effective he was as a promoter of his Church – by example, not by preaching, because he did none of the latter except in chapel meetings. By comparison the Protestant chaplain, his colleague and competitor, was left in the dust.

There were sailors who were neither Catholic nor Protestant. Me, for instance, and a few others were totally secular, but there were also a number who were Jewish. One was a friend of mine, a yeoman, and a reader of books. We sometimes swapped books we had finished reading. He had little sustenance for his faith most of the time, but once when we were in a cluster of many ships, there was a notice that anyone wishing to go to a Jewish service would be transported to another ship where a Jewish chaplain awaited them.

We landed troops on Leyte Island in the central Philippines. The fighting was soon over. Some enterprising Filipino took over a house near where the ships were anchored, found some women, and opened a brothel. We had a Filipino steward aboard. He came back sadly announcing in the stewards' quarters that he had been turned away from the brothel. The girls were earning their dowries and they did not want any customers who might later recognize them when they were married. The black stewards offered sympathy but their mood was gleeful – they were familiar with the problem of being refused entry by a white Madame – this time they had been accepted.

Off duty, I was out on deck with "Red," our teenaged pharmacist mate, when out of nowhere, it seemed, a Japanese plane came in low, just over the top of trees on a slight rise of land, and out over the water toward us. Gunners on a ship near us opened fire and one of the slugs hit Red, inches away from me, in the chest. We got him below into the sickbay. A doctor operated on him. I gave blood for a transfusion and so did others. He was bleeding internally, into his lung cavity. Red was transferred to a hospital ship and we never heard whether he survived or not.

If the plane was a *kamikaze*, it had not been targeting us. If it had intended to hit us, it could have crashed into the *Callaway*. It was headed for a battle ship further out from shore and it never made the extra distance, shot down either by the gunners on the APAs or those on the battleship.

We did on another occasion have a *kamikaze* crash onto our bridge. The Filipino steward was on the bridge, probably bringing coffee to the officers, and ran from the bridge, his clothes ablaze from the petrol splattered from the crash. Some gunner thought he was the Japanese pilot and shot him. My friend the signalman, who had been transferred from the *Cavalier* along with me, and who had lingered on deck with me the night before the assault on Kwajalein, was on the bridge too, and he was one of the mortalities. One of the bunks in my compartment had a hole in it where a bullet from the plane, fired as it was coming toward us, had penetrated the metal skin of the ship and the bunk next to it. Of course none of us had been in our bunks; we were all at battle stations -- nevertheless it gave me a jolt to see the holes.

Leyte was a notable stop on my itinerary. As we were leaving, the *Callaway* was hit by a torpedo. It was at night; most of the crew was asleep, with some on deck because it was so hot below. As the ship buckled under the impact, some heads were pushed up and as they came down on the hard metal deck, they got minor scalp wounds. It was a source of humorous discussion later whether such injuries counted for an award of a purple heart.

The torpedo almost missed the ship, hitting it only a foot or so from the propeller. The underwater section of the ship at that point was so narrow that the explosion occurred as the torpedo was already emerging on the far side of the ship, and much of its impact was on the water. Nevertheless, the shaft to the propeller was buckled and we could not proceed under our own power. But aside from a few cracks on the sides of the ship, the torpedo had not done much damage and there was no loss of life. The explosion of the torpedo, had it been a few feet forward, would have had its major impact on an ammunition storage compartment and that was right under my sleeping compartment. At the time I was unaware of the close proximity of explosives. We only learned that later in discussions of the damage to the ship.

We were stopped in the water, unable to move and in danger of receiving another torpedo. The destroyers escorting the fleet soon reported the submarine had been sunk by depth charges. The convoy, of course, had never halted, and was soon disappearing from sight. A sea tug was obtained from somewhere and took us in tow. With a single DE ("destroyer escort," a ship smaller than a destroyer) circling around us using its sonar to detect subs that would find the crippled ship an easy target, we made our slow way halfway across the Pacific to Pearl Harbor.

An aerographer's mate, third class, on his first ship had had it easy in convoy, with meteorologists on every ship, he told me, but now, on his own with no back-up from more experienced specialists, he was uneasy about the data he was getting. It seemed to indicate a typhoon, but he had never actually dealt with these indicators before and he was unsure how to read them. He went to the captain, showed him the information, stated his uncertainty, but said he felt there was a big storm heading toward us. The Captain looked at the charts, found an atoll not too far off course and gave the command to head for it. Not long after getting into the lagoon, inside the ring of coral, the typhoon caught us. The ship rocked wickedly, but it was not as bad as it would have been outside on the open ocean. The aerographer's mate said he was probably the only one who was happy to see the storm.

When the ship got back to Pearl Harbor, Chandler and I would go bowling on the base on days we did not have liberty and could not go into town. Workmen were all over the ship repairing the damage, and we had to be out of their way, so we were sent ashore, either on liberty to go into Honolulu, or to use the facilities of the base. In addition to bowling alleys, there was beer available after noon, and one of the ship's bands would play while we drank our brews. "Torpedo Junction" was one of the current favorites. I also associate this time with a song with lyrics that began "Caledonia! What makes your big head so hard?"

We bowled in the mornings and drank beer in the afternoon. Chandler was a good bowler and coached me, a novice, to improve. The only time I had ever bowled before was when I was with Harry, the "rubber tramp," and that had been merely an introduction to the game. Now it was more than just a pastime, it was a temporary escape from the reality of war, and from remembering we were in the military. Achieving a little skill, I began to enjoy it.

With the ship out of service, why couldn't we get leave? Fitz had written that he was going to get married and wanted me to be best man. I re-enforced my request for stateside leave. No news came to me of any decision on my request. I was getting angrier by the day. Gus White, one of my fellow pharmacist mates, and I were walking on the base. Coming toward us, in a column of twos, were newly minted ensigns in brand new uniforms. Everyone knew the war was practically over, and here was this new batch of "90-day wonders" just arriving as the job was done. I didn't like officers in general; I had nothing against these particular officers, but somehow the sight of them made me more annoyed than I had been, and that was plenty. I walked into the file, pushing my way between each of the twos, hitting both with my elbows. It was a nutty thing to do. No one said a word or took any action. I suppose they were in formation and too afraid to break formation, and too inexperienced in the exercise of their authority to deal with an unexpectedly trepidatious enlisted man. Gus said when I rejoined him, "You're crazy." At the moment he was correct.

The war was winding down, and we heard rumors of a "G.I. Bill" that would provide government loans to veterans to start businesses. Chandler said, "Dan, why don't we each get a loan, put them together and start a bowling alley in Baltimore?" Chandler was from Baltimore. I didn't care whether it would be Baltimore or somewhere else. It sounded an attractive idea, and I said, "Yeah! We could do that."

Chandler would be demobilized as soon as the government could process him and other draftees, but I was an enlisted man and had nearly a year to go before I would be discharged. That would be a postponement, not a permanent obstacle, as we both realized.

The fact that Baltimore was a Southern city had briefly flitted through my mind. How would a business partnership of a white man and a black man fare in a southern city? Well, how did any partnership fare whatever the nature of the individuals? It was always a gamble. Why not take a chance. And gamble? Didn't I know from my long ago travels with Harry that people gambled over bowling? What king of a business, really, was I getting myself into? Aw, don't begin imagining trouble! What better offer did I have?

"Sure," I shook Chandler's hand. "Let's do it."

The version of the G.I. Bill I had heard from the mouth of a shipmate was incomplete. He had no interest in going to college, so he didn't mention that the law would also provide tuition and support for college. The next day I found Chandler and said: "Sorry, Chandler. I'm going to college." And thus I set off on the path to my academic career.

Made in the USA
San Bernardino, CA
14 December 2012